THE BOOK OF

NAVIGATION

TIM BARTLETT

Edited by

Bob Armstrong

Purchased with funds from the
Allegheny Regional Asset District

Mt. Lebanon Public Library
16 Castle Shannon Boulevard
Pittsburgh, PA 15228-2252
412-531-1912
www.mtlebanonlibrary.org

SKYHORSE PUBLISHING

Copyright © 2009 by Tim Bartlett

All Rights Reserved. No part of this book may be reproduced in any manner without the express written consent of the publisher, except in the case of brief excerpts in critical reviews or articles. All inquiries should be addressed to Skyhorse Publishing, 555 Eighth Avenue, Suite 903, New York, NY 10018.

Skyhorse Publishing books may be purchased in bulk at special discounts for sales promotion, corporate gifts, fund-raising, or educational purposes. Special editions can also be created to specifications. For details, contact the Special Sales Department, Skyhorse Publishing, 555 Eighth Avenue, Suite 903, New York, NY 10018 or info@skyhorsepublishing.com.

www.skyhorsepublishing.com

10 9 8 7 6 5 4 3 2 1

Library of Congress Cataloging-in-Publication Data

Bartlett, Tim.
  The book of navigation : traditional navigation techniques for boating and
yachting / Tim Bartlett.
      p. cm.
Includes index.
ISBN 978-1-60239-621-0
  1. Navigation--Handbooks, manuals, etc. 2. Boats and boating--Handbooks,
manuals, etc. 3. Yachting--Handbooks, manuals, etc. I. Title.
  VK559.B33 2008
  623.89--dc22

2008055259

Printed in China

The author and publisher would like to express their thanks to all the following people and organizations who have assisted with the illustration of this book:

Photographs and equipment
Amberley Marine: pages 111 and 112
Garmin: pages 41–43
National Aeronautics and Space
  Administration: page 113
Raymarine: pages 44 and 108
Suunto: pages 28 and 31

Thanks also to:
Adlard Coles Nautical for permission to use
  the quotation from *Channel Harbours and
  Anchorages*
Bill Anderson
Linda Jermy
Hydrographer of the Navy (UK) for
  permission to use extracts from Admiralty
  charts and publications
NOAA for permission to use extracts from
  U.S. charts and publications
U.S. Coast Guard for permission to use
  information on Aids to Navigation and
  Local Notices to Mariners
Fisheries and Oceans Canada for permission to
  use information regarding Canadian Notices
  to Mariners
National Geospatial-Intelligence Agency
  (NGA) for permission to use information on
  updating charts
Reed's Nautical Almanac for permission to use
  extracts from their publication
Alison Noice

Original illustrations by the author

Contents

Foreword

When Bob Dylan first sang "The Times They Are a Changin'" back in 1963, I doubt he had any idea just how *much* change would occur over the ensuing decades. While we've seen great changes in many aspects of our lives, perhaps the most spectacular have been in the world of electronics, where TV has grown from three networks offering mostly black and white programming that was often sort of fuzzy despite the relatively small image (a 26-inch picture tube was HUGE!), to hundreds of them showing everything in sparkling digital color, many in high definition that remains spectacularly sharp on some very large screens. TV audio has progressed from tinny monaural to rich, theater-like 5.1 surround sound.

We now can carry more computing power in a laptop than we had in room-filling mainframes back then.

And in marine navigation, progress has been equally phenomenal. For centuries, navigation was strictly hands-on: We mariners had to plot everything on paper charts using data obtained through various means that always involved some sort of painstaking physical activity. Even the limited electronic aids we had until just a couple of decades ago—primarily the Radio Direction Finder (RDF) and Loran A—required considerable manipulation of their controls only to produce marginally better results than we could get without them. Over the years we saw steady improvement as first Loran C, and then a satellite-based system known as Transit and most recently, the also satellite-based NAVSTAR, which is better known as the Global Positioning System (GPS), entered the scene. Each new system required less and less

manual and/or mental effort to produce better results more quickly. Now, thanks to electronic charts and GPS, a modern chart plotter can show us where we are and how to get to where we want to go while we do little more than push a button or two and glance at its screen. And if the GPS has the Wide Area Augmentation System (WAAS), its accuracy can be within a boat length. It's wonderful! But this progress has its downside: Many people have become so reliant on these magic boxes that they never bother to learn what the electronic devices are doing for them, much less how to do it for themselves. That you are looking at this book—even if you are still just contemplating reading it further—would suggest that you may not think this way, which begs two comments: First, congratulations! You apparently have an active, inquisitive mind. Second, read on. If you want to learn about marine navigation in a most uncomplicated, straightforward fashion, you'll find exactly what you are looking for in the following pages.

I can make that latter statement without bias (or bragging) because I didn't write the book but merely edited some good work that already existed. As you can plainly see, this volume originated in England, where it was initially a Royal Yachting Association (RYA) text. I've long admired the Brits for their no-nonsense approach to boating education, particularly the training/certification programs offered by the RYA. We Yanks would do well to emulate them. Indeed, books written for RYA courses are excellent sources of nautical knowledge. When brought to this side of the pond, however, these books often suffer from two rather aggravating problems: One, though we and the English ostensibly speak the same language, we really don't! The Queen's English is actually quite foreign to us and on occasion requires "translation" in order to be better understood. Two, expressing the same sort of obstinate determination to go our own way that started the whole independence flap back in 1776, we often do things quite differently over here. This didn't make the original form of this book "wrong," but rather created the need for some adaptation to bring its content in line with our American practices, situations and phraseology. That was my task: to "Americanize" an excellent British publication and make it suitable for U.S. consumption. I hope you'll conclude that I've done the job well and wish you fair winds and following seas as you embark on a voyage in quest of knowledge.

Bob Armstrong

Foreword by the Author

Bill Anderson, in his foreword to the original incarnation of this book as *The RYA Book of Navigation*, wrote "The technology of navigation is under-going considerable change at the moment." He was dead right. Already, we have seen the demise of three of the electronic navigation systems that were described in the first edition, published eleven years ago. Position fixes from the Global Positioning System (GPS), on the other hand, are nearly ten times more accurate than they were then, because the American government has removed the deliberate errors that were originally used to degrade the accuracy available to civilian users. Satellite-based differential systems promise even greater accuracy in the not too distant future, and it is quite likely that a European version of GPS will be operational within the next few years. At the same time, the cost of electronic navigation equipment has fallen, and the level of sophistication available has risen. Chart plotters, in particular, have developed from being little more than toys to the stage at which they really can be regarded as serious navigational tools, with potentially life-saving advantages. Despite these technological changes, of course, traditional navigation techniques survive. They may be less important now than they once were, but they are still available as backups to modern technology, and as a means of understanding or cross-checking the information available from the electronics . . . or even as an interest in their own right, that can be just as consuming and rewarding as boatbuilding, sail trim, or the racing rules.

Tim Bartlett FRIN

Introduction

We are all navigators. We have to be, because navigation is the art or science of controlling or directing travel. So as soon as we start learning to walk or crawl we also start learning to navigate. Of course, our first "journeys"—from wherever we happen to be toward a favorite toy—are pretty simple; we can see our destination before we set off. Gradually though, we build up a mental picture or model of our surroundings until we are able to navigate to unseen destinations.

By the time we have grown to adulthood our individual territories are likely to have become quite large, but there will still be times when we find ourselves in unfamiliar surroundings. On vacation it might be quite fun to start the exploration process all over again, but in the hurry of everyday life we are more likely to ask someone else for directions.

Following directions based on someone else's local knowledge can be very effective, and it is almost certainly the way many of the earliest seafarers "navigated." They engaged local pilots to navigate for them in unfamiliar waters, or used information handed down by word of mouth or in the form of written sailing directions. At sea, as well as on land, we still sometimes use these techniques today. But simply following instructions is hardly navigation—there is no decision-making involved; you have no freedom to vary the route, and no real control other than to stop or go. More importantly it has serious limitations: handed-down instructions work only for one particular route, so you need different instructions for every combination of starting point and destination; they depend on your being able to recognize key landmarks from someone else's description; and they rapidly become useless if you get lost or have to deviate from the route for some reason or other.

To overcome these shortcomings, some of the old written sailing instructions were illustrated with drawings, and then with simple maps or charts. The first recognizable charts were probably produced in China about the tenth century AD, with Europe following suit two or three centuries later. In both cases, charts were developed about the same time as the magnetic compass—and not purely by coincidence. Those early map-makers needed some means of measuring direction in order to produce their maps in the first place, and their customers equally needed the compass in order to use them to best advantage, because although maps may have been developed to overcome the difficulty of describing the appearance of a particular headland or the precise location of a rock, their big advantage was that they could be used as universal sailing directions. They gave navigators the information required to plan their own passages from anywhere to anywhere. It was this facility that made the compass so important. You can see why if you think of a simple land-based example. If you are following directions, "turn left at the crossroads" is all you need, because whoever gave you the directions knows which road you are on in the first place. If you could have approached the crossroads from any direction, a much more positive indication is needed—north, south, east or west.

Art or science?

Whether navigation is an art or a science is a moot point, and in fact it is probably a bit of both. Like most other sciences it involves a certain amount of mathematics—nothing complicated, but the abilities to do simple arithmetic and to draw and measure accurately are important—and it requires hard facts if it is to be put to practical use. Some of those facts have to be learned by heart, but others are too complicated or variable to commit to memory, so you need to know where to find the necessary information.

The scientific side of navigation can be taught in a classroom or learned from books. What makes it an art are those things that can only be developed through practical experience at sea—knowing how to get the best out of your equipment when conditions are against you; being able to make a "best guess" when some key piece of information is not available; and being able to decide when—and when not—to use approximations and shortcuts.

Electronics

Much of this book is concerned with what have become known as "trad-nav" (traditional navigation) techniques. This is not just because "they're in the syllabus," nor is it to pretend that modern electronics do not exist. Increasingly, electronics have a part to play in sailing yacht navigation, and an even greater role in motorboats. But to depend on them totally not only means pinning your faith on the reliability of the equipment itself and on its power supply and antenna connections, but also on your own ability to operate it correctly. If you have ever dialed a wrong telephone number or recorded the wrong program on your DVR, there is a sporting chance that one day you will make a similar mistake with an electronic navigator.

A good knowledge of trad-nav will serve as a backup in the event of electronic failure and serve as a double-check against operator error. No less important: it can be interesting and rewarding in its own right and form part of the reason for going to sea in the first place.

Charts and the Real World

1

Maps, or charts as they are called at sea, are the navigator's prime tool. They provide much of the information you require, serve as worksheets for calculations, and as temporary records of what has happened. First and foremost, however, a chart is a representation of part of the real world, so it makes sense to start by looking at the earth as a whole. Our earth is an uneven, slightly flattened ball of rock spinning through space. To simplify the job of defining directions, distances and positions (the navigator's term for locations) on its surface, it is divided up by a grid of imaginary lines of latitude and longitude. It is somewhat like the grid on a street map, but with the important difference that the grid of latitude and longitude is not purely arbitrary.

Latitude and Longitude

The fact that the earth is spinning gives us two natural reference points, at the ends of the axis of spin, called the North and South Poles. Exactly midway between them, and at right angles to the axis, is the equator, running around the fattest part of the earth. Latitude can be defined as angular distance from the equator measured at the center of the earth.

Of course, lots of places are exactly the same distance north of the equator. If you were to join together all the points that are, say, 50° north, the result would be a circle running around the earth, parallel to the equator; so it is called a parallel of latitude (Figure 1–1). Parallels of latitude are equivalent to the horizontal lines in the grid on a street plan,

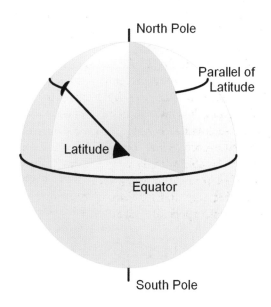

Fig 1-1 The latitude of a place is its distance from the equator, expressed in degrees, measured at the center of the earth.

and appear as horizontal lines on most navigational charts.

The corresponding vertical lines on the chart are called meridians. They run from Pole to Pole. The equator was a reasonably obvious baseline from which to measure latitude, but you could draw any number of meridians between the Poles, none of which has any particularly strong case for being singled out as a starting point for measurements of longitude.

For historic reasons, though, the meridian that passes through the Greenwich Observatory in London is internationally accepted as the prime meridian. So the longitude of somewhere can be defined as the angular distance between its meridian and the prime meridian, measured at the center of the earth (Figure 1–2).

Latitude and longitude are both angles, so they are normally expressed in degrees. Latitude is measured as 0° at the equator and increases until it becomes 90° north or south at each Pole. Longitude is 0° at Greenwich increasing to 180° east and west. The earth is so big, however, that one degree measured at its center corresponds to up to 60 miles at its surface. For this reason each degree is usually broken down into 60 minutes, while for even greater precision, each minute can be further

subdivided—either into 60 seconds, or into decimal parts.

Nowadays decimal parts are much more common, so you are likely to find the position of Portland Head Light—the very first lighthouse built by the fledgling U.S. government back in 1791—for instance, given as 43° 37.38' N, 070° 12.47' W. Note that, by convention, latitude is always given first followed by longitude and that their directions (north or south, and east or west) are always included. They are important, because 43° 37.38' N, 070° 12.47' E is a desolate hillside northwest of Kyrgyzstan in Russia, hundreds of miles from the sea, while 43° 37.38' S, 070° 12.47' W is another remote and inhospitable spot in the Andean foothills of Argentina. Note also that since latitude only goes to 90 degrees while longitude extends to 180, by convention we always use two digits for the whole degrees of latitude while longitude requires three, even though the first one is normally zero here in the U.S.

Geodetic Datums

The working definitions of latitude and longitude given earlier in this chapter are something of an over-simplification, because the earth is not a perfect sphere and does not actually spin around a fixed axis. It is slightly flattened, uneven in shape and composition, and it wobbles. This means that it has several "centers" depending on which part of its surface you are most interested in, so cartographers use slightly different grids of latitude and longitude for different parts of the world (Figure 1–3). Until recently this was of purely academic interest to yacht navigators, but with the advent of satellite positioning systems it has assumed much greater significance, because positions obtained from GPS (see Chapter 3), are normally based on the World Geodetic System of 1984 (WGS-84) Datum.

Current U.S. charts are drawn using the North American Datum of 1983 (NAD 83). Though it is actually slightly different, this

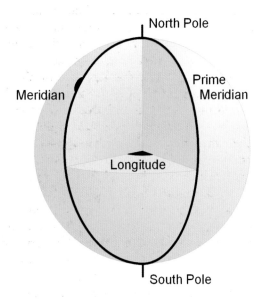

Fig 1–2 The longitude of a place is the angle between the meridian that passes through it and the prime (Greenwich) meridian.

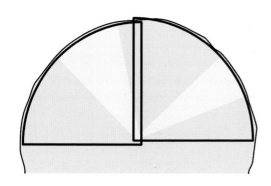

Fig 1–3 The earth is not a perfect sphere, so it has many possible "centers," giving us many possible grids of latitude and longitude—or "horizontal datums."

datum is navigationally equivalent to the WGS 84. Some old charts, however, are still based on the North American Datum of 1927 (NAD 27), though they are steadily disappearing. Be aware that the differences between NAD 27 and NAD 83 paper charts can possibly range from 100 feet in Maine to 1,500 feet in Hawaii. In other parts of the world, charts are based on yet different formats such as WGS 72, European Datum 1950 (ED50), or possibly on their local and regional datums. For example, in the Bahamas and the Caribbean, some of the paper charts are extremely old and contain errors of 500 feet or more. In other parts of the world, the errors may be several miles. Although this is enough to be significant when navigating close inshore, traditional navigators need not be concerned by it; they will be changing from charts drawn on one datum to charts drawn on another so far from land that the discrepancy will pass unnoticed. It is important, however, for those using satellite navigators; although most sets can be adjusted to give positions referenced to any of the most widely used datums, they do not change over automatically; it is up to the

operator to select the appropriate datum for the chart in use. Eventually, the problem will disappear. Most new charts are now drawn on WGS84 or on a datum such as ETRS89 (European Terrestrial Reference System) or NAD 83, which are effectively identical to it.

Direction

The grid of latitude and longitude also gives us a reference for our measurement of direction—north being the direction of a meridian heading toward the North Pole, while south is the direction of a meridian heading toward the South Pole. East and west are at right angles to these two, with east being the direction of the earth's rotation and west the opposite.

Cardinal Notation

Directions between these four cardinal points can be given names too: The four half-cardinal points are called northeast, southeast, southwest and northwest. Continuing this process of sub-division produces eight quarter-cardinal points, each of which takes the name of the nearest cardinal point followed by the name of the nearest half-cardinal: north-north-east, east-north-east, east-south-east and so on. A third sub-division introduces sixteen by-points—so called because their names include the word "by," as in "north by east," meaning "a little bit east of north"; "north-east by north" meaning "a little bit north of north-east" and so on.

This cardinal system served seamen and navigators well for centuries, but the names are unwieldy, and even using the full 32 points and by-points gives precision no better than 11¼°, so for most navigational purposes it has now been superseded. Cardinal, half-cardinal and even quarter-cardinal points still have their place in applications such as weather forecasts, where any more precise notation would give the listener a misleading impression of accuracy.

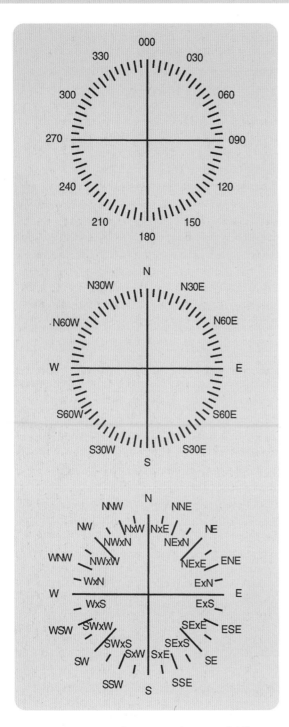

Fig 1–4 Direction can be expressed in several different ways: modern, three-figure notation (top); obsolete, quadrantal notation (middle); or traditional, points notation (bottom).

Quadrantal Notation

One way of defining directions with greater precision involves using the four cardinal points to split the compass into four quadrants, then specifying the direction within each quadrant in terms of degrees, from north or south toward east or west. So "north-east" became "north 45° east," "south-south-west" became "south 22½° west," and so on. This has the merit of precision, and was reasonably easily understood by seafarers who were used to the old points notation, but the names are still cumbersome, and any calculation that involves adding or subtracting angles is decidedly tricky.

Three-figure Notation

Almost all navigators now use the three-figure notation, in which directions are referred to as angles, measured clockwise from north, so east is 090°, south is 180° and west is 270°. As the name "three-figure notation" suggests, they are always written and spoken as three distinct figures, so you might say "steer zero two zero" but never "steer twenty degrees."

Distance

The standard unit of distance used at sea is the *nautical mile*, now internationally defined as 1,852 meters (6,076 feet or 2,025 yards), making it about 15% longer than a statute mile. It is not a purely arbitrary figure, but is based on another older unit of distance called the sea mile—which is the length of one minute of latitude at the surface of the earth. Unfortunately, because the earth is not a perfect sphere, the length of a sea mile varies slightly from place to place, ranging from 1,843 meters (6,047 feet) at the equator to 1,862 meters (6,109 feet) at the Poles. The discrepancy between these two and between either of them and the international nautical mile is so small that for most practical navigation purposes it can be ignored, and a minute of latitude taken to be a nautical mile. A minute of longitude is useless as a measure of distance because it varies from 1,855 meters (6,086 feet) at the equator to zero at the Poles. So to sum up: When measuring distance in nautical miles, use the latitude scale down the side of your chart: e.g., 6 minutes of latitude equals 6 miles. Distances less than a mile are nowadays often given in meters or sometimes yards (we're still taking to metrification rather slowly!), but you may still come across distances given in cables. A cable is a very old nautical unit of measure that equals one tenth of a nautical mile or about 200 yards.

Speed

Speed, of course, is distance covered divided by the time taken, so at sea the most common unit of speed is a nautical mile per hour, known as a knot. The name, incidentally, comes from the days when speed was measured by throwing a "log chip" overboard. The log chip was a small, flat piece of wood, ballasted so that it floated upright in the water to serve as a miniature sea anchor. Attached to it was a long piece of string with knots at 100-foot intervals. The number of knots that were dragged overboard in one minute as the ship sailed away from its log chip gave its speed in nautical miles per hour.

Navigational Terminology

Direction is so important in navigation that navigators have many different words for it, just as Eskimos have many different words for snow. Each has a precise meaning, so they are not interchangeable:

Bearing is the direction of one object from another, e.g., "the lighthouse is on a bearing of 270," or "the lighthouse bears 270" means "the lighthouse is to the west of us."

Course is the direction in which the boat is being steered, and is ideally (but rarely) the same as . . .

Heading which is the direction the boat is pointing at any given moment. So if the

navigator asks the helmsman "what is your heading?" he means "what direction is the boat actually pointing now?" rather than "in what direction is it supposed to be pointing?"

Track Angle is the direction in which the boat is moving—as opposed to the direction in which it is pointing. The word "angle" is most often omitted. For some purposes it is useful to differentiate between the water track sometimes called the wake course, meaning the direction in which the boat is moving through the water, and the ground track—the direction in which it is moving over the seabed. To help make this distinction, the water track is often simply called the track, while the ground track is called the course made good (CMG) or the course over ground (COG).

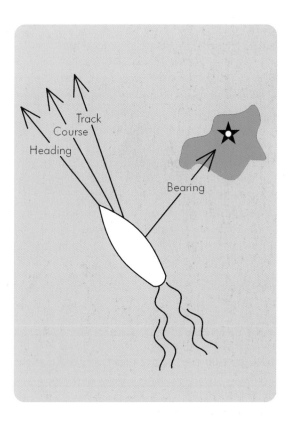

Fig 1–5 Navigators have several different words for "direction," each with its own distinct meaning.

Charts

Every major maritime nation has a government department or agency responsible for producing official charts of its own waters, and in some cases of the waters around former colonies or dependencies. In the U.S., the National Ocean Service (NOS), a division of the National Oceanic and Atmospheric Administration (NOAA), is responsible for providing nautical charts for most of the nation, with a suite of over 1000 charts encompassing the coasts of the U.S., the Great Lakes, and the U.S. territories. NGA, the National Geospatial-Intelligence Agency (formerly the National Image and Mapping Agency—NIMA) is responsible for producing deep water charts and charts for foreign waters. The U.S. Army Corps of Engineers produces charts for the Mississippi River and other inland waterways. The activities of the various national agencies are coordinated (though not directly controlled) by the International Hydrographic Organization. Thanks largely to the efforts of the IHO, there is a fair degree of standardization among the official charts of different countries, so if you can navigate on a U.S. chart you should not find it too difficult to work with a British, French or Norwegian one. Whether you will ever need to is largely a matter of choice, because, as noted above, the National Geospatial-Intelligence Agency (NGA), is one of few agencies to publish its own charts of the whole world; you'll rarely ever need foreign charts.

In some respects the requirements of the yacht navigator are quite different from those of his counterpart onboard a ship. In particular, a yacht may not have room to spread a full sized chart, nor the stowage space available for a large stock. For this reason, some Hydrographic Offices—including NOS—produce special small craft charts, as do commercial publishing houses. In the U.S. you'll find a number of sources of privately-produced charts, including books in which a whole region's worth of charts is presented in one convenient and economical package—individual paper charts are becoming exceedingly expensive. You'll undoubtedly discover a wide variety at your favorite marine store, whether it is "brick and mortar" or online. There are also waterproof charts, which are excellent for navigating small, open fishing and dive boats on which the probability of getting thoroughly soaked often extends to just about everything aboard! Many waterproof charts are available with additional notations of special interest to fishing and/or diving.

Chart Projections

A chart is intended to be an accurate representation of part of the earth. Unfortunately, despite the best efforts of surveyors and cartographers, it can never be absolutely perfect, because the earth's surface is curved while a chart is flat. There are many different ways of projecting a curved surface onto a flat one, but they all introduce distortions of one kind or another, so which projection the cartographer decides to use is determined by which distortions are acceptable and which are intolerable. In other words, it is determined by the chart's intended purpose. On a political map of the world in a school atlas, for instance, the main requirement may be for the whole map to be at the same scale, so that all countries appear to be the right size compared to each other. For navigation, the most important requirement is usually that direction should be undistorted, so that north appears to be in the same direction everywhere on the chart, and that a straight line (such as a bearing or a constant course) appears to be straight when it is drawn on the chart. Although, strictly speaking, projections are defined mathematically, it can be quite useful to visualize them as the picture that would be cast on a sheet of paper wrapped around a transparent globe with a light somewhere in the middle.

Mercator Charts

One of the most useful projections for navigation is the Mercator projection, which—using the globe and paper analogy—would be the result of rolling the paper into a cylinder, centered on the earth's axis so that it touched the globe only at the equator, while the globe is lit internally by an all-around light at its center (see Figure 1–6). The effect is to make meridians appear on the chart as vertical parallel lines, and the parallels of latitude as horizontal parallel lines.

From the coastal navigator's point of view, this meets the main requirement of making a straight course appear as a straight line on the chart. Its relatively minor disadvantage is that distances are distorted. On the real world the meridians converge toward the Poles, so making them parallel on the chart involves "stretching" land masses near the Poles. Having stretched east–west distances to account for the distorted meridians, north–south distances have to be stretched as well, to preserve the shape of land masses, so the parallels of latitude are not evenly spaced, but are moved farther apart toward the Poles. On a chart covering an area that reaches from

the Bay of Fundy to Cape Cod (NOAA Chart 13260) this change of scale is large enough to be apparent with normal plotting instruments, but for most coastal navigation it can be almost entirely ignored.

Gnomonic Charts

You are quite likely to come across references to charts drawn on the gnomonic projection, because this was once widely used for ocean routing charts and charts covering polar areas. Although polar charts are no longer drawn on the gnomonic projection, polar areas provide perhaps the most obvious example of why the Mercator projection is not always appropriate. On the real world, the meridians come together at the Poles, yet the parallel meridians of a Mercator chart, by definition, can never meet. This paradox can only be resolved by using another projection.

Going back to the globe and paper analogy, gnomonic projection can be seen as the image that would be cast by a translucent globe, with a point source of light at its center, standing on a flat piece of paper (Figure 1–7). The globe and paper will be in contact with each other at

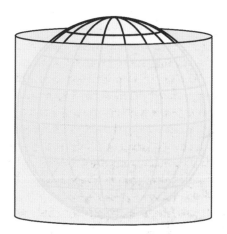

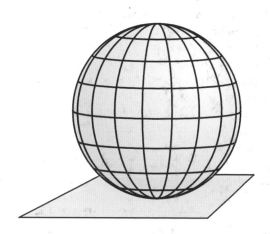

Fig 1–6 A Mercator chart can be seen as the image that would be cast on a paper cylinder by an illuminated globe inside it.

Fig 1–7 A gnomonic chart is the image that would be cast by an illuminated globe standing on a flat sheet of paper.

only one point (called the tangent point). This could be anywhere, though for polar charts the obvious place to choose is the Pole itself. The result is a pattern of meridians and parallels that looks rather like a spider's web, with meridians radiating outwards from the Pole, and the parallels forming a pattern of concentric rings. One obvious drawback of this arrangement is that north appears to be in a different direction on different parts of the chart: on a chart showing the North Pole, for instance, north would be straight upwards from the middle of the bottom edge, but straight downwards from the middle of the top edge. This, however, is inevitable on any chart that attempts to represent polar areas, and the main reason that gnomonic projection has fallen out of favor for polar charts is that the scale changes as you move away from the Pole in much the same way as the scale of a Mercator chart changes as you move away from the equator. This effect is minimized, though not completely eliminated, by the projection now used for polar charts called the Universal Polar Stereographic, for which the point source of light in our globe and paper analogy has been moved from the center of the earth to the opposite pole.

Transverse Mercator Projections

Very rarely, you'll see a chart based on the transverse Mercator projection, which can be visualized as the image that would be cast on a roll of paper wrapped around the globe so that it touches both poles (see Figure 1–8). The transverse Mercator projection is mathematically complicated, has curved meridians and parallels, and suffers distortions of scale in much the same way as a Mercator projection, but has technical advantages for surveyors and mathematicians specializing in precise positioning and the shape of the earth. Here in the U.S. you'll rarely encounter a nautical chart based on the Transverse Mercator projection. But if you should happen to encounter one in some other part of the

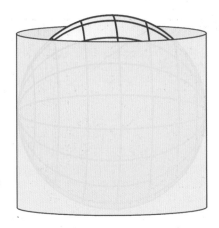

Fig 1–8 A transverse Mercator chart is like a regular Mercator chart, but with the globe's north/south axis running transversely.

world, realize that as far as practical navigation is concerned, charts drawn on the transverse Mercator projection cover such small areas that the distortions involved are negligible, and you can treat them as normal Mercator charts.

Rhumb Lines and Great Circles

The only charts still being drawn on a true gnomonic projection are those used for planning ocean passages. To appreciate the reason for this, imagine that you plan to sail from Newport, Rhode Island to Bermuda so you want to find the shortest distance. You might do it by sticking pins in a globe—one in Newport the other in Bermuda—and stretching an elastic band between them. The elastic band will naturally shorten itself until it lies along the shortest possible route. This is called a great circle route because it is part of a great circle whose center coincides with the center of the earth. It would not, however, cross every meridian at the same angle, so if you transfer a great circle route to a Mercator chart you find it forms a curve, bulging away from the equator (see Figure 1–9). The longer, constant-course route that appears as a straight line on

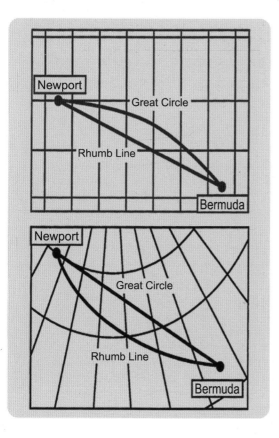

Fig 1–9 A Mercator chart (top) is most useful for navigation, except that the shortest distance between two points (a great circle) appears as a curve. On a gnomonic chart, the great circle route is straight.

a Mercator chart is called a rhumb line. For practical yacht navigation on passages less than about five or six hundred miles in length, the difference between the two is negligible; so coastal and offshore navigators can reasonably refer only to Mercator charts and rhumb line courses.

Scale

The representation of the earth's surface depicted on a chart is, of course, considerably smaller than the corresponding area on the earth itself. We are quite used to thinking of road maps being drawn to a scale of perhaps three miles to the inch, or of U.S. Geological Survey (USGS) topographic maps at one and a quarter inches to the mile, meaning that one and a quarter inches on the map represents one mile on the real world. Another way of expressing this is to say that distances on the map are one fifty-thousandth of the corresponding distance on the earth's surface, or that the map is drawn to a scale of 1:50,000.

All chart projections involve some degree of distortion; in particular the scale of a Mercator chart changes between its top and bottom edges, so the quoted scale of a chart is true only at a certain specified latitude, usually the one at the middle.

The expressions "large scale" and "small scale" often seem to be a source of confusion, but it may help to remember that the larger the number shown in the scale's ratio, the smaller the scale of the chart. Also remember that although a chart can cover a large geographical area or be drawn to a large scale, no single chart can ever be both: large scale equals small area. Alternatively you can think of charts as being divided into four main groups:

Sailing Charts are the smallest scale charts. They cover a lot of territory and are used for planning, fixing position at sea and for plotting dead reckoning while proceeding on a long voyage. The scale is generally 1:600,000 or smaller. The shoreline and topography are generalized and only offshore soundings, the principal navigational lights, outer buoys, and landmarks visible at considerable distances are shown.

General Charts are intended for coastwise navigation outside of outlying reefs and shoals. The scales range from about 1:150,000 to 1:600,000.

Coastal Charts are intended for inshore coastwise navigation, for entering or leaving bays and harbors of considerable width, and for navigating large inland waterways. The scales range from about 1:50,001 to 1:150,000.

Harbor Charts are intended for navigation and anchorage in harbors and small waterways. The scale is generally larger than 1:50,000, and can be as large as 1:2,000.

The Chart Title Panel

All charts are identified by a number and a name, or title, such as *Salem and Lynn Harbors*, to give some indication of the area covered. The title is printed somewhere on the face side, but its position varies from chart to chart so as not to obscure important detail. Immediately under the title is a lot of small print including specifications of the chart itself, such as the units of measurement of depths; the datum levels from which depths are measured; the scale, geodetic datum, and the projection used (see Figure 1–10).

Finally, there may be several notices and warnings. Do not dismiss these as being irrelevant to yachts, because, although most concern bigger vessels and commercial shipping, it is becoming increasingly common to find references to harbor regulations and other details that affect small craft.

Each NOAA chart, with the exception of international charts, has a 5-digit number in addition to its name or title. The numbers can be found in the lower left hand corner of paper charts (and often also in other corners so the number will be visible no matter how the chart is folded or rolled for stowage). Charts are numbered in sequence, though there are often continuity gaps within any given series of charts, a potentially confusing reality caused by there often being several types of charts available for that area. A perfect example would be the Small-Craft Charts issued for the Atlantic Intracoastal Waterway being

UNITED STATES - EAST COAST

MASSACHUSETTS

SALEM AND LYNN HARBORS

Mercator Projection
Scale 1:25,000 at Lat. 42° 29'
North American Datum of 1983
(World Geodetic System 1984)
SOUNDINGS IN FEET
AT MEAN LOWER LOW WATER

Fig 1–10 The title panel for NOAA chart No. 13275

interspersed with Coastal Charts (which also include more of the offshore waters) for the same region. Above the chart number is the edition number followed by the month and year that the chart was printed (see Figure 1–11). Charts printed in 2003 and later show the exact dates that charts were corrected for corrections published in the USCG Local Notice to Mariners and also in NGA's U.S. Notice to Mariners. Mariners should update their charts by applying corrections that appear in those publications after the dates appearing on the chart (see below). This area of the chart will also display the meaning of any latticed overprinting such as "D" for Decca; "Loran-C Overprinted" for Loran C; and "Omega Overprinted" for Omega.

Metrification

Traditionally, the numbers indicating depth on U.S. charts have represented feet or, in some cases, especially with older surveys, fathoms, an ancient nautical measure that equals 6 feet. At the present time, NOAA is in the process of converting charts from traditional units to metric units—except for the nautical mile, which is too convenient to change. This conversion to metric units is a multiyear effort that will take a while to complete. In the meantime, just remember this: Every chart clearly states the depth units it employs, and in several prominent places, at that. Be sure you note this carefully every time you change

L

26th Ed., Jul. /04 ■ Corrected through NM Jul. 31/04
Corrected through LNM Jul. 13/04

11439
LORAN-C OVERPRINTED

Fig 1–11 This chart's title is *Sand Key To Rebecca Shoal*, which is an area just west of Key West, Florida.

charts; there is too wide a discrepancy between a foot, a fathom and a meter to risk using the wrong measurement unit simply because it is what you *were* using with the previous chart.

Chart Symbols

There are numerous features in the real world that may be of navigational interest, but are too small or complicated to be accurately represented at the same scale as the rest of the chart. Reduced to 1/75,000 of its real size to appear on a coastal chart, for instance, a prominent church would be barely a millimeter long, a lighthouse would be smaller than a period in this book, and a buoy reduced to a microscopic speck. Symbols overcome this problem, and NOAA uses the same ones to represent the same objects on all its charts, though there are some variations to account for different scales. There are too many of them for any chart to include a comprehensive key such as you might find on a road atlas. Instead, NOAA publishes a booklet called Chart No. 1. Officially titled *United States of America Nautical Chart Symbols, Abbreviations and Terms*, it is no longer printed by the government, but is still available in printed form from private publishers. You'll probably find it at your favorite marine store. The easiest way to obtain a copy, however, is to download it in Portable Document Format (PDF) from: http://www.nauticalcharts.noaa.gov/mcd/chartn o1.htm. It is wise to memorize the more common symbols, but equally so to keep a copy on hand for quick reference whenever you run into that curious new chart symbol you've never seen before, as you certainly will if you ever cruise beyond your local waters.

COLREGS Demarcation Lines

On all NOAA charts that include both inland and offshore waters, lines have been established to delineate those waters upon which mariners must comply with the Inland Navigational Rules Act of 1980 (Inland Rules).

The waters inside of the lines are Inland Rules waters, and the waters outside of the lines are COLREGS (International Rules) waters. In most cases, the line is drawn across the mouths of inlets and rivers, though this is not always so. In *every* case, it will be clearly shown as a magenta line that's labeled: "COLREGS Demarcation Line."

Acquiring Charts

NOAA has about 1,200 authorized agents—probably including your nearest marine supply store—that will undoubtedly also stock charts in various forms from private publishers as well. Of course, you can also go directly to the Office of Coast Survey's Web site at http://www.nauticalcharts.noaa.gov/. The "How to Obtain Charts" link will take you to the NOS page with several more source options to click on in addition to charts, including where to find some of the various publications we'll discuss later in the chapter. This Web page can be most helpful. The "View Charts" link will take you to NOAA's On-Line Chart Viewer, where you can select charts to preview in their entirety, with considerable ability to zoom in to check out smaller details. These views are not intended for navigation, and trying to print screen captures is usually less than satisfactory for navigational purposes, but they can be a great help in deciding which particular charts will best serve your needs and can even aid in cruise planning when you aren't aboard your boat.

Chart Corrections

The real world is constantly changing. On land, buildings are put up or knocked down, road layouts are changed, and new roads built, so most people have probably found themselves driving along a road that does not appear on their road map. Much the same happens at sea: the shape of the coastlines and seabeds can be changed by the action of wind and water, deep water channels can be dredged or harbors silt up, and buoys or navigation

marks can be installed, moved, or taken away altogether. On land, where we often navigate mainly by signposts and where the consequences of getting lost are seldom disastrous, an out-of-date map is merely annoying, but at sea we are so much more dependent on charts that it is important to keep them up to date.

There are three ways of achieving this, of which the most drastic is for the issuing agency to publish a new chart or a new edition of an existing chart. This may happen when an area has been re-surveyed, when it has been affected by several major changes or by a very large number of minor ones. The vast majority of changes, however, are nowhere near important enough to warrant the production of a new chart and can be written on to an existing chart by hand, in pen and ink.

In U.S. waters, a mariner using paper charts can rely on three publications to provide update information: the USCG Local Notice to Mariners (LNM); National Geospatial-Intelligence Agency (NGA) Notice to Mariners (NtM); and in the Great Lakes and St. Lawrence Seaway, the Canadian Coast Guard Notice to Mariners (NOTMAR).

The USCG's LNM are published weekly by each of 9 individual Coast Guard Districts. They are the primary source of information for most detailed chart updates. If you choose no other source of update information, be sure to include your appropriate LNM on your weekly critical reading list. LNMs used to be sent by mail to all who had signed up to receive them. Now, however, they are available only on line as downloaded PDFs, though you can sign up for weekly e-mail reminders. The URL is: http://www.navcen.uscg.gov/LNM/default.htm, which will lead you to links for LNM from the district(s) of interest to you.

The NGA NtM is also published weekly and, for the most part, contains the same information published in the USCG LNMs. However, the NGA NtM is primarily intended for deep ocean vessels and typically does not carry LNM chart updates that affect waters shallower than 18 feet. Occasionally, an NTM will contain information that was not originally published in the USCG LNM, therefore it is wise to check both publications routinely. NGA NtMs are also available only on line—to either view or download—through a "Notice to Mariners" link on NGA's Web site at http://www.nga.mil/portal/site/maritime. The Notice to Mariners page also offers the opportunity to search a database of corrections by chart number.

Since some U.S. and Canadian charts overlap, the Canadian Coast Guard's Notice to Mariners will sometimes contain unique information not found in the USCG LNM. NOTMARs are published monthly and are also available on line. The URL is: http://www.notmar.gc.ca.

Sometimes there are changes that are too big or complicated for pen-and-ink corrections, but which affect only a relatively small area of the chart. In these cases the NGA publishes a block correction, often called a "patch," which is a new section that can be pasted on to the existing chart, to replace the affected area.

When correcting a folio (set) of charts it is a good idea to begin by arranging the charts in numerical order, because the searchable database requires you to list the charts by number, rather than by name. It will then show you all the relevant notices affecting each chart. Each Notice gives simple but very specific instructions about the correction to apply to each chart: in most cases you are told to "insert," "move" or "delete" a symbol at some specified position. Convention dictates that pen and ink corrections should be made in violet ink using a fine nib drawing pen, but in practice any waterproof ink—such as a fine red ballpoint—will do. Block corrections, or patches, are also included in the *Notices to Mariners* and are simply printed and then cut out and pasted in place. It is worth rounding off the corners slightly to prevent them lifting when the chart is in use, and it is a good idea

to mark the exact position of the block on the chart before applying any paste. "Wet" paste is best applied to the chart, as this is less likely to distort than the block, but with modern "dry" paste this precaution is unnecessary.

Finally, once the correction (pen-and-ink or block) has been applied, write the year, and the number of the *Notice to Mariners*, in the bottom left-hand margin of the chart. The virtue of this is that it will later provide a double-check that all the relevant corrections have been applied, because each *Notice to Mariners* (NtM) includes a note of the last Notice affecting that chart. NtMs also include temporary notices giving details of short-lived changes, and preliminary Notices giving advance warning of changes that are about to occur or for which full details are not yet available. It would be pointless to mark these on the chart in indelible ink so they should be applied in pencil.

Updating "New" Charts

You'll often have to apply updates to charts you've just purchased. You might ask, "Why? They're brand new aren't they?" Well, consider this reality: NOAA currently maintains over a thousand charts. They are printed in batches and stored and then issued from inventory through a worldwide network of 1,200 authorized agents. Chart agents can have thousands of dollars of capital tied up in stock. As a result, charts can be two or more years out of date by the time they are sold. Charts are not corrected while in stock awaiting sale (though this was common practice years ago, it is no longer economically viable), so the purchaser must check all Notices to Mariners subsequent to the print-date and make all applicable corrections. This can be a time-consuming process, but it is important enough to bear with it nonetheless.

There is an alternative, however: Print On Demand (POD) charts. As the name suggests, a POD chart is a paper chart that isn't printed until the time of purchase and thus it can contain all the updates that have been made up until then. For example, let's say you buy a paper chart that has an edition date one year prior to the purchase. Traditionally, the chart must be brought up to date by manual corrections. If you purchase a POD chart, however, all updates that have been published in the year between the edition date and the purchase date have already been applied. (Of course, once you've purchased a POD chart, all future corrections are up to you.) POD charts are produced by NOAA's private partner, Ocean Grafix, and are available through licensed agents, many of which have the ability to print the charts on site, so you can receive them immediately on purchase. You can also order them directly from the Ocean Grafix Web site at http://www.OceanGrafix.com.

Other Publications

Navigation can require a mass of other information that cannot be shown on a chart without cluttering it or confusing the picture, so a large, long-distance cruising yacht may well carry quite a library of reference books including:

n *The United States Coast Pilot*® covers a variety of information important to navigators of coastal and intracoastal waters and the Great Lakes. Issued in nine volumes to fully cover our extensive coastlines, Coast Pilots contain supplemental information that is difficult to portray on a nautical chart. Coast Pilots include channel descriptions, anchorages, bridge and cable clearances, currents, tide and water levels, prominent features, pilotage, towage, traffic separation schemes, small-craft facilities, and federal regulations that are applicable to navigation. Coast Pilots are available online for purchase or download (as PDFs) at http://www.nauticalcharts.noaa.gov/nsd/cpdownload.htm. The Coast Guard's LNMs usually contain info on new editions when they become available and also include

corrections to apply between editions. If you sign up for the LNM e-mail notices, this info will be included when appropriate. Corrections to date are also available as a PDF download as well. Coast Pilots are geared more (though not entirely) toward commercial shipping, but much of the valuable information will be available nowhere else, so they can be well worth having aboard yachts.

n *Light Lists* contain detailed information about every currently active aid to navigation (ATON) from lighthouses to unlighted "daybeacons" and more. The lists include descriptions that will help identify each ATON by day, and where appropriate, the ATON's "characteristics," the light pattern that identifies it by night (see Chapter 6), as well as the geographic coordinates of each individual ATON, which is also identified by a unique "Light List Number." Because this information can be much more detailed than could possibly fit on any chart, regardless of its scale, having a light list aboard will provide invaluable data that are often very helpful to the navigator. Light Lists for the U.S. are published by the Coast Guard in 7 volumes. They are available in printed form (for about $40 to $50 each) from chart agents and the other usual sources, or they can be downloaded as PDFs at http://www.navcen.uscg.gov/pubs/LightLists/LightLists.htm. As we saw with LNMs, this site contains links to the 7 different individual volumes as well as to a summary of corrections to date and other related matter.

n *NOAA Tide Tables* are produced in two volumes. One covers the east coast of North and South America including Greenland, while the other covers the west coast of North and South America including the Hawaiian Islands. As we saw with *Chart No. 1*, these volumes are no longer printed by the government, but have been assigned to private publishers. We'll discuss Tide Tables in greater detail in Chapter 5.

n *Tidal Current Tables* show the times of Slack Water, and both Maximum flood and Maximum ebb currents, plus the predicted velocity of each, as well as the directions of the flood and ebb, for a number of critical locations on the Atlantic and Pacific coasts of the U.S. and Canada from New Brunswick around to British Columbia. These, too, are generated by NOAA but published privately.

n **Yachtsmen's Almanacs** Although much of the above information is almost indispensable, the format of the official publications—generally substantial books giving considerable detail and covering wide geographic areas—is inconvenient and can be expensive for most pleasure craft, so several commercial publishers produce yachtsmen's almanacs, dealing with smaller areas and in slightly less detail. Of these, the best known and most popular is the *Reed's Nautical Almanac* published in 3 editions to cover the east and west coasts of the U.S. plus the Caribbean. As well as providing data about lights, fog signals, radio services and tides, most yachtsmen's almanacs offer a compendium of other useful information such as the collision regulations, notes on radio procedure and seamanship, and brief details of harbors. Another well-known publication with similar, though slightly less extensive, information is *Eldridge's Tide and Pilot Book*.

n **Cruising Guides** are produced by a number of specialist publishers and by some clubs and associations. They vary considerably in scope, content and style: Some concentrate on hard factual information; some give detailed directions on routes in and out of harbors, and complete listings of available facilities,

such as marinas, fuel docks and "pump-out" stations; while others are more like tourist guidebooks, so choosing which to use is very much a matter of personal taste and preference. No matter what their focus, hard facts or fancy, they all provide information geared to yachtsmen, rather than shipping interests, but, unfortunately, even the more fact-oriented volumes can vary in the quality of their updating. For U.S. and Bahamian waters, most guide books are updated annually. Some are less accurate than others, however, though these inaccuracies usually vary with the location being considered and even from year to year. Fortunately, a few of them seem to be spot on every year for every item printed therein. Until you learn for yourself the overall accuracy of any particular publication, always double check its information with another source, if possible. That said, understand that these cruising guides, even if occasionally wrong on a detail or two, still provide information you probably won't find anywhere else and are invaluable for cruising.

n *Sailing Directions,* a 47-volume set of navigation books published by the National Geospatial-Intelligence Agency (NGA). There are 37 Enroute volumes and 10 Planning Guides. Planning Guides describe general features of ocean basins; Enroutes describe features of coastlines, ports, and harbors. *Sailing Directions* are either totally unnecessary or absolutely priceless, the qualifying factor being whether you leave U.S. waters. As long as you stay close to home (though the term "U.S. waters" covers a vast area) you simply don't need *Sailing Directions*. If you "go foreign," however, you most certainly do as they are dedicated to foreign waters: with detailed information on how to get "there"—the different volumes cover different areas—and what to expect when you arrive.

2 Measuring Direction and Distance

Chapter 1 concentrated on the chart as a source of information, but it has an equally important role as a work sheet on which passages can be planned and the boat's position monitored. Both of these involve measuring direction and distance.

Measuring Distance at Sea

The old type of log that gave us the knot as a unit of speed (page 7) has long since given way to more sophisticated mechanical and electronic devices.

Walker Log

One of the oldest is the Walker log. This uses a torpedo-shaped spinner a few inches long, towed behind the boat on a length of braided line. As it moves through the water, spiral fins on the torpedo make it spin, twisting the line. The onboard end of the line is hooked onto the back of the log instrument, where it turns a shaft connected to a reduction gearbox. This in turn moves the hands on a series of dials, somewhat like those of an old-fashioned gas meter, to give a direct reading of the distance the spinner has moved through the water. Advantages of the Walker log are its rugged simplicity and the ease with which weed or debris can be cleared from the spinner. Its disadvantages are that its display has to be mounted right at the back of the boat; that the log line (usually 30 or 60 feet in length) has to be streamed before the log can be used, and recovered before entering harbor; it tends to

under-read at very low speeds; and at speeds over about ten knots the spinner is inclined to jump out of the water and skitter along the surface.

There are definite techniques for streaming and recovering a mechanical trailing log, intended to reduce the risk of the line tangling. To stream the log, first attach the onboard end to the hook on the back of the display unit. Then, keeping the spinner in hand, feed out all the line to form a long U-shaped loop astern before dropping the spinner overboard, well off to one side of the loop. Some owners like to hold on to the line just astern of the display unit for a few seconds, just to absorb the snatch as the load comes on to the line. When recovering the log, speed is essential, especially if the boat is moving fast. Unclip the inboard end from the hook on the back of the display, and drop it overboard, allowing it to trail out astern while you pull in the log line. Then holding the spinner, gather in the line, coiling it as you go. Trailing the line astern like this allows any kinks to unravel.

Electrical Trailing Log

The electrical trailing log is superficially similar to a Walker log, inasmuch as it uses a spinner towed astern of the boat on a long line. In this case, however, the spinner is in two parts, and the "log line" is an electrical cable. The front part of the spinner is attached to the cable and only the rear part is free to rotate. As it does so, an electronic sensor in the front part makes and breaks an electrical circuit, so the onboard display unit receives a short pulse of electricity each time the spinner rotates. These pulses are counted electronically and are presented as a digital display of speed and distance run. The advantages and disadvantages of this type of log are much the same as for the mechanical Walker log except that it is dependent on electrical power from internal dry batteries, which in return allows the display unit to be mounted almost anywhere onboard, and that because the line itself is not twisting, it is easier to stream and recover.

Hull-mounted Impeller Logs

On cruising boats, hull-mounted logs are by far the most popular type, though in principle they are much the same as the electrical trailing log: a rotating impeller sends a stream of electrical impulses to a display unit mounted in the cockpit or near the chart table. The impeller—which can be either a miniature version of the trailing log's spinner, or a paddle wheel an inch or so in diameter—is mounted in a fitting called a transducer, which either protrudes through the bottom of the boat or hangs down below the transom. The disadvantages of this system are that an impeller so close to the hull can be affected by the water flow around the hull itself, and that it is difficult and potentially dangerous to withdraw the transducer to clear weed or debris from it at sea. The reason in-hull logs are so popular is primarily the convenience of not having to stream and recover 30 feet or more of log line at the beginning and end of each passage.

Other Logs

At the top of the scale of price and sophistication are several alternative methods of measuring speed through the water:

Electromagnetic logs are based on the same principle as generators and electric motors: that electricity is created if you move a magnetic field past an electrical conductor. In this case the conductor is sea water and the magnetic field is created by the transducer. As the transducer moves through the water a small electric current is set up, measured by sensors on the transducer.

Sonic logs use accurate measurements of the speed of sound between two transducers mounted one ahead of the other. Each transducer emits a continuous stream of clicks, inaudible to the human ear, while listening for clicks transmitted from the other. When the boat is moving, the movement of the water past the hull slows down the clicks traveling forward while speeding up those traveling aft. The instrument accurately measures the time taken for each click to make the trip, compares them, converts the results into a display of speed through the water, and from this calculates the distance run. Another type of sonic log uses sophisticated echo sounder technology to measure the rate at which plankton and debris are moving past its transducer.

The big advantages of all three types are that they are much less susceptible to fouling than ordinary in-hull logs and that they can go on working at very high speeds or in rough sea conditions, when turbulence or air bubbles make impeller logs unreliable.

Calibrating Logs

No log can be relied upon to be 100% accurate. This is particularly true of hull-mounted logs because—quite apart from any inherent inaccuracies in the instrument itself—the gradual build-up of fouling as the season progresses means that the boat is dragging an ever thickening layer of water along with it, so the water flow past the impeller will be slower than the boat speed through the water. Conversely, around some parts of the hull, such as alongside a sailboat's keel or near the propellers of a motorboat, the water flow may actually be accelerated, making the log over-read. Errors can always be allowed for if you know about them, and most electronic logs have a calibration facility that allows them to be adjusted to take account of these variations. Finding, and if necessary correcting, log error is known as calibration. In principle it involves measuring the time taken to cover a known distance, using this to calculate true speed, and comparing this with the speed indicated by the log. Any accurately-known distance can be used, though the best are undoubtedly the "measured distances" set up specially for the purpose. They consist of two (or sometimes three) pairs of range markers marking the start and finish of a precisely-measured distance (generally one nautical mile), and shown on the appropriate chart. The course to steer to cover the measured distance is also shown. Settle the boat on course and at a steady speed before crossing the first range line; note the time at which you cross the start line and hold that course and speed without making any allowance for wind or current until you cross the finish line, and note the time taken. Note the actual log reading at intervals of, say, 15 seconds so that you can work out the average log speed for the whole run.

The principle is that distance ÷ time = speed. The snag is that the distance is fixed, but the log is measuring speed through the water. If the water were perfectly still, it would be no problem, but still water is so rare that in practice it is important to repeat the process in the opposite direction. You can use the distance and time taken to work out the speed in each direction. From that, work out the average speed by adding the two speeds together and dividing by two, and compare the average with the averaged log speed.

A more accurate result can be obtained by making four or six runs, but this can be a very time-consuming process, especially as log errors are not necessarily the same at all speeds, so the calibration runs need to be carried out at a range of different speeds, and repeated as a double check after the log has been adjusted. A common mistake is to work out the average time taken and divide the distance by this. The result invariably understates the boat's speed, because it must have been traveling in the "slow" direction longer than in the "fast" direction.

Example

Measured distance: 1 nautical mile (1,852 m)

Time (First run):	2 min 36 sec
Time (Second run):	2 min 55 sec
Logspeed:	23.2 kts

First run:	36 sec ÷ 60 = 0.60 min
	2.60 min ÷ 60
	= 0.043 hrs
	1 mile in 0.043 hrs
	= 1 ÷ 0.043 = 23.25 kts

Second run:	55 sec ÷ 60 = 0.92 min
	2.92 min ÷ 60
	= 0.049 hrs
	1 mile in 0.049 hrs
	= 1 ÷ 0.049 = 20.41 kts

Average speed:	(23.25 + 20.41) ÷ 2
	= 21.83 kts

Error:	23.2—21.8 = 1.4
	over-read
	1.4 ÷ 23.2 × 100
	= 6% over-read

Measuring Distance on the Chart

Some large scale charts (harbor charts, and small-craft charts for example) have a clearly marked scale of distance—like the one you might find on a road atlas. These scales usually include both nautical miles and statute miles as well as yards (and henceforth, meters). But this is not always the case, and on the smaller scale charts used for offshore navigation it would be impractical to provide such a scale because the scale of the chart varies slightly from top to bottom. One sea mile, however, is by definition one minute of latitude, so the latitude scales on each side of the chart constitute a scale of distance. The slight difference between a sea mile and an international nautical mile is so small that for normal navigation it can be ignored: what is important, on small scale charts, is the distortion caused by the Mercator projection, which means that distance has to be measured at the latitude at which it is to be used—the latitude scale nearest the area you are measuring. The longitude scale on the top and bottom edges of the chart is useless as a scale of distance. It is relatively rare to find ourselves faced with the job of measuring distance in an exactly north–south line, so we need some means of transferring the distance between any two points on the chart to the latitude scale.

Dividers are the tool for the job. For classroom navigation the kind of dividers used in technical drawing are perfectly adequate, and their sharp needle points give a reassuring sense of precision, but for practical navigation, traditional bow dividers have the big advantage that they can be opened and closed with one hand, by squeezing the bow to open them, and squeezing the legs to close them. Sometimes it is necessary to draw arcs of measured radius on the chart, for which it is useful to have a drawing compass. Again, the type intended for technical drawing can be used so long as it is big enough, but it is generally better to use the larger and less sophisticated versions intended for marine navigation.

Fig 2–1 Bow dividers, which can be used with one hand, are ideal for measuring distances on a chart.

Measuring Direction at Sea

Direction at sea is measured using a compass—essentially an instrument that points north, and goes on pointing north regardless of the movement of the boat around it. In practice most yachts carry at least two compasses. One, the steering compass, is relatively large, fixed to the boat, and used to measure heading. The other is usually smaller, portable and is used to measure the direction (bearing) of distant objects, so it is called a hand-bearing compass. Sometimes one compass can do both jobs: on many ships and a few large yachts an attachment called a pelorus allows the steering compass to be used for taking bearings, while on very small craft, a hand-bearing compass clipped into a bracket can serve as a steering compass.

There are many ways of making an instrument that will stay pointing in one direction, including gyroscopes, and what are called "ring laser gyros," but although these have their advantages, they are much too sophisticated, and therefore expensive, to be of practical interest for most yachts. The overwhelming majority of yacht compasses depend on magnetism, and in that respect can be seen as direct developments from instruments that were probably in use several thousand years ago. Compasses make use of the earth's magnetic field, which acts very much as though a huge bar magnet were embedded in its core and aligned with its north–south axis.

Any magnet that is free to swing tends to line itself up with the earth's magnetic field. This effect is particularly obvious in the small, flat compasses used for orienteering on land, in which a single straight needle-like magnet gives a direct indication of north. In marine compasses, several such magnets, or a single magnet in the shape of a ring, are mounted underneath a circular "card," with a scale of degrees or compass points marked on it. The whole thing is suspended in a bowl filled with a mixture of water and alcohol, which slows down the movement of the card, to reduce the swinging that would otherwise be caused by the pitching and rolling of the boat. Compasses intended for fast motorboats are much more heavily damped than those intended for sailing craft; the rapid slamming of a planing boat can be enough to make the card of a sailboat compass rotate continuously.

Steering Compasses

On a steering compass the fore-and-aft line of the boat is marked by a line or pointer on the compass bowl, called the lubber line, against which the boat's current heading can be read from the card, so it is obviously important for the compass to be installed so that the lubber line is accurately aligned with, or parallel to, the centerline of the boat. Many compasses have supplementary lubber lines offset by 45° and 90° on each side, intended mainly for use in situations such as tiller-steered boats where the helmsman is likely to be looking at the compass from one side or the other. Of course, there are variations intended to suit particular applications. On many small and medium sized sailing yachts, where cockpit space is at a premium, the compass is set into the aft bulkhead of the superstructure, so that the rear edge of the card is visible, rather than its upper surface. A compass intended for this type of mounting has an aft lubber line and a scale of degrees marked on the downturned rim of the card. An even more extreme variation is occasionally found in compasses intended for steel craft, whose structure effectively masks the compass from the earth's magnetic field. This problem can be reduced by mounting the compass as high above the hull as possible, so compasses have been produced that can be mounted on the wheelhouse roof, with mirrors or prisms arranged so that the helmsman effectively looks upwards at the bottom of the compass card.

Grid compasses, intended primarily for aircraft navigation, enjoyed a surge of

Fig 2–2 A bulkhead-mounted steering compass on a sailing cruiser

popularity after the Second World War, when many boats were fitted out from Army surplus stores! The claim that they were easier to steer by maintained their popularity for at least 20 years and several marinized versions were produced. A grid compass has a card with a particularly prominent north mark, set in a flat-topped bowl. On top of the bowl is a transparent cover, marked with a grid of parallel lines and with a scale of degrees around its edge. The required course is "set" by rotating the cover, and the helmsman then steers so as to keep the north mark on the card lined up with the grid.

Hand-bearing Compasses

A hand-bearing compass is basically a small, portable version of a steering compass, fitted with some form of sighting arrangement that allows it to be accurately lined up on a distant object (Figure 2–4). They can be subdivided into two groups: those intended to be used at arm's length, which are usually fitted with a handle; and those intended to be held close to the eye, which are usually supplied with a neck strap. Which kind is best is very much a matter of personal preference, but anyone who wears glasses or a hearing aid is well advised to go for an arm's-length compass because even small pieces of ferrous metal such as the hinges of glasses can cause compass errors if they are only inches away. Sighting arrangements vary. The classic Sestrel Radiant, for instance, has a prism mounted above the bowl, with a V-shaped notch on top. When the compass is held up at arm's length and eye level the lubber line and compass card can be seen in the prism. To take a bearing of a distant object, you line up the "target" with the notch, rotate the compass until the lubber line appears in the prism immediately below the target, and then read off the bearing. Another common

Fig 2–3 A flush-mounted steering compass on a fast sportboat

Fig 2–4 A hand-bearing compass. On this type, the fore sight and back sight are inside the compass bowl.

arrangement has two sights on top of the bowl, like the fore sight and back sight of a gun, and an edge-reading compass card.

Close-to-the-eye compasses do not have such obvious sighting arrangements; instead they have a small prism mounted on top, whose optics are arranged in such a way that when you look at a landmark across the top of the compass, its bearing appears in the prism immediately below.

Fluxgate Compasses

A new type of compass is rapidly gaining in popularity. Unlike a conventional "swinging card" compass, a fluxgate compass has no moving parts, but instead uses electronics to detect the earth's magnetic field and present that information on some kind of display. A fluxgate depends on the phenomenon of electromagnetic induction—as used in

transformers and the ignition coil of a gasoline engine that doesn't have electronic ignition. If you pass an electric current through a coil of wire wound around a suitable metal core, the core becomes a magnet. Which end is the north pole, and which the south, depends on the direction of the current flow in the wire, so if you apply an alternating current to the wire, the north and south poles of the core change places each time the current reverses. If you have a second coil of wire wound around this whole assembly, the constantly-reversing magnetic field induces an electric current in the secondary winding (Figure 2–5).

In a fluxgate there are two cores side by side, with their primary windings receiving alternating current from the same source, but wound in opposite directions. This means that in a magnetically "clean" environment (with no external magnetic influences) the induced

25

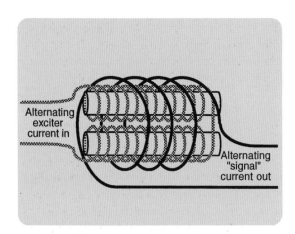

Alternating
exciter
current in

Alternating
"signal"
current out

Fig 2–5 A fluxgate element—one of several at the heart of the most popular types of electronic compass

magnetism in the two cores would be equal and opposite, so they would cancel each other out and produce no current at all in the secondary winding that surrounds both of them. The presence of an external magnetic field upsets the balance, causing a short surge of electricity in the secondary winding each time the primary current reverses. This effect is most pronounced if the two cores are parallel to the external magnetic field. In a practical fluxgate compass, several fluxgates are arranged in a circle. By comparing the voltages induced in the various secondary windings it is possible to deduce where north is relative to the ring of fluxgates.

At present, the most common use of this technology is to provide heading information for other electronic equipment such as autopilots or radars, but it can also be used to provide a steering display for the helmsman or as the heart of an electronic hand-bearing compass. Apart from the ease with which fluxgate compasses can be connected to other navigational electronics, their big advantages are that they can be fitted with an automatic correction facility to minimize the effect of deviation (see page 28); and that because the sensor and display are usually separate from

each other, the sensor can be mounted anywhere onboard and well away from distorting magnetic influences.

Their main disadvantage is that very large errors can occur if the fluxgate ring is not kept perfectly horizontal. There are electronic solutions to this problem, but the fact remains that "the compass with no moving parts" actually requires more sophisticated gimbal arrangements than its swinging card counterparts.

Variation

All magnetic compasses—fluxgate or swinging card—measure direction relative to the earth's magnetic field. This is almost in line with the earth's north–south spin axis, but not quite. At present, the north magnetic pole is among the islands of north Canada, some 600 miles from the true North Pole. This creates a discrepancy called variation between magnetic north (shown by a magnetic compass) and true north corresponding to the meridians on a chart. Variation varies from place to place, and from year to year: in the central Mediterranean, for instance, it is negligible, and in the Gulf of Mexico the numbers are small. But variation is in the neighborhood of 15° W or more in New England and about 14° E off the coast of southern California.

Variation is always shown on the navigational chart, usually printed in the center of the compass roses in the form VAR 14° 15' W (2006) ANNUAL DECREASE 3'. This means that in 2006 magnetic north was 14° 15' west of true north. The statement "ANNUAL DECREASE 3'" means that it was moving east at three minutes per year, so in 2011 it should be 14° 00' W. For practical purposes variation can be rounded off to the nearest degree, which means that mariners can consider the variation for the chart we're quoting to be effectively 14° W now and for several years to come.

For various reasons it is impossible to predict the rate of change with any accuracy in

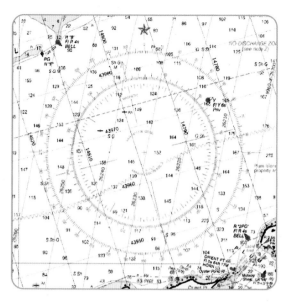

Fig 2–6 A compass rose shows direction on the chart: notice the inner rose showing magnetic directions and the note about variation, which in this case is 14°15′ West.

advance, so the information given on charts more than five years old should be treated with some suspicion, even if the rest of the chart has been kept up to date. Isogonic charts showing variation and its annual change over very wide areas are published at five-yearly intervals, but a more practical approach is simply to take the variation from the most up-to-date chart of the area you have available, even if it is not the one you are navigating on at the time.

If you know about an error you can always allow for it—in this case by a simple arithmetical process.

To convert from Magnetic to True, easterly variation should be added, or westerly variation subtracted.

Converting from True to Magnetic is the reverse: Westerly variation should be added and easterly variations subtracted.

So if the variation is 14° W and you want the helmsman to steer a course of 200° T (True), you should give him a course of 214° M (Magnetic): 200° (T) + 14° W = 214° (M) Conversely, if you have taken a bearing of 150° with a magnetic compass, it should be plotted on a chart as 136° T (True): 150° (M) – 14° W = 136° (T). There are various mnemonics (see page 32) to help remember whether to add or subtract variation, but one of the best ways of all is to lay a straight edge across the center of a compass rose and see whether the numbers on the magnetic ring are higher or lower than the corresponding numbers on the true ring. If the variation has changed less than one degree since the chart was published, comparison of the true and magnetic rings can even be used to give a direct conversion, completely eliminating the risk of arithmetical errors.

Magnetic Anomalies

In some areas, large naturally-occurring deposits of magnetic rock cause local distortions of the earth's magnetic field. Manmade features, including some power cables or large metal structures such as wrecks or pipelines, can have a similar effect. The manmade ones are usually so localized that you would have to be extremely unlucky for them to have any real significance. The natural ones are less common but cover larger areas:

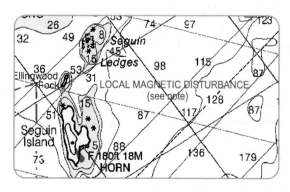

Fig 2–7 Wherever there's a local magnetic anomaly, you will see a clear warning on your chart.

they are marked on charts with a note giving any available information.

Deviation

Metal structures and electrical cables within the boat itself are much closer to the compass, and can therefore have a much greater distorting effect on it, giving rise to an error called deviation. Beyond the simple statement that deviation is caused by electricity, magnetism and ferrous metals onboard the boat itself, a full explanation of it would be surprisingly complex—some idea of just how complex can be gained from the fact that although magnetic compasses have been in use for thousands of years, as late as the mid-nineteenth century the British Admiralty felt it necessary to set up a committee to investigate what they described as this "evil so pregnant with mischief." Only 100 years before, Captain Cook had regarded the compass binnacle as a handy place to keep his iron keys! We can laugh at that now, but many modern yachtsmen and boat builders commit even worse magnetic blunders by surrounding their steering compasses with loudspeakers, electronic displays, power distributionboards and engine monitoring instruments, all of which can set up powerful magnetic fields.

Deviation can be minimized by taking care to site such equipment as far from the compass as possible. In the case of electronic instruments the equipment usually carries a label indicating its "compass safe distance"—the distance at which that particular item will deviate the compass by less than one degree. Almost inevitably though, on a modern boat there will be some deviating components, such as engines and keels, that cannot be moved. These deviating influences can be counteracted, at least to some extent, by a compass adjuster, who places a combination of small needle-like magnets and soft iron rods around and inside the compass casing in an effort to cancel out the boat's own magnetism. He will then draw up a deviation card showing the remaining deviation.

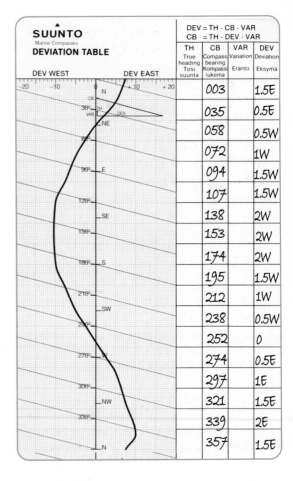

Fig 2-8 A deviation card, like this, is drawn up by a compass adjuster, giving details of the deviation affecting a fixed compass.

Because deviation is caused by the boat's magnetic field, its direction and extent depend on which way the boat is pointing: it will be negligible when the boat's magnetic field is parallel to that of the earth and greatest when the two are at right angles to each other. For this reason the compass adjuster presents his results in the form of a table, showing the deviation on various headings.

Compass adjustment is a specialized job, and not one for the do-it-yourselfer. Measuring deviation, however, is a relatively straightforward task that should be done at least once a year, and after any repair or maintenance work that may have affected the magnetic characteristics of the boat.

Swinging for Deviation

There are many possible ways of measuring deviation but they all involve comparing the direction indicated by the compass with the actual direction known by some other reliable means. This process is called swinging the compass. Perhaps the most straightforward method is known as the "swing by distant objects." This involves taking the boat to an accurately known position, then turning it round to point straight at each of several distant landmarks in turn. The true bearing of each mark can be found from the chart and converted to a magnetic bearing by applying variation. Comparing the known magnetic bearing with the corresponding compass heading gives the deviation. If the compass heading is less than the magnetic bearing the deviation is named east; if the compass bearing is greater the deviation is named west.

Exactly how distant the "distant objects" should be depends on the precision required and the accuracy of your known position. It is normal to aim for an accuracy of about one degree, in which case every 100 meters (328 feet) of possible error in position requires at least three miles distance between the boat and the landmarks.

Suitable position fixing methods include the intersection of two ranges (see next section), circling very close to a charted wooden pile or around a navigational buoy. Buoys are much easier to find than suitable piles or ranges, but they are not nearly as good for the purpose, partly because they are usually made of steel and can therefore induce their own local magnetic anomaly if you get too close to them, and partly because they can lie some distance down current of their charted positions. If you have to use a buoy, stay at least 50–100 yards away from it to minimize the effect of deviation, and take care to use landmarks that are far enough away to minimize the effect of any possible position error.

Compass Check by Ranges

Any two objects that appear to be in line with each other form a range (not to be confused with the term range when it means "distance away," as in determining the range and bearing of an object by radar (see Chapter 8) or by GPS (see next chapter). Your line of sight along the range line can be drawn on a chart simply by ruling a straight line through the two landmarks concerned. Ranges have many navigational uses; indeed, the Coast Guard often installs range markers where there are no natural ranges, such as at the ends of channels to aid mariners in lining up on them properly. But in this context they are useful because it is easy to point a boat straight along a range and it is equally simple to measure the true bearing of the range on a chart. One drawback of this method is that it is not always easy to find enough ranges in different directions to draw up a complete deviation card, though even a single range can be useful as a quick check.

Swing by Comparison

If you know the deviation on one compass, it can be used as a reference against which to measure the deviation on another. A common application of this is on flybridge motor cruisers. The upper steering position usually has excellent visibility and few sources of deviation, so producing a deviation card by distant objects or ranges is a relatively straightforward matter. The deviation on the lower compass can then be found by comparing it with the indicated heading on the upper compass.

Deviation of Hand-bearing Compasses

A hand-bearing compass can be used anywhere onboard, in positions that can have very different effects on its deviation. This makes it impractical to correct a hand bearing compass by fitting corrector magnets, and equally

29

impractical to draw up a deviation card for it. Because it is better to apply no correction than risk adding deviation when it should be subtracted, it is normal practice to assume that its deviation is nil.

It cannot be stressed too strongly, however, that this is only a convenient assumption: when using a hand-bearing compass it is important to be aware of possible sources of deviation in the vicinity including equipment such as anchors, gas bottles, galvanized rigging, radar scanners and other compasses, to name just a few. It also follows from this that a hand-bearing compass can only be used as a standard against which to measure the deviation of the steering compass if you can be absolutely certain that it is in a spot completely free of deviating influences.

Deviation and Fluxgate Compasses

Fluxgate compasses, too, are affected by deviation, though they have the advantage that the sensor can be located anywhere onboard— even on top of a mast. Most also include an auto-correction facility. Different models have different correction procedures for which you should consult the manufacturer's manual.

Heeling Error

Compasses are usually corrected and deviation cards drawn up with the boat upright, even though sailboats in particular do not always operate in this position! When the boat heels, its magnetic geometry changes: the keel, for instance, may be vertically below the compass when the boat is upright, but moves out to port when the boat heels over on port tack. In some cases this can have a noticeable effect on the steering compass, known as heeling error. Heeling error can be measured and reduced, but it is a job for a professional compass adjuster.

Allowing for Deviation

Once you know the deviation, it can be allowed for in exactly the same way as variation:

To convert from Compass to Magnetic, easterly variation should be added, or westerly variation subtracted.

Converting from Magnetic to Compass is the reverse: westerly variation should be added and easterly variations subtracted.

So if the deviation is 3° W and you want the helmsman to steer a course of 204°M (Magnetic), you should give him a course of 207°C (Compass). 204°(M) + 3°W = 207°(C) Despite the similarity, it is worth getting into the habit of regarding the conversion between compass and magnetic as quite separate from the conversion between magnetic and true, and carrying them out as two distinct processes, rather than adopting the "short cut" of adding variation and deviation together and regarding them as a single error.

The reason for this becomes particularly apparent if you imagine yourself navigating a boat with an uncorrected compass in an area with a large variation (20°W). Suppose you want to steer a course of 070° (T). From the deviation card in Figure 2–7, the deviation on a heading of 075° is 1°W, and on 060° it is 5°W—so on 070° one might expect the deviation to be about 2°W. Adding this to the variation of 20°W produces a "total error" of 22°W—giving a compass course of 070° + 22° = 092° (C).

Applying variation and deviation separately gives a different—and more accurate— result, because 070° (T) + 20° = 090° (M). The deviation card shows that on a heading of 090° the deviation is 3°E, so the compass course required is: 090° – 3° = 087°.

Second Error Correction

When the deviation is large, a further refinement is needed in order to achieve an accurate result. Suppose, for instance, the course required is 120° (T). Allowing for variation converts this to

120° + 20° = 140° (M). From the deviation card in Figure 2–7, the deviation for 140° is 13°E, suggesting a compass course of 140° – 13° = 127°(C). On a course of 127°(C), however, the deviation is only 11°—giving a compass course of 140° – 11° = 129°(C). Checking, by converting it back to true, reveals that this is, indeed, the right answer. The reason this apparently tortuous process is required is that the deviation card is referred to compass heading: so a first, approximate, calculation is needed in order to find an approximate compass heading before the deviation card can be used to find the appropriate figure for deviation.

Measuring Direction on the Chart

Direction is indicated in two ways: by the grid of intersecting north–south meridians at

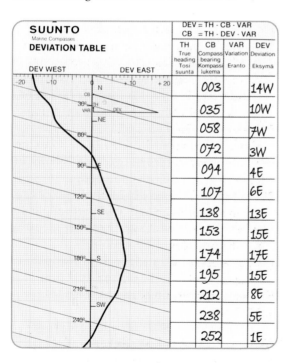

Fig 2–9 An unadjusted compass, or one in a magnetically "difficult" position, may have very large amounts of deviation, and calls for particular care (see text).

east–west parallels; and by compass roses each with a graduated ring of 360 marks at 1° intervals. Some, though not all, have a second, inner ring, slightly skewed from the outer ring, showing directions relative to magnetic north (see page 24).

Just as the distance you want to measure seldom runs north–south, so directions seldom run conveniently through the middle of a compass rose, making some means of transferring directions around the chart just as important as dividers. There is quite a choice of devices available for the purpose.

Traditional Parallel Rulers

Traditional parallel rulers consist of two straight rulers, joined together by pivoting arms that allow the rulers to be moved apart while keeping their edges parallel, so that they can be "walked" across the chart while preserving their alignment. Using them quickly and accurately takes practice and demands a flat unobstructed chart table but they are still the preferred choice of many experienced navigators.

Rolling Parallel Rulers

A rolling parallel ruler is a single wide ruler fitted with a pair of rollers fixed to a single shaft. This means that the ruler can be rolled from one place to another while preserving its alignment. A rolling parallel is much quicker and easier to use than the traditional type, but in order to be effective it has to be bigger and demands an even larger chart table, so they are really only of practical use on ships or very large pleasure craft.

Douglas Protractor

An alternative way of measuring directions on the chart is by using one of many different types of protractor. These have their own scale of degrees so they do not rely on compass roses and do not, therefore, have to be moved around the chart. Using them calls for less manual dexterity than parallel rulers, but in

MNEMONICS

"True Virgins Make Dull Companions" gives the letters TVMDC, as a reminder that Variation (V) separates True (T) and Magnetic (M), and that Deviation (D) separates Magnetic and Compass (C).

"CAdET" is a reminder that to go from Compass (C) to True (T) you have to Add (Ad) Easterly (E) errors.

"Error east, Compass least; Error west Compass best" is an alternative to the "Cadet" rule that is particularly useful as a double check, or to work out deviation after a compass swing. It says that easterly errors make the compass heading smaller (least) than the true heading, while westerly errors make the compass heading bigger ("best").

Another common mnemonic for converting from compass to true is "Can Dead Men Vote Twice At Elections." CDMVT for the conversion itself; with AE as a reminder to add easterly errors.

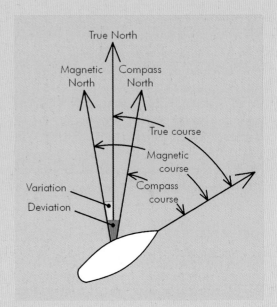

Fig 2–10 Variation is the difference between true and magnetic north; deviation is the difference between magnetic and compass north.

most cases more mental dexterity. The Douglas protractor has long been popular with air navigators, though it was originally devised for marine use. It consists of a square of stiff transparent plastic—five inches or ten inches for a genuine Douglas protractor, though other sizes are available from different manufacturers. Around its edge are two rows of markings from 0 to 360°, with an outer scale reading in a clockwise direction and an inner scale running counterclockwise. Inside these is a grid of equally-spaced lines, parallel to the edges of the protractor; and right in the center is a small hole.

The most intuitive way of using a Douglas protractor to measure the direction of a line on the chart is simply to place it on the chart, with the central hole on the line and its grid aligned, by eye, with the nearest meridians and

parallels. The direction of the line can then be read directly from the clockwise scale.

A similar technique can be used to draw a line in a particular direction: Place the central hole of the protractor over the starting point of the line, ensure that the protractor's grid is lined up with the meridians and parallels, and make a light pencil mark on the chart alongside the required direction on the outer (clockwise) scale. Then move the protractor and use its edge to rule a straight line from the starting point through the pencil mark.

An alternative method makes use of the inner (counterclockwise) scale. This time the central hole is placed on the meridian and the protractor rotated until the mark corresponding to the required direction lies on the same meridian. Two edges of the protractor now lie in the required direction—the two

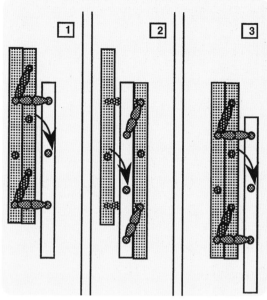

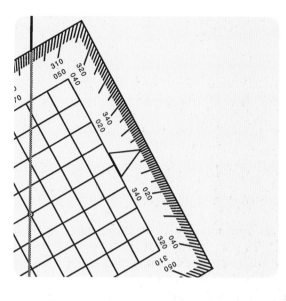

Fig 2-13 A Douglas protractor is a popular alternative to parallel rulers, especially on small boats.

Fig 2-11 "Walking" parallel rulers are the traditional tool for transferring direction to and from the compass rose.

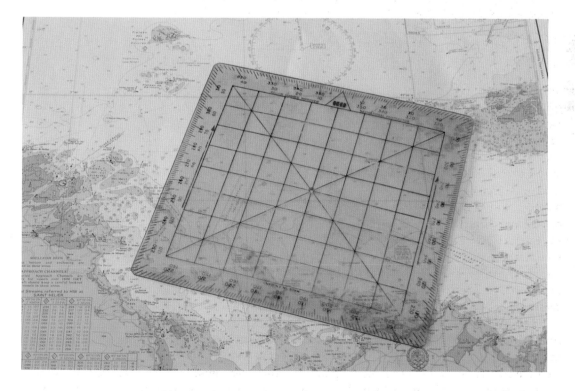

Fig 2-12 A Kelvin Hughes protractor—a larger and thicker variant of the Douglas protractor

parallel to the protractor's north–south line. Keeping this alignment, slide the protractor up or down the meridian until one of these edges passes through the starting point of the line you wish to draw, and then pencil it in. This method sounds tortuous, but with practice it often turns out to be quicker and slightly more accurate than the other.

Breton Plotter

The Breton plotter and its several variants are a more recent development, but have gained enormous popularity among amateur navigators. It consists of a rectangular piece of transparent plastic with a circular protractor fixed to it, but free to rotate. In the center of the protractor is a squared grid. Once the grid has been aligned with the meridians and parallels on the chart, the main body of the protractor can be rotated and the direction of

its long edges read off directly from the protractor scale. In practice, when using the plotter to measure the direction of a pre-drawn line, it is easier to get the plotter base lined up with the line first and then rotate the protractor, and when drawing, to set the required direction on the instrument before placing it on the chart and sliding it around as necessary to get the grid aligned with the chart.

One advantage of the Breton plotter is a supplementary scale on the base plate. Variation (see page 26) can be allowed for by aligning the rotating protractor with the appropriate mark on this scale, rather than with the plotter's center-line.

Hurst Plotter

The Hurst plotter (and its variants) is another type of protractor-based plotting instrument. This one has a square base-plate, on top of

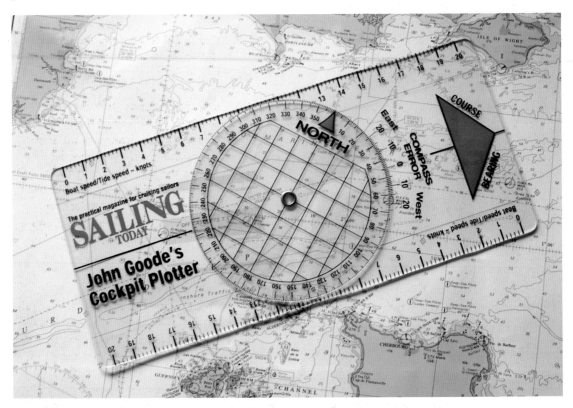

Fig 2–14 One of the many variations on the Breton-style plotter

Fig 2–15 A Breton plotter incorporates a rotating protractor that can be aligned with the meridians and parallels to serve as a mobile compass rose.

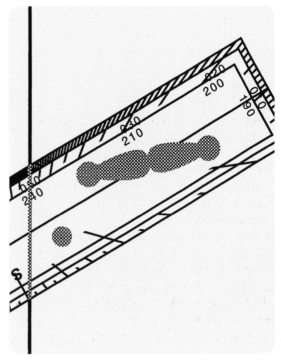

Fig 2–16 Captain Field's pattern parallel rulers combine some of the advantages of parallel rulers and protractors in one instrument.

which is a 360° protractor that can be clamped firmly in place. Between the base-plate and the protractor is a pivoting arm. The protractor can either be lined up with the grid, to work in "True" directions, or it can be deliberately offset to work in "Magnetic" (see page 27), and then locked in place. A grid on the base-plate allows it to be aligned with the meridians or parallels on the chart, so the protractor then serves as a compass rose that can be positioned anywhere on the chart, while the arm forms a straight edge that can be swung around to point in any direction, but which always lines up with the center of the protractor.

Captain Field's Pattern Parallel Rulers

Many of the parallel rulers in use nowadays, whether of the "walking" or rolling type, are of the "Captain Field's pattern," marked with a counterclockwise scale of degrees. This combines the advantages of both parallel rulers and protractors, because when the rulers are in their closed position, they can be placed directly on the chart in much the same way as a Douglas protractor. The only difference is

that the protractor's central hole is replaced by a mark on the middle of one of the rulers—usually identified by the letter S or an arrow.

Keeping the S mark on any convenient meridian, rotate the rulers (keeping them closed) until the required direction on the scale crosses the same meridian. The rulers are now lined up and their precise position can be adjusted if necessary by opening or closing them.

Choosing a Plotter

There is an enormous variety of plotting tools available, of which parallel rulers, Douglas protractors and Hurst and Breton plotters are only the most popular. It is worth mastering at least one or two of these common plotting tools, if only because they are the ones you are most likely to come across on friends' boats, charter craft, or deliveries, but it is also worth experimenting with others whenever the opportunity arises, because "which one is best?" is very much a matter of personal opinion.

Chartwork

It almost goes without saying that chartwork should be as accurate as possible: the precision expected during most shore-based courses—0.1 mile and 1°—may not always be practical at sea in a small boat, but it is a good target to aim for. Even this degree of precision can be achieved without resorting to the engineering draftsman's hard and super sharp pencil: soft (2B) pencils leave a much clearer line, are less damaging to the chart, and are much easier to erase. On charts made of synthetic, plastic paper it can even be worth using a softer pencil

still, up to 4B. Hard pencils and ballpoint pens have no place anywhere near a chart other than for chart correcting! In the interests of clarity it is also important to be able to remove superfluous lines so an eraser is essential, and in the interests of the chart, this too should be as soft as possible.

The skipper who does all his own navigating can use any signs, symbols and abbreviations he likes on the chart. But on larger boats or longer passages, where there is the slightest possibility that more than one person may be involved, it is essential that all the members of the navigating team are able to understand each other's chartwork. So it is worth getting into the habit of using the standard chartwork symbols such as those shown in Figure 2–18.

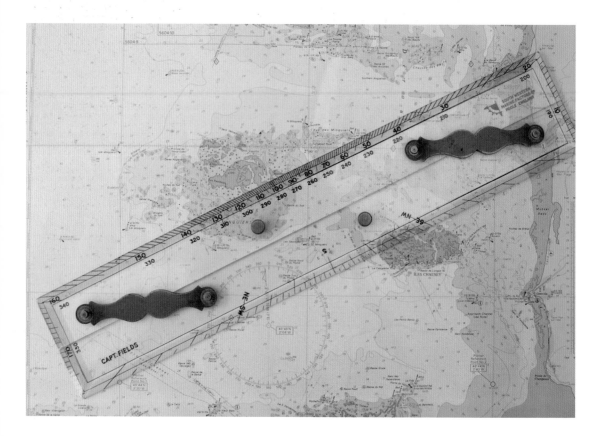

Fig 2–17 Captain Field's pattern parallel rulers

The Chart Table

The size, shape and surroundings of a chart table are usually determined by the designer and builder of the boat, and sadly nowadays often seem to take second place to more superficially attractive features such as stereo systems and cocktail cabinets. But there is no doubt that a good chart table makes navigation considerably easier. Whether it faces fore-and-aft or athwartships does not seem to make much difference: what is important is that the navigator should be able to brace himself in position against the motion of the

boat while leaving both hands free. It should be flat, without hinges or joints to interrupt the movement of plotting instruments, and as big as possible. It needs something to stop the chart falling off, stowage for pencils, erasers and instruments, reference books and other charts—and for night passages, a light. Traditionally chart table lights are red, as this was thought to have a less damaging effect on night vision than any other color, but this is not, in fact, the case and a white or green light is perfectly acceptable as long as it is sufficiently dim.

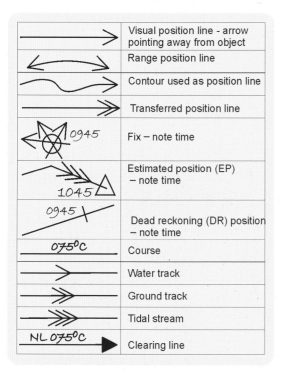

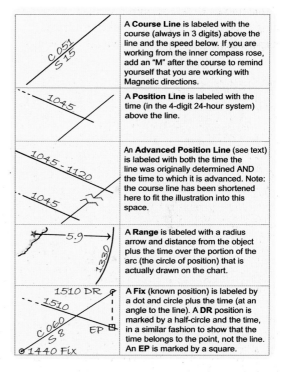

Fig 2-18 Standard chartwork symbols are always useful even if you are the sole navigator—they help eliminate confusion when you look at something you plotted earlier. Standardization becomes essential if there is more than one navigator onboard. Those on the left are from the original UK editions. The ones on the right are more common here in the U.S. and are taught in all navigation classes from the Naval Academy at Annapolis down to your local USPS or USCG Auxiliary safe-boating courses. Just remember: The main consideration is not the particular symbols you use, but rather that you and any other navigators aboard always use the same ones consistently.

Electronic Navigation Equipment

Marine electronics have boomed over the last thirty years or so, with equipment becoming more sophisticated, more reliable, more compact and yet less expensive. Fifty years ago (about the time the first fiberglass boats were being built) an echo sounder was rather large, could weigh upwards of 50 pounds and cost nearly as much as a new small car. So it should be no surprise that only commercial fishermen used them and most yachtsmen relied on the lead and line for measuring depth. Now, you can buy a fish finder that will show the shape of the seabed as well as its depth for less than $200, while another $200 or so will buy you a satellite "navigator" that can give you your position accurate to a matter of yards anywhere in the world by day or night and display that position on a screen that also includes the details of an electronic chart.

Fig 3-1 A compact and user-friendly digital echo sounder

So available and reliable are modern electronics that it is tempting to wonder whether so-called traditional navigation is still of any value. But while modern electronics very rarely "fail" in the technical sense of the word, they are still vulnerable to broken or corroded wiring, to external influences such as radio interference and—perhaps most common of all—to human operators who either press the wrong buttons or misread the information on their displays.

A seamanlike approach to electronics is neither to ignore them altogether nor to be totally dependent on them, but to regard them as additional sources of information with their own strengths and weaknesses that—like those of a compass—need to be understood and kept in mind.

Echo Sounders

An echo sounder, for measuring depth, is now virtually standard equipment on all but the smallest and simplest of boats. It works by transmitting pulses, or clicks, of ultrasonic sound from a transducer mounted onboard, down to the seabed, and then receiving the returning echoes. Although the speed of sound in water varies slightly, it is always in the order of 1,400 meters (4,593 feet) per second, so the time taken for each pulse to complete a down and back trip depends on the depth of water.

The most readily-understood timing system is that used in the "rotating neon" type of sounder, in which the heart of the display unit is a fast-spinning rotor with a neon lamp or light-emitting diode (LED) at its end. Each time the rotor passes the upright position, the light flashes and the transducer is triggered to transmit its pulse. When the returning echo is detected by the transducer, the light flashes again, but by this time the rotor has moved on.

How far it has moved depends on the time interval between transmission and reception, so the depth of water is indicated by the position of the second flash. It can be read directly off a scale marked on the face of the instrument around the window that covers the rotor. For operation in deep water, the rotor speed can be slowed down, increasing the range of time intervals that can be measured and increasing the time between successive pulses, but reducing the accuracy and precision of the depth measurement. With practice the appearance of the returning flash gives a clue to the nature of the seabed: a hard seabed such as rock produces a crisp echo that appears as a short flash; while a very soft bottom such as mud or weed gives a more drawn-out echo and produces a more diffuse or drawn-out flash. Sometimes, however, the echo sounder can be misleading.

Air bubbles are good reflectors of sound waves, so turbulence caused by the wash of passing ships can produce a mass of shallow flashes. The swim bladders of fish also contain air, so a single large fish can produce a brief flash, while a dense shoal of small fish produces a more consistent flash at a depth corresponding to the depth of the shoal. Fishermen find this useful and the echo sounder principle has been developed into fish finders, but for navigation purposes such echoes are simply a nuisance. Luckily, they are usually easy to identify because they are short-lived and erratic.

Another type of spurious flash can sometimes be seen in shallow waters over a hard bottom, and is caused by the returning echo reflecting back from the sea surface to make a second trip down to the seabed and back. If this second echo is strong enough to register on the echo sounder, it is called a reflection echo and appears as a relatively weak flash at twice the true depth.

A particularly worrying type of spurious echo can be produced by hard bottoms when the water is so deep that the echo does not return until after the rotor has completed one full revolution. The returning echo produces a flash on the display which is considerably shallower than the true depth. If, for instance, the echo sounder is set to an operating range of 0–25 meters (0–82 feet) and the true depth is 30 meters (98 feet), the indicated depth will be 5 meters, or about 16 feet. Fortunately these second trace echoes can easily be identified by switching to a deeper operating scale which will indicate the true depth.

Recording Paper Sounders

Although they look very different and are much more expensive, recording paper echo sounders use much the same timing system as rotating neons, except that instead of a flashing light the timing display is a stylus or "electric pen." This is mechanically swept across a moving roll of special paper—similar to that used in older fax machines—producing a mark each time a pulse is transmitted and each time an echo is received. Like the flashes of a rotating neon sounder, the distance between these two marks corresponds to the depth. Over a period of time as the recording paper unrolls, successive traces build up to produce a continuous permanent record. Although they have their uses for some commercial operations and for surveying, recording paper sounders have no particular merit for pleasure craft, especially as the need to keep them supplied with recording paper can be an expensive nuisance.

Electronic Displays

Electronics manufacturers are seldom keen on mechanical components, and whatever the merits of rotating neon echo sounders, their dependence on fast moving mechanical parts makes them potentially unreliable and power hungry, while possible variations in motor speed can make them inaccurate. As technology developed and electronic timing devices became a practical proposition, most of the more up-market manufacturers offered display units that indicated the depth by means of a moving pointer on a graduated dial. Some of these units have survived, but they have been almost completely superseded by all electronic displays giving either a digital readout or a graphical presentation similar to the trace of a recording paper sounder.

Added Features

An echo sounder is basically a simple instrument measuring a single quantity—depth—so there are few added features that can usefully be incorporated. Most, however, include a shallow water alarm that can be set to sound a beep when the indicated depth is shallower than a chosen limit, and many have a deep alarm that beeps or flashes when a preset depth is exceeded.

A carefully-set shallow alarm has an obvious value as a warning function when operating in shoal water, and a deep alarm can be useful when anchored, as a reminder to let more cable out to cope with the rising tide. Used together, they can play a part in piloting or in fog navigation, when they can be used to guide you between two contour lines (see page 164).

Installation and Calibration

For an echo sounder to work, the transducer has to be able to send its pulses down to the seabed. Wood is a very effective insulator of sound, so in wooden boats a through-hull installation is essential, with the transducer mounted in a watertight housing so that its transmitting face is in direct contact with the sea water below. A similar set-up can be used in fiberglass or metal boats, but it is not essential because these materials transmit sound. In-hull mountings can be used, as long as there is no air gap or bubbles between the transducer and the hull skin. The transducer can be bonded directly to the hull with a layer of epoxy glue or (better) mounted in a tube bonded to the hull and filled with vegetable oil to exclude the air.

The location of the transducer needs to be chosen with some care to avoid turbulence and air bubbles caused by the boat's own movement. Manufacturers' manuals invariably offer advice on this, but on sailboats and low speed motorboats it generally boils down to "about one third of the way back from the stem but not too close to the keel."

On planing motorboats this would be the worst possible position and may even be out of the water altogether, so the transducer should be farther aft—at least two-thirds of the way back.

The sound from the transducer is not transmitted equally in all directions, but is concentrated into a funnel-shaped beam, about 30° across—part of which has to point straight down to the seabed. This is seldom a problem for motorboats as long as the transducer is vertical, rather than at right angles to the hull skin. It can be more difficult to achieve in a sailboat, either because the keel gets in the way, or because the boat heels more than 15°. If these problems cannot be overcome by careful siting of a single transducer, the usual solution is to have two transducers, one on each side of the boat, with a manual or gravity-operated changeover switch to select the lower of the two.

The speed of sound in sea water is not absolutely constant, so survey ships calibrate their echo sounders by lowering an iron bar to a measured depth below the transducer and adjusting the display to show the correct depth. This is impractical and unnecessary for yacht navigation, but most yacht sounders include a simpler calibration facility or "keel offset" to allow either for the depth of the transducer below the waterline or for its height above the keel. Both have their advantages: depth below the keel errs on the side of pessimism, and it is easy to remember that if the echo sounder reads zero you are aground; depth below the waterline is of more use for navigational purposes, which may require the true depth of water.

On boats that can safely go aground, the most direct way of setting the keel offset to show depth below the keel is to put the boat aground deliberately, and adjust the keel offset to give an indicated depth of zero. On other boats, or to set the echo sounder to show depth below the waterline, the true depth can be found by lowering any suitable weight to the bottom on a piece of string, and the keel offset adjusted accordingly so that the indicated depth matches the measured depth.

Fig 3–2 A compact fish-finder showing the shape of the seabed, and with arch-shaped mid-water echoes probably representing fish

Satnav

The expression "satnav," or satellite navigation, covers a number of electronic positioning systems. Of these systems, the only one that is currently relevant to yachtsmen is GPS. It is quite likely, however, that GPS may be joined by two similar systems (the Russian Glonass and the European Galileo) within a few years.

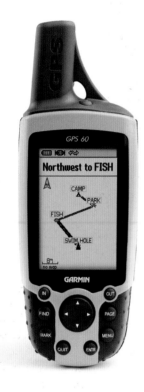

Fig 3–3 Economical hand-held GPS receivers have revolutionized navigation.

GPS

Development of the Global Positioning System (GPS) began in 1973 and by the time the system was officially operational in 1995, thousands of yachts already carried GPS receivers. Since then, the numbers have only increased. In many respects GPS has solved the problems of position fixing in an instant,

giving continuous worldwide coverage with an accuracy of a few yards. The GPS constellation consists of about two dozen satellites—the actual number varies as old satellites break down and new ones are launched—in orbit at an altitude of almost 11,000 nautical miles. Each satellite continuously transmits a coded signal on two microwave frequencies—roughly ten times higher than marine VHF—including a message that says "I am here" and "the time is now." The codes used on the two frequencies are different and only one, called the CA code (for Coarse Acquisition), is available to civilian receivers, but their messages are essentially the same. The signal takes time to travel from the satellite to the receiver, so it is received slightly later than it was sent. Microwaves, like any other radio waves, travel at an almost constant speed of 162,000 nautical miles per second, so the difference between the time of transmission and the time of reception corresponds to the distance between the satellite and the receiver.

If the signal arrives one-tenth of a second after it was sent, the receiver is 16,200 miles from the satellite—that is, it is on the surface of a sphere with a radius of 16,200 miles, centered on the satellite. Doing the same with another satellite gives a second sphere intersecting with the first to produce a circle. The only place where the receiver can be on both spheres at once is somewhere on that circle. Repeating the process with a third satellite narrows the possible position down to two points, and a fourth satellite removes any possible ambiguity.

That, at least, is what would happen if the receiver's internal clock was precisely synchronized with the atomic clocks in the satellites, but in practice this is not the case. When we are dealing with radio waves, timing errors of as little as a millionth of a second produce large errors of distance, so the position spheres do not initially intersect at a point, but form a three dimensional version of the traditional navigator's "cocked hat" (see page 55). The GPS receiver's computer is

Fig 3–4 Stand-alone GPS sets have become relatively rare, but products such as this Garmin 152 are still available, and provide simple and cost-effective position fixing and basic navigation information.

designed to recognize this problem, identify its most likely cause as clock error, and adjust its own clock accordingly until all the position spheres intersect as they should.

The Geometry of GPS Receivers

In order to produce a fix, a GPS receiver requires signals from four satellites. Most, however, can manage with only three, by using the surface of the earth as one of the position spheres. This is called a 2D (two-dimensional) fix, and while it may be acceptable for most navigational purposes, it is generally less accurate than a full 3D fix, because the earth is not such a neat geometric shape as the satellite range spheres.

There are a number of ways in which the GPS set's computer can be supplied with three or more satellite signals, of which the most obvious is to connect it to several separate microwave receivers. An alternative is to rely on a single receiver "listening" to each

of several satellites in turn—called multiplexing.

Accuracy and Selective Availability

The inherent accuracy of CA code GPS is about 50 feet (2σ). But it is owned and operated by the Department of Defense, which did not want potential enemies to derive the full benefit of a system that had cost them over five billion dollars. Getting that five billion dollars out of us taxpayers, however, involved making a commitment to Congress that the system would be available to civilians. This posed a dilemma that was solved by a policy known as Selective Availability (SA). SA was not selective, nor did it have anything to do with availability; it involved the introduction of deliberate errors into the time and position information carried by the CA signal, to produce position errors of about 100 meters (328 feet) (2σ). SA was switched off in May 2000, with an assurance from the government

43

Fig 3–5 As the price of computing power and displays has fallen, chart plotters such as this Raymarine C70 have largely taken over from stand-alone GPS receivers.

that there was "no intention" of reintroducing it. The fact remains, however, that SA has only been switched off; the capability remains.

Differential GPS

All errors can be allowed for, as long as you know about them. The snag is that many of the errors afflicting GPS are apparently random and constantly changing, so calibration (as for logs) or correction tables (as for compasses) do not work. The solution is to use fixed shore-based reference stations to monitor the GPS signals and broadcast correction messages that can be received and automatically applied by any suitably-equipped GPS receiver. This supplementary system is generically known as differential GPS (DGPS).

In theory, DGPS corrections can be broadcast by almost any means, but in practice, most DGPS reference stations are on the sites of old radio direction finding beacons, and transmit on the same frequencies. DGPS corrections can also

be broadcast through communication satellites. At present (2009) a system called WAAS (Wide Area Augmentation System) pools the data from a network of reference stations and broadcasts the corrections to most of the Atlantic, part of the Pacific, and the whole of the U.S. mainland. Interestingly, WAAS was initially developed for air navigation but we mariners were able to take advantage of its accuracy even before it was approved by the FAA.

Accuracy

In everyday language one might take "an accuracy of 50 feet" to mean that "all fixes are within 50 feet of the true position." A more detailed look at a succession of fixes largely taken from a stationary "navigator" shows that this could be misleading because they are likely to be scattered (Figure 3–7). Sometimes different types of error cancel each other out, giving fixes very close to the true position. Sometimes errors add together to produce bad fixes, and occasionally a number of unusually large errors accumulate to produce a rogue. It would be unreasonable to quote the accuracy of the system on the basis of the worst fix, because that ignores the vast majority that are very much better, but it would be equally unrealistic to refer only to the lucky fix that happens to be correct. For most purposes accuracies are quoted either in terms of percentage error circles or by means of a statistical measure called "sigma" (σ).

The circular error probable (CEP) is the radius of a circle that contains 50% of all fixes. The CEP 95% is the radius of a circle containing 95% of fixes. σ is the standard deviation or "root mean square error" (dRMS), and it can be found by measuring all the errors, squaring them, adding the squares together, dividing by the number of fixes to find a mean square error, and taking the square root of the mean.

For statisticians this is useful as a basis for further calculations, while for navigators it is a good indication of the practical value of a navigation system, because it tends to "reward" a consistent performer with a lower error figure than an erratic one.

Doubling the standard deviation gives a measure called 2σ (2 sigma), which for a system with random errors, like those produced by SA in GPS, closely matches the CEP 95%. For navigation purposes, you can regard these as levels of confidence. GPS, for instance, may be described as being "accurate

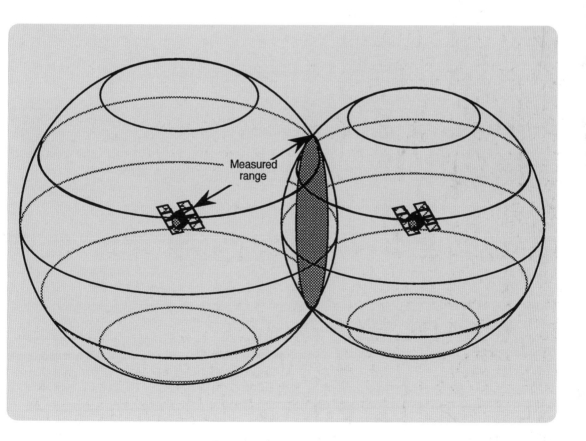

Measured range

Fig 3–6 A GPS receiver uses precise time measurement to determine its distance from each of several satellites. One range fixes its position as being on the surface of an invisible sphere; two narrows the position down to the perimeter of a circle; four produces a 3-D "fix."

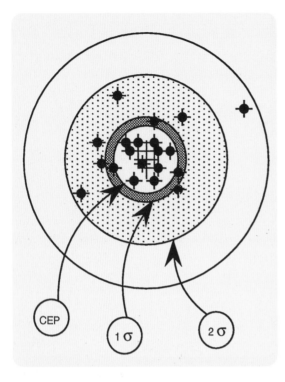

Fig 3–7 Random errors produce a scattering of fixes around the true position, so accuracy can be expressed at several different "levels of confidence."

to 50 feet (2σ)." This means we have a 95% chance of being within 50 feet of where it says we are, or a one in twenty chance of being more than 50 feet away.

Three Kinds of Accuracy

As well as different measures of accuracy, there are also different kinds of accuracy.

- *Absolute accuracy* is a measure of how your fix compares with your true position. It is what you need to find the entrance to an unfamiliar harbor.
- *Relative accuracy* is an indication of consistency throughout an area, and is of more concern to surveyors than to navigators because it is what is required if, for instance, you want to measure the distance between two landmarks.

- *Repeatable accuracy*, or repeatability, refers to a system's consistency over a period of time, and it is particularly useful to people like fishermen who have laid a string of crab pots and want to get back to precisely the same spot to collect them, but do not necessarily need to know the true position.

Waypoint Navigation

For centuries navigators had to devote most of their time and effort to finding their position, even though this is seldom an end in itself. Navigation is much more concerned with where you are going than where you are. For an instrument that is capable of working out where three spheres intersect on the surface almost instantaneously displaying the result in terms of latitude and longitude, many of the routine navigational tasks that follow from knowing your position are extremely simple. Using this extra capability of electronic navigators has led to the development of a range of new techniques that are often collectively called waypoint navigation.

Entering Waypoints

There is nothing magical about a waypoint: it is simply a position that has been stored ("entered") into the navigator's memory. Usually a waypoint is either your intended destination or some intermediate point that you want to pass through on the way there—hence the name "waypoint."

When entering waypoints it is important to be aware that many electronic navigators require latitude and longitude to be given in a very rigidly defined format. It is quite common, for example, for a navigator to demand that the degrees of longitude be given as three figures. So if someone in the UK were to enter 1°26.10' W as "1 26 1," the navigator might store this as 126°10.00' W. Of course, here in the U.S. we're not likely to be entering such a low number for longitude. But if your navigator is programmed to accept only "0" or "1" as the first digit of longitude (as many are), you would have a hard time entering 76° as anything but "076." Alternatively, it may insist on the minutes being given to two (or three) places of decimals, in which case entering anything but the proper number of digits could also provoke an error message and probably result in the unit's failure to accept entry of the desired waypoint.

The third, and very common, pitfall is to neglect to enter the direction of latitude (N or S) or longitude (E or W). Though we can often get lazy in our thinking here in the U.S., because we normally deal only with north latitude and west longitude, your navigator may not be so "narrow minded." On the other hand, many nav units sold in the U.S. have N and W as the defaults for their respective entries. But because they must be able to also accept S and E, sometimes all it takes to "flip" the direction, is an additional press of a button. Do this inadvertently without paying attention and you could find your navigator displaying a very interesting, but totally wrong course to steer when you select the "Go To" mode. Just look back at Chapter 1 if you need a reminder of the vast differences the correct numbers but wrong directions can make to any Lat/Long position.

One or more waypoints that you intend to pass through in a particular order is called a route. Some of the simplest navigators demand that you enter the waypoints in the correct order, but most allow you to pick, choose and rearrange. This is particularly useful for racing boats whose (human) navigator can store the lat and long of all the local race marks in his (electronic) navigator's memory at the start of the season, and quickly assemble the relevant ones into a route when the course is displayed at any time up to the five-minute gun.

Pre-prepared Waypoints

In planning a route for waypoint navigation it is easy to concentrate solely on the waypoints and to forget that the only reason they are

there is because you are intending to travel from one to the other, and that—circumstances permitting—you will be doing so in a series of straight lines. Rather than putting a waypoint off each main headland along the way, and at a few buoys in between, it is much better to draw the route as a series of straight lines first, and then put a waypoint at each corner.

If you decide to start with the waypoints, either because they are already stored in the navigator's memory or because you have chosen to use waypoints from one of the many published lists, it is important to draw the route in on the chart as well, to check that it does not pass dangerously close to any hazards.

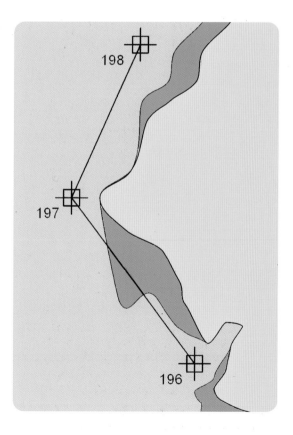

Fig 3–8 Let your route decide your waypoints, not vice versa! Pre-loaded waypoints, or those taken straight from a published list, should be used with care.

Basic Navigator Functions

Six basic functions are common to almost all electronic navigators, though the terminology used to describe them, and the operating procedures required to achieve them, vary from one manufacturer to another. The most fundamental of all is position, given in terms of latitude and longitude. If you plot your position on a chart it is a relatively straightforward matter to measure the range and bearing to a waypoint. An electronic navigator can do this too, except that it uses trigonometry, rather than geometry.

Alternatively, by comparing your position now with your position a few minutes ago, you could work out the direction and distance you have traveled and, from that, work out your speed over the ground. These two are standard functions on electronic navigators and are usually called COG (course over ground), and SOG (speed over ground). CMG and SMG for course made good and speed made good are common variations, as are TRK and VEL for track and velocity.

In practice, most GPS receivers use a rather more sophisticated technique for working out COG and SOG, but both functions can be badly affected by positioning errors, and become increasingly suspect at low speeds. On a stationary boat, in particular, the COG display is likely to fluctuate at random.

One way to improve the accuracy of COG and SOG is to take an average over a period of time, and most of the better electronic navigators have a damping facility based on this principle. "High" damping uses a long time interval and gives a steadier and generally more accurate reading, but is less responsive to genuine changes of COG and SOG.

The final standard function is known as cross track error, usually abbreviated to XTE. XTE can only be used when the navigator is used in the "Go To" mode (or following a route), because it is an indication of how far

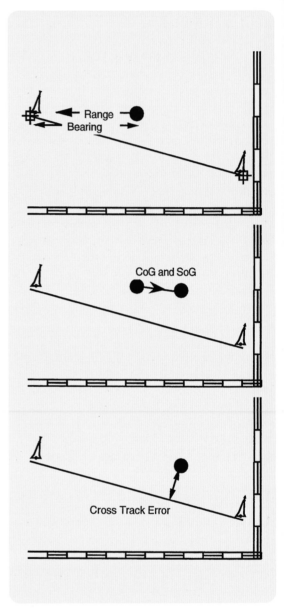

Fig 3–9 As well as position, most electronic navigators offer range and bearing to waypoint (top); course and speed over ground (middle); and cross track error (bottom).

your present position lies from the straight line track between your starting point (where you chose the "Go To" function) and the selected waypoint you are headed toward.

Other Functions

Most electronic navigators offer a range of other functions, including a "man overboard" facility, and "time to go"—both of which have their limitations.

On all but a few particularly sophisticated instrument systems, the man overboard facility effectively "freezes" the position at which the man overboard button is pressed, and stores it as a waypoint. It may be tempting to use this to guide the boat back to the spot at which the casualty fell overboard, but you should bear in mind that by the time you get back to that spot the person in the water will have drifted away from it with the current. The real value of the man overboard facility is that it can allow you to give the Coast Guard an accurate time and position, from which they can calculate the casualty's most likely movement.

The time to go facility is invariably based on the range and bearing of the waypoint, and the assumption that the boat's course and speed will be constant. For a motor cruiser, in good conditions, that may be a valid assumption, in which case the time to go should be reasonably accurate. Sailing yachts, by contrast, hardly ever maintain a constant course or speed, so the time to go is likely to fluctuate, and will hardly ever be more than a very rough estimate.

Quick Plotting

No matter how seductive the display of an electronic navigator, its information is of very limited value until it can be related to the real world. The most obvious way to do this is to take the latitude and longitude readout, and plot them on a chart, but this involves manipulating parallel rulers, dividers and a pencil—and this, in itself, can be difficult in bad conditions. An alternative is to use some of the other functions "backwards."

Plotting by Range and Bearing

In your home waters it can be useful to draw a "spider's web" of bearing lines and range rings on the chart, centered around some key

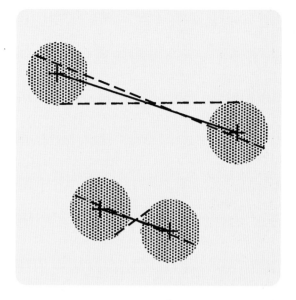

Fig 3–10 Small errors in successive position fixes (represented by the shaded circles) affect the accuracy of an electronic navigator's course and speed display. The effect is exaggerated at low speeds (bottom).

feature, such as the harbor entrance. Draw the bearing lines at 5°- or 10°-intervals, and label them, and use a compass to draw concentric circles with radii of 1/2, 1, 1 1/2 miles and so on (Figure 3–11).

When the chosen feature is the navigator's "active" waypoint, it is easy to relate the displayed bearing to one of the pre-drawn bearing lines, and the displayed range to one of the range rings, so that a position can be plotted very quickly and with no need for plotting instruments. The accuracy of a position plotted by this means depends largely on the distance between the boat and the waypoint: at 6 miles, an error of 1° represents about 200 meters (656 feet or 219 yards), but at 60 miles you'd have to move at least a mile to change the bearing by 1°. On a short sea passage, one way to reduce the distances involved is to pick a reference position roughly halfway along the intended route.

Another variation is to store the center of a compass rose as a waypoint, even if you have no intention of going there. The bearing can then be plotted quickly and easily, just by laying a straight edge across the rose.

Plotting by Range and XTE

Rapid fixing by range and bearing gives flexibility to putter all over an area, but it is less useful on a passage from A to B, because its range limit is about 5–10 miles, and it requires a lot of preparation.

An alternative is to use range in conjunction with cross track error, by marking the chart at regular intervals (e.g., 1/2 mile or 1 mile) along the track, working backwards from each waypoint, and drawing lines parallel to the track at some convenient distance (such as 1 mile) each side of it (Figure 3–12). When the navigator shows that you are, for instance,

5 miles from the waypoint with an XTE of 0.7 mile to port, it should be easy to find the 5-mile mark, and measure or estimate 0.7 miles away from the track.

Chart Plotters

For centuries navigators had to devote most of their time and effort to working out their position. Now, to a very large extent, GPS can be relied upon to take care of that. The snag is that even with quick plotting techniques, a human navigator working on a paper chart can't hope to keep up with the flow of information available from the GPS receiver.

One solution is to use a chart plotter to display the boat's current position on an electronic chart. Of course, plotters have their

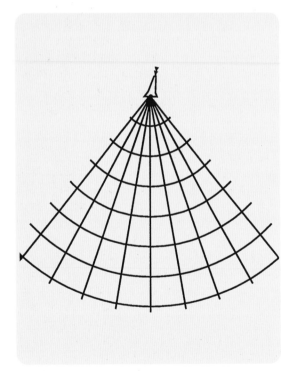

Fig 3–11 The range and bearing display can be used to plot positions quickly, by drawing a "spider's web" on the chart around a chosen waypoint.

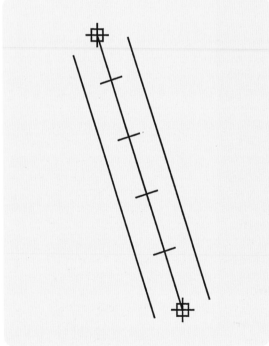

Fig 3–12 On long passages, range and cross track error can be used for quick plotting, so long as the chart has been marked up in advance.

drawbacks, but their great strengths are that they update the position continuously, without human intervention, and without introducing such very human errors as plotting 38°45.6'N instead of 38°46.5'N.

Even the simplest plotters, however, do more than this, allowing you to mark waypoints, plan routes, and measure directions and distances, while some can work out the course to steer to allow for tidal current, or even plan the optimum route to follow to allow for forecast changes in wind strength and direction. They can then show how your actual position compares with your plan, give simple steering instructions to a human helmsman, or control an autopilot.

Any chart plotter is a combination of three main groups of components:

- the hardware
- the cartography
- the software

The hardware is the physical equipment (the casing, display, control panel, and so on) and the internal electronics, such as the power supply, processor and memory. It may be designed from the outset as a chart plotter; it may be combined with some other equipment such as a radar or autopilot; or it may be a desktop or laptop PC or even a PDA (Personal Digital Assistant).

The cartography refers to the electronic charts. They are available from various sources, in different formats and on different media, such as CD-ROMs, floppy discs, PCMCIA cards, flash memory cards, or custom-made cartridges of various shapes and sizes.

The software is the link between the two, converting the electronic cartography into a form that can be displayed on the screen, enabling us to carry out navigational tasks, and communicating with other electronic equipment such as a GPS receiver and autopilot.

Dedicated Hardware vs. PC

In general terms, most dedicated hardware plotters are produced by specialist marine electronics companies, and are supplied with their own software already installed. Dedicated hardware is good because it is rugged and waterproof (at least to some extent) and is designed to operate from an unreliable 12-volt supply. Its control panel and operating procedures are likely to have been designed specifically for use as a chart plotter, and although the choice of cartography is limited—usually to one particular supplier and one particular type of cartridge—the coverage is generally good and cartridges are readily available.

PC plotters consist of specialist plotting software that can be loaded into almost any personal computer, though laptops are the most popular for the job. PC plotters are good because the initial outlay is relatively low (especially if you already own a suitable computer) and because the computer itself is very much more versatile than a dedicated plotter. Some PC software can use cartography from a variety of different suppliers, but additional or updated charts are not always easy to come by.

Raster vs. Vector

Although there are many suppliers of electronic charts, the charts themselves can be divided into two main groups: raster and vector. Raster charts can be regarded as electronic photocopies of paper charts, produced by scanning a master copy of a paper chart, in much the same way as a fax machine scans a document that is about to be sent. The chart is broken down into a vast number of tiny dots (pixels), and the position and color of each pixel is recorded. Instead of sending this information down a telephone line, as a fax machine does, the chart scanner stores it on the cartographer's computer, from where it can be copied onto CD-ROMs, or proprietary cartridges and supplied to customers.

Raster charts are relatively cheap and simple to make, but each chart uses up a lot of memory or disc space. Because they are electronically copied straight from the paper chart, they are familiar in appearance, and contain exactly the same information; nothing is added or taken away. The drawback of this is that they can only be used effectively at about the same scale as the original chart; if you zoom in, then letters and symbols become huge, but without any extra detail becoming visible; while if you zoom out, names and symbols become illegible.

Vector charts are produced by electronically tracing raster charts. The fundamental difference is that lines are not stored as strings of darkened pixels, but as lines. Vector charts originally became popular for small boat hardware plotters because although they are more expensive to produce, they occupy much less memory. The vector format also allows more flexibility in the way the chart is used: A vector chart can be zoomed in or out much further than a raster chart, but the letters and symbols always stay the same size.

"Unfolding" Electronic Charts

At present, electronic charting is still in the process of rapid development; different manufacturers use different types of cartridges and discs, with different software and different keyboards and control panel layouts. Even so, there are a number of processes that are more or less common to all chart plotters—analogous, in some ways, to the process of unfolding a paper chart ready for use.

Zoom in / zoom out are self-explanatory terms referring to the way in which the scale of the displayed image of the chart can be changed. From the user's point of view, zooming is usually a very simple process.

Scrolling and panning are ways of moving the screen image to make different areas visible: scrolling generally refers to a north–south movement and panning to an east–west movement. Many programs also include different "centering" options which allow you (for instance) to lock the center of the display to your own position. Other options allow the user to choose whether to view the chart in the conventional "north-up" mode, or to turn it round to "course-up" mode.

De-cluttering is only available on vector charts. In effect, each type of information is stored in a different database: contour lines in one; spot soundings in another; major lighthouses in another; buoys in another; and so on. The effect is as though a paper chart were built up using many different layers of tracing paper, each of which can be removed or replaced at will. Most software programs add and remove some layers automatically as you zoom in and out, in order to stop the screen becoming cluttered. Many, however, allow you to choose "more detail" or "less detail," or to make your own selection of exactly what kind of information you want to see. It's important

Fig 3–13 A typical small-boat chart plotter

to appreciate, though, that the accuracy of information depends on the scale of the original chart, not on the zoom level you happen to have chosen, and to be aware that it is possible to inadvertently hide information that could turn out to be important.

Chart Databases

On a raster chart, a feature such as a buoy is represented by a cluster of colored pixels that together make up the shape of the buoy symbol exactly as it appears on the original paper chart. On a vector chart, however, the buoy's position is linked to a database of information about the buoy. The software can use this database in various ways. Some programs, for instance, represent all navigation aids by means of the same diamond-shaped symbol. When you select one (by "pointing at it" with the cursor) the data is revealed in a text panel somewhere on the screen. Other systems use the database information to display a symbol showing the shape and color of the buoy itself.

More sophisticated versions of this are used on some electronic charts to provide graphic representations of the changing height of tide at particular places, to provide additional information such as lists of port facilities, or to superimpose arrows showing the tidal current on top of the main chart.

Updating Electronic Charts

Human nature being what it is, we tend to regard things electronic as being always dead-on-time. After all, we see many things on the TV news at the very moment they are happening, don't we? But the reality is that electronic charts are effectively "printed matter," too, and as such, are as prone as paper charts to becoming outdated after a while. In short, they need updating from time to time, also. The good news here is that the process can be ever so much easier than updating paper charts; no hand-drawn corrections or paste-on patches required.

Updating Raster Charts

Since raster charts are simply electronic images of NOAA's paper charts, the same update system described for POD charts also applies to them. Once NOAA cartographers update the master electronic versions, the digital differences between the updated chart and the base edition are isolated into an update or patch file. NOAA posts these updated files on the Internet where they are available for free download. Electronic chart companies offer an update service for mariners who have purchased their charts. The update or patch files (considerably smaller than the entire chart file) can more easily be sent by e-mail or downloaded by subscribers. Software is available to apply the update patch to the base version of the raster chart.

Updating Vector Charts

Currently, NOAA has over 600 vector charts available for free download. Updates for these charts are also available for free download. Each NtM and/or LNM chart correction must be applied independently to the electronic master version. NOAA's goal is to post vector chart updates weekly for its entire suite of charts. The simplest, least expensive, but the most laborious way, is to hand enter the updates from the Notices to Mariners into the navigation computer—*if* the navigation software you select is annotation-capable, as well as user friendly. Each program handles this option in different ways, so be sure to check this out before you buy. And remember, some GPS plotters may not offer this capability. Of course, the fastest, easiest, but more expensive, way to keep your charts current is to subscribe to your chart vendor's update service.

Planning on a Plotter

Almost all plotters include the same kind of facilities for creating and storing waypoints as are found in position fixers. They have an important advantage, though, in that you don't have to enter waypoint positions in terms of their latitude and longitude coordinates; there is a much simpler procedure for creating waypoints graphically, in effect by just pointing at the chart image and telling the plotter where you want to go.

Creating routes is usually almost as easy: It's just a matter of pointing at a succession of waypoints in turn. Most plotters now include a useful feature that is sometimes known as "rubber banding," by which you can add a waypoint between two existing waypoints, and then move it, to "stretch" the route like a rubber band to avoid obstacles.

This allows you to take a broad-brush approach to passage planning, perhaps starting off with a straight line route from your departure waypoint to your destination, then adding extra waypoints to stretch your route around major headlands, before zooming in to look at each leg of the trip in more detail, and perhaps adding more intermediate waypoints to deal with minor hazards that didn't show up on the small-scale, large-area picture.

4 Position Fixing

Finding out where you are, or "fixing" your position, is seldom an end in itself. It is, however, a vital first step in making a great many navigational decisions: You cannot decide which way to go until you know where you are starting from. There are many ways of "getting a fix" other than by electronic means, of which one of the commonest and most useful is by compass bearings.

Compass Bearings

If you take a bearing of a landmark by looking toward it across the top of a hand-bearing compass, your line of sight can be represented on the chart by a pencil line drawn along that bearing and passing through the symbol that represents the landmark. As that line represents your line of sight, your position must be somewhere along it, so it is called a position line—often referred to as a "line of position," which can be abbreviated as LOP. Doing the same with the bearing of another landmark produces a second LOP. There is only one place where you can possibly be on both position lines at once, and that is where they cross. If everything in a navigator's life were reliable, then two intersecting LOPs would be enough for a fix, but in practice it is normal to take yet another bearing, of a third landmark. The third position line does not make a fix more accurate: its sole purpose is to guard against a gross error, such as a landmark wrongly identified or a bearing wrongly read or plotted.

In theory, one might expect all three position lines to cross at a single point—each one

confirming the accuracy of the other two. Such perfect fixes happen so rarely in real life that when an experienced navigator produces one he is more likely to ask himself what has gone wrong, than to pat himself on the back! More often the three lines intersect to form a triangle known as a "cocked hat" (see Figure 4–1). Strictly speaking, it would not be true to say that a small cocked hat is more accurate or reliable than a large one, but you can generally

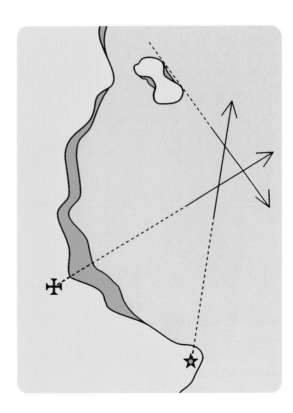

Fig 4–1 Three position lines rarely intersect at a single point, but form a triangle known as a "cocked hat."

be a lot more confident about a compact cocked hat. One that straggles around all over the chart shows that something is wrong. Erase the lines and start again!

Improving the Fix

There are a number of things you can do to minimize the size of the cocked hat. The most obvious of these is to make sure that the landmarks are correctly identified, i.e., that the features you have taken bearings of do indeed correspond with those on the chart. It is also a good idea to make sure the bearings are measured as accurately as is practical by, for example, trying to take bearings with the compass in a spot that is relatively free of deviating influences. No matter how carefully you take the bearings, though, some error is almost inevitable.

The effect of bearing errors can be minimized by a careful choice of landmarks. Ideally they should be spaced around the horizon, to give the largest possible angle of cut between the position lines. For a fix using two position lines, this means choosing objects that are, as nearly as possible, 90° apart. For a three-position-line fix the optimum angles are 60° or 120°.

The reason for this is shown in Figure 4–2: if two position lines cross at a shallow angle, a small bearing error creates a much larger position error than it would if the two position lines intersected at a larger angle.

Close objects are better than more distant ones, even if the distant ones are more conspicuous. As Figure 4–3 shows, the position error caused by a small bearing error is far greater when the landmark concerned is a long way away than if it is close at hand. The order in which you take bearings can also make a difference, particularly on a fast moving boat or with landmarks at close range. Because the boat is moving while the fix is being taken, its position will be slightly different at the beginning of the fix than at the end. The bearing of objects directly ahead or astern will

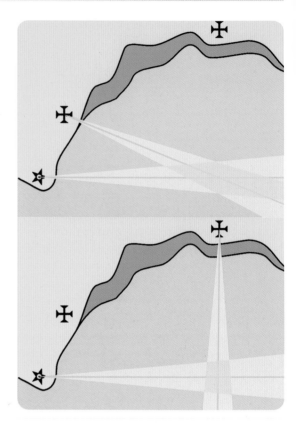

Fig 4–2 Small errors in bearing produce an exaggerated error in the fix if the position lines intersect at a shallow angle. So choose well-spaced landmarks for visual fixing.

not change very much, but those abeam will appear to be moving aft. For this reason you should take bearings ahead or astern first, followed by those over the bow or quarter, and finish up with those which are almost abeam. Taking bearings in this order not only minimizes the effect of the boat's own movement on the size of the cocked hat, but also means that the final fix is as up to date as possible.

Accuracy vs. Speed

Suggesting that bearings should be taken as accurately as is practical, and then that the boat's own movement affects the size of the cocked hat, begs the question, "Which is more

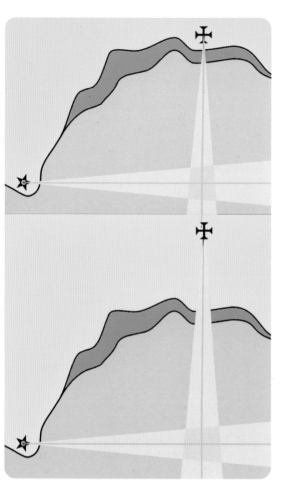

Fig 4–4 Steeply-sloping headlands are good landmarks. On shelving coastlines it can be difficult to decide where the edge of the land really is.

Fig 4–3 The effect of small bearing errors is exaggerated if the landmarks are far away. Choose near landmarks rather than distant ones.

important—accuracy or speed?" The answer is that it depends on the distance of the landmark concerned. You should always wait until the compass card has stopped spinning, but for landmarks at very close range speed is much more important than precision and it may be sufficient to take a rough mental average of the bearing while the card is still swinging, to an accuracy of perhaps five or ten degrees. For a landmark one mile away, an accuracy of 5° corresponds to a position accuracy of about 150 meters (492 feet; 164 yards), or about the

distance a five-knot sailboat would cover in one minute. If the landmark was 15 miles away, a bearing accurate to ±5° would produce a position uncertainty of 1.25 miles, equivalent to 15 minutes worth of movement for the same five-knot boat. So for distant landmarks it may be worth spending a minute or more on each bearing to take a more careful average of several swings of the compass card.

Choosing Landmarks
Any charted feature can be used as a landmark for a fix by visual bearings. The best are compact, conspicuous and easily-identified, such as lighthouses, beacons, churches, and water towers. But natural features such as headlands and rocks can also be used, and in many of the most attractive cruising areas are

far more plentiful. The main requirement is the same as for man-made landmarks—that they should be positively identified. There is no point taking a bearing of a rock if you do not know which rock it is!

Headlands can be very useful landmarks indeed, because they are generally conspicuous and—as long as you know roughly where you are in the first place—are usually easy to identify. But there are a couple of pitfalls to be avoided. Gently-sloping headlands look as distinct on the chart as near vertical ones, but when it comes to taking a bearing of the real thing it can be very difficult to identify exactly where the headland really ends: at low water a considerable expanse of foreshore may be uncovered, extending the visible land farther to seaward than it appears on the chart; conversely, at any distance more than about two miles or so, the edge of the land may be below the horizon, so that what appears to be the end of the headland is actually a point somewhere inland. Steeply-sloping headlands or cliffs give neither of these problems. When plotting the bearing of a headland on a chart it can often be difficult to tell exactly which part of the headland you are seeing. The solution is to set the parallel rulers to the correct bearing, and then gradually move them in from seaward until one ruler just touches the coast. That first point of contact is the particular point you took a bearing of. Buoys also have their limitations as marks on which to base position lines, because they are not truly "fixed" objects, but are free to drift to the extent of their mooring chains, and have been known to drag their anchors or break adrift altogether. On the credit side, however, they are often easy to identify, and may well be much closer than any fixed landmark. These two advantages usually more than make up for their drawbacks: a position line based on a buoy a mile away is likely to be more accurate than one based on a distant headland or lighthouse, even if the buoy is 50 meters (164 feet) out of position.

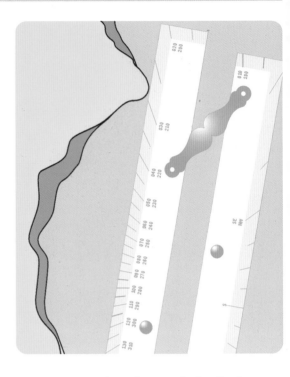

Fig 4–5 Having taken a bearing of a headland, move the parallel rulers in from seaward until they just touch the coastline.

Range Lines

One definition of range is "two or more objects on the same bearing from an observer." The other definition involves distance away (see page 60). While this could be a source of confusion, it helps to distinguish the meanings by the article used. Having two objects in line is usually called *a* range, but when referring to a distance, it is usually stated as *the* range. Our concern here is that "A Range" occurs whenever two objects appear to be in line with each other. Ranges make ideal position lines because:

- they are instant; there is no need to wait for a compass card to settle.
- they are accurate and independent of errors such as deviation.
- they are quick to plot, because a range can be drawn on the chart simply by ruling a straight line that passes through the two landmarks.

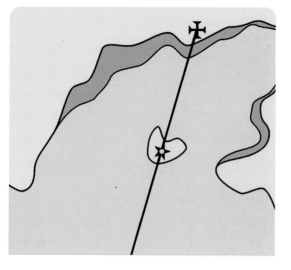

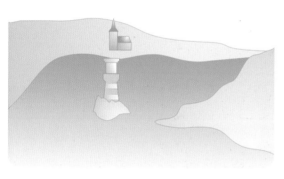

Fig 4–6 Two objects in line form a range—and a charted range is a very accurate, very simple position line.

Ranges are so useful that many have been set up deliberately, with conspicuous marks positioned to indicate a safe route through narrow channels (see "A Visual Buoyage Guide" on page 169) or to accurately mark the ends of a measured distance. These, and naturally occurring ranges, are often shown on charts or mentioned in pilot books. A range does not have to be purpose-built to be of use for navigation, though: Any two objects can be used as long as they can be positively identified and are shown on the chart. Their virtues make ranges well worth looking out for, but it is most unlikely that you will find yourself on two or three ranges at once. A range can often

be found that will provide one position line, but the other one or two position lines required for a fix will have to be derived by other means, such as compass bearings.

Plotting Direction-based Fixes

You should very rarely find yourself in a situation in which you do not have at least a rough idea of where you are, so there is no need to draw the full length of every position line on the chart. For the first one, a couple of inches or so in the vicinity of where you expect the fix to be should be enough. And the second and third position lines can be even shorter— just enough to produce the cocked hat. The boat's assumed position within the cocked hat is marked by a spot surrounded by a circle (see Figure 2–18 on page 37). Finally, and perhaps most important of all, the fix should be labeled with the time at which it was taken.

Assessing the Quality of a Fix

Although one cannot say for certain that a fix given by a compact cocked hat is reliable, it is certainly true that a large cocked hat gives an unreliable fix. So as a general rule of thumb, it is fair to use the size of the cocked hat as a means of assessing the quality of the fix. In one particular situation, however, this rule fails: that is where the boat and all three landmarks lie on the perimeter of the same circle. Although this sounds unlikely it can easily happen when crossing a bay (Figure 4–7). The geometry of this situation is such that if all the bearings are subject to the same error, such as deviation, they will still produce a good looking fix but in the wrong position.

Am I Inside the Cocked Hat?

Any fix that produces a cocked hat begs the question "where is the boat's true position?" Clearly it cannot be at all three intersections at once. It is usual to assume that the true position is in the center of the cocked hat, equidistant from all three position lines. All things being equal that is a reasonable "best guess," but it is

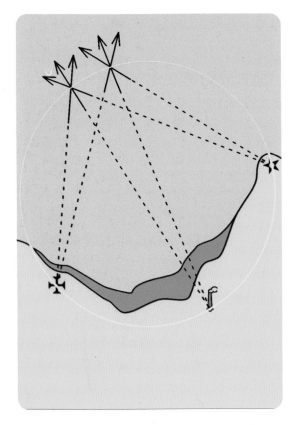

Fig 4–7 A small cocked hat can give a misleading impression of accuracy if you happen to be on or near the circle that passes through all three landmarks.

important to appreciate that the probability of your true position being inside the cocked hat is only 25%! In other words, there is a three-to-one chance that you are outside it. For this reason, if one corner of the cocked hat is a considerably more dangerous place to be than any of the others, it is as well to assume your position to be in the worst corner, and to bear in mind that there is a small but distinct possibility that even that is unduly optimistic.

Position Lines by Range Measurement

Visual bearings and range lines both produce straight position lines because both are based on direction. Range measurements—your distance away from an object—produce equally valid position lines, but they are circular in shape. If, for instance, you know you are two miles from a lighthouse, then your position must lie somewhere on the circumference of a circle with a radius of two miles, centered on the lighthouse. There are several reasonable ways of measuring range from a yacht, but the most common are: radar and "rising and dipping distances."

Radar
The use of radar is covered more fully in Chapter 8, but essentially radar is an electronic device that measures the range of objects by measuring the time taken for a short pulse of microwave energy to make the there-and-back trip between its antenna and the object in question. By using a directional antenna it can also measure the object's bearing. So over the course of a couple of seconds, a radar set can build up a map-like picture of its surroundings on a screen. Regularly-spaced range rings can be superimposed on the picture to give a sense of scale and a quick way of estimating the distance of objects. Alternatively a variable range marker (VRM)—an adjustable range ring, can be used to give a more precise measurement of range.

Dipping Distances
Another easy method of measuring ranges requires no equipment whatsoever. It relies on the curvature of the earth, which makes distant objects dip below the horizon as you move away from them, or rise above it as you move toward them. Unfortunately, it can only be used at night, on brightly-lit objects such as lighthouses, and only over certain ranges. As you move toward a major lighthouse at night you will first see the "loom" of its light, like a searchlight sweeping across the sky. As you get closer still, the loom appears more intense, but the beam looks shorter until, quite suddenly, the light itself appears as a bright pinpoint with no perceptible loom at all.

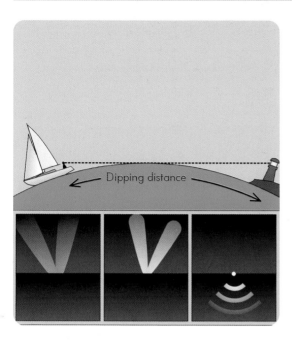

Fig 4–8 The dipping distance of a light is the range at which it first appears above the horizon or drops below it.

Going away from the light the reverse happens—the pinpoint flash gives way to the loom.

The distance at which that transition from flash to loom takes place is called the light's "rising" or "dipping" distance. The rising or dipping distance depends on two factors: the height of the light above sea level; and the height of the observer's eye above sea level. The height of the light can be found from the chart or from the Light List. Strictly speaking, the quoted height (called the elevation) should be corrected to allow for the effect of tide (see Chapter 5), but except in the case of short lighthouses or very large tidal ranges this seldom makes much practical difference. Once you know the height of the light and your own height of eye, the dipping distance can be found either from tables published in some yachtsmen's almanacs, the distance of visibility tables published in Coast Pilots (Figure 4–9), "Table 13" (from NGA's Publication 9), which is available on-line in PDF form at http://pollux.nss.nima.mil/NAV_PUBS/APN/

Tables/T-13.pdf or by calculator using the formula:

Range in miles = $1.15 \times (\sqrt{Ht_{eye}} + \sqrt{Ht_{object}})$ where both heights are in feet
or
Range in miles = $2.08 \times (\sqrt{Ht_{eye}} + \sqrt{Ht_{object}})$ where both heights are in meters.

To use table 13, find the row corresponding to the height of the light and the column corresponding to your height of eye. The rising or dipping distance is shown in the square where the row and column meet. To use the table shown in Figure 4–9, find the distance of visibility for the height of your eye (above sea level) and then the distance of visibility for the height of object. Add the two to get the total distance of visibility, i.e., the "dipping" distance. For example, if your height of eye is 12 feet, your distance of visibility (to the horizon) is 4.1 nautical miles. If the elevation of the lighthouse is 160 feet, it will be visible when it is 14.8 nm beyond the horizon, which means the transition from loom to flash will occur when your distance from the lighthouse is 18.9 nautical miles.

Plotting Fixes Based on Range

Plotting any kind of range-based fix requires a drawing compass. This is set to the measured range and used to draw an arc, centered on the object from which the range was measured. As with direction-based fixes there is no need to draw in the complete position line—an inch or two is enough.

Just like a fix by visual bearings, the boat's assumed position should be marked with a spot surrounded by a circle, and the whole fix labeled with the time at which it was taken.

Position Lines by Depth

For most of the time in coastal navigation the closest solid land is directly below you. It too

Distance of Visibility for Objects Having Various Elevations

Height (feet)	Distance (nautical miles)	Distance (statute miles)	Height (meters)	Height (feet)	Distance (nautical miles)	Distance (statute miles)	Height (meters)
1	1.2	1.3	0.3	120	12.8	14.7	36.6
2	1.7	1.9	0.6	125	13.1	15.1	38.1
3	2.0	2.3	0.9	130	13.3	15.4	39.6
4	2.3	2.7	1.2	135	13.6	15.6	41.2
5	2.6	3.0	1.5	140	13.8	15.9	42.7
6	2.9	3.3	1.8	145	14.1	16.2	44.2
7	3.1	3.6	2.1	150	14.3	16.5	45.7
8	3.3	3.8	2.4	160	14.8	17.0	48.8
9	3.5	4.0	2.7	170	15.3	17.6	51.8
10	3.7	4.3	3.1	180	15.7	18.1	54.9
11	3.9	4.5	3.4	190	16.1	18.6	57.9
12	4.1	4.7	3.7	200	16.5	19.0	61.0
13	4.2	4.9	4.0	210	17.0	19.5	64.0
14	4.4	5.0	4.3	220	17.4	20.0	67.1

Fig 4–9 Geographic Range tables show the dipping distance of a light, based on its height and the observer's height of eye above sea level. The two distances are determined individually and then added. (Source: *NOS Coast Pilot 2*)

can be used to give a position line based on a well-defined depth contour.

Like all fixing methods this has its limitations and its strengths: position lines based on depth are unreliable in very deep water, where the echo sounder's inaccuracies may be significant, or on soft or moving seabeds where the chart may not accurately represent the true depth, but on the other hand, in poor visibility the echo sounder may be the only source of information available on a boat without other electronic nav-aids.

The depths shown by spot soundings (numbers) or contours on a chart represent the depth when the tide is at its lowest, so they very rarely represent true depth of water, but have to be "adjusted" to allow for the height of tide (see Chapter 5). If, for example, the height of tide is 3.4 meters (11 feet) then the depth of water over the 5-meter (16-foot) contour will be 8.4 meters (27 feet). To put this another way, when the height of tide is 3.4 meters (11 feet) and the echo sounder shows a depth below the water line of 8.4 meters (27 feet) you must be on the 5-meter contour. This in turn means that the 5-meter contour itself is a position line—even though it may turn out to be a very wiggly one!

Line of Soundings

An alternative way of using an echo sounder to find your position—though it is really almost a last resort, and can only be used effectively when you are crossing a number of well defined contours—is known as a line of soundings. Again, being based on depth measurement it requires the height of tide to be taken into account.

Record the depth and log reading each time you cross a contour, remembering to subtract the height of tide from the depth shown by the echo sounder: If you are looking for the 10-meter (33 foot) contour, for instance, and the height of tide is 3 meters (10 feet), you will be crossing the contour when the echo sounder displays a depth of 13 meters (43 feet). It may help later if you also record a few intermediate depths at regular intervals.

Mark all these adjusted depths on the edge of a strip of paper, at intervals corresponding to the distance you have traveled between each reading. Then draw your approximate track on to the chart, and move the strip of paper around the area, keeping it parallel to the penciled track, until the depths shown on the paper correspond with the soundings shown on the chart. The position of the last sounding on the chart corresponds with the boat's position at the time.

Mixed Fixes

Although it is tempting to think in terms of "a visual fix" or "a radar fix" it is worth remembering that most fixes are simply a combination of several position lines. There is no rule that says all the position lines have to come from the same source, so it is quite possible to combine two or three different types of position line in a single fix, as long as you stick to the principle that they should cross at as large an angle as possible.

A good example of the kind of situation where a mixed fix might be used is at night, after an offshore passage, ready to enter harbor in daylight later in the morning. The range and bearing of a single lighthouse—range based on its rising and dipping distance and bearing by hand bearing compass—with a check on the depth by echo sounder, gives a fix as much as 20 miles offshore.

Running Fixes

A landfall fix using a range and bearing is one example of how you can fix your position

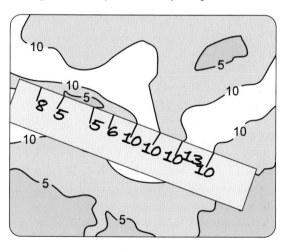

Fig 4–10 As a last resort, a position can sometimes be found by marking up a strip of paper with echo sounder readings corrected for height of tide, and moving it around until it matches up with the chart.

when there is only a single landmark in sight, but there is an alternative, called a running fix. In Figure 4–11 the navigator has taken a bearing of the lighthouse, but for some reason or another has not been able to cross it with another position line in order to produce a fix. Sometime later the boat has moved on. If he had been starting with a fix instead of with a single position her navigator could work out her estimated position (see Chapter 7). But he did not: he knows only that he was somewhere along the position line A B C.

If he had been at A, his estimated position would be D; if he had been at B, then his estimated position would be E; and if he had been at C, his estimated position would now be F. D, E and F all lie on a straight line, parallel to the original position line but separated from it by the distance and direction the boat has moved since the original bearing was taken. The line D E F is called an "advanced position line," and once it has been worked out it can be treated like any other position line and crossed with a new bearing of the same object (or the range of that object) in order to produce a running fix.

You do not, in practice, have to work on three points along the original line of bearing: one is enough. It can be anywhere, though it is usual to choose the point nearest to where you believe yourself to be. From this point, plot an EP (see Chapter 7), then draw in the transferred position line parallel to the original line of bearing and passing through the EP.

A running fix is not only subject to all the usual errors that afflict any other fix based on visual bearings, but is also highly dependent on the accuracy of the estimated position used to transfer the position line. That, in turn, is dependent on the accuracy of the boat's log and compass, on the tide tables, sea state, and on the ability of the helmsman and navigator.

With so many things that could go wrong a running fix is not to be relied on, but neither should it be dismissed as useless: Even a rough position can be very useful in the middle of a longish passage. Besides, if there is only one thing in sight at a time, then the chances are that you do not need a high degree of accuracy because there is unlikely to be anything around to hit! You do not, incidentally, have to use the same landmark for both position lines, so a running fix can be equally useful when following a relatively featureless coastline, where the only recognizable landmarks are too far apart for more than one to be visible at once.

Doubling the Angle on the Bow

A special case of the running fix is known as "doubling the angle on the bow." If you note the log reading when a landmark is, say, 30° off the bow and then again when the yacht has sailed on far enough for the landmark to be 60° off the bow, then your distance off the landmark is the same as the distance traveled (see Figure 4–13).

This technique is really only a rule of thumb: it hardly justifies the name "fix" because it completely ignores so many significant factors such as the effect of wind and current. But for a boat on a steady course and in an area of weak tidal currents, it can be a useful quick check.

Four Point Fix

This special case occurs when the initial angle on the bow is 45° ("four points," in the old "points" notation), because when this is doubled it becomes 90°—and the landmark is therefore abeam. Again the distance off corresponds to the distance traveled between the two bearings.

The Simplest Fix of All

The simplest fix of all is inherently more accurate than any of the others, yet it requires no measurement, no arithmetic, and no plotting apart from marking it on the chart and labeling it with the time. It is achieved

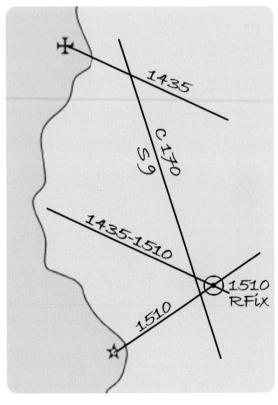

Fig 4–12 A running fix does not have to use only one landmark: An advanced position line can be particularly useful if you lose sight of one landmark before sighting the next.

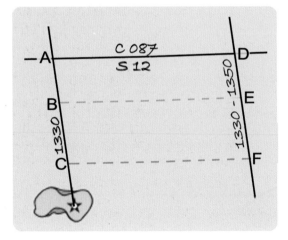

Fig 4–11 A position line can be "advanced" to allow for the distance the boat has traveled since the bearing was taken.

simply by passing very close to some fixed and charted object.

Of course such a simple fix has its drawbacks—nothing can be quite that perfect. It depends on there being a suitable object precisely positioned, with safe water on at least one side and in a convenient location. Ideally this calls for a post or beacon driven into the seabed, in water deep enough for the yacht. Buoys and the Large Navigational Buoys (LNBs) that have replaced lightships are slightly less perfect objects because—like any anchored object—they usually drift a few yards away from their designated position, and can occasionally break loose altogether or drag off station.

The value of "the simplest fix of all" should not be understated, though: its accuracy is generally on a par with that of the most sophisticated electronic position-fixing devices, and the ease and speed with which it can be plotted make it invaluable in rough weather or when sailing short-handed. For high speed

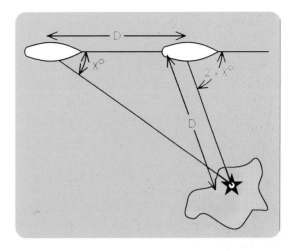

Fig 4–13 A special case of a running fix, known as doubling the angle on the bow, can be a useful rough check.

craft, in particular, it is often worth making a slight detour to pass close to a buoy or beacon, rather than trying to obtain a fix by any other means.

5 | Tides

It is almost impossible to spend more than a few days anywhere on any coast of North America without becoming aware of the effect of the tide—the regular raising and lowering of sea level—so it must have been common knowledge even to prehistoric sailors.

Even land-locked waters, such as the Great Lakes or the Mediterranean Sea, are tidal to some extent, but their tides are so much smaller that they are easily masked by the effects of wind and barometric pressure. This is probably why tides failed to arouse the curiosity of the ancient Greek philosophers. Not until the Roman invasion of Britain were they the subject of any kind of scientific analysis. A proper explanation of them, however, had to wait until Newton "invented" gravity.

The Causes of Tides

Tides are caused by the gravity of the sun and moon. Although the sun is much bigger and heavier than the moon, it is so much farther away that its effect is less, so it is worth getting to grips with the moon's effect first.

The Moon's Tides
Imagine the world as a uniform ball of solid rock covered by a layer of water. Although it is usually said that the moon orbits around the earth with the earth's gravity stopping it from flying off into space, that is something of an over simplification; the two bodies really make up a single system held together by the mutual attraction of each other's gravity, and spinning about a point somewhere between the two.

The effect of gravity decreases with distance, so the water closest to the moon is attracted toward it somewhat more strongly than is the solid mass of the earth itself. The water on the far side, being farther from the moon, is attracted less strongly. The overall result is to produce two bulges, or tidal waves, one on each side of the earth, but both moving round it to follow the moon in its 28-day orbit. Meanwhile, of course, the earth is still spinning on its own axis, so any given point on its surface will pass the crest of one tidal wave, then the trough, then the crest of the other and so on. The moon goes round the earth in the same direction as the earth's own rotation so it takes slightly longer than twelve hours for a fixed point to go from one high tide to the other, but even so, these tides are called half daily or "semi-diurnal."

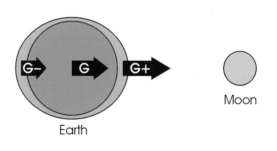

Fig 5–1 Tides are caused by the moon's gravity pulling on the water nearest to it more strongly than on the earth itself, while leaving the water on the other side of the earth behind.

Diurnal Tides

This straightforward picture of two more-or-less equal semi-diurnal tides per day would hold true only if the moon's orbit were permanently lined up with the equator—which it is not. The earth's axis is at an angle to the moon's orbital plane, so the moon appears to wander from north to south and back again every month. This skews the picture of the earth with its two symmetrical tidal waves: A stationary observer anywhere north of the equator would see one hump as being much bigger than the other. In other words, he would see a major high tide roughly once every 25 hours. This is called a diurnal tide.

Tides in the Real World

All this theory suggests that if the world were really completely covered with water, we would experience semi-diurnal tides twice a month (while the moon crosses the equator), and diurnal tides the rest of the time. The reason that this is not the case is because of the presence of land, which divides this huge body of water into separate seas and oceans, each of which behaves as if it were a huge bowl, with the water sloshing around inside it.

If you were to fill a wash basin with water and gently rock it, you would find that the water would slosh back and forth with a certain natural rhythm, and that if your rocking

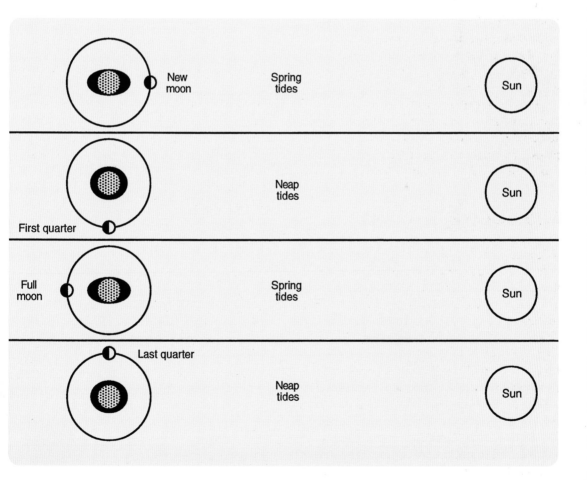

Fig 5-2 Big tides (springs) occur when the gravitational forces of the sun and moon are together or directly opposed. Small tides (neaps) occur in between.

matched that rhythm, small but regular movements would be enough to build up an exaggerated surge of water in the bowl. Exactly how fast your rocking action would need to be depends on the size of the bowl: A small bowl needs faster movements than a big one. Much the same thing applies to the world's oceans, though it is complicated by their irregular shapes and the reality that each ocean is not one large individual basin but rather is made up of several smaller ones. The Atlantic responds strongly to semi-diurnal tides. This means that in northern Europe and along the eastern seaboard of the U.S. and Canada, the most obvious characteristic of tides is a pattern of 2 highs and 2 lows that are quite similar in their respective heights with about 12 hr 25 min between successive highs (or lows). The Gulf of Mexico displays mostly diurnal tides with one high and one low each day. And our Pacific ports react most strongly to mixed tides in which there are also two highs and two lows each day, but one set of highs and lows is of a substantially lesser range than the other: There's one high followed by a low and then a "higher high" followed by a "lower low" (see Figure 5–3).

The Sun's Tides

The effect of the sun's gravity alone on a water-covered world would be very much the same as that of the moon, except that because it is so much farther away the tides it produces would be about half the size. When the sun and moon are in line with each other, the sun's tide-raising forces supplement those of the moon, causing bigger than average tides. A week later, when the moon has moved round 90°, so that the sun's gravity is at right angles to the moon's, the tide-raising forces of the sun and moon are opposing each other. The sun's gravity isn't enough to cancel out the lunar tide altogether, but it reduces it, producing a smaller high tide.

A week later still, at full moon, the sun and moon are in line again, and although they are on opposite sides of the earth their

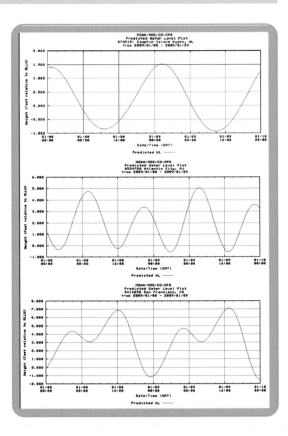

Fig 5–3 Graphic representations showing Diurnal tides on the Gulf of Mexico at Mobile, AL (top), Semi-diurnal tides at Atlantic City, NJ (middle) and Mixed tides on the Pacific coast at San Francisco, CA. (bottom) (Source: NOAA)

tide-raising forces are again supplementing each other to produce another period of big tides.

Springs and Neaps

To sum up the story so far: the Atlantic Ocean is primarily affected by the moon's gravity, which produces a half-daily pattern of alternating high waters and low waters. On to this basic rhythm, the sun superimposes a half-monthly pattern of bigger-than-average tides (with high highs and low lows), interspersed by smaller-than-average tides, with relatively low high waters and relatively high low waters. The big tides are called springs and the small ones are neaps.

It is worth noticing, incidentally, that at any given place, high water spring tides always occur at about the same time of day—give or take an hour. In Miami, Florida, for example, HW springs are always about breakfast and supper-time, while half a world away in Honolulu, Hawaii they are always around midday and midnight.

Other Factors

There are numerous other factors that superimpose even slower rhythms onto these half-daily and half-monthly patterns. Although the sun and moon are in east–west alignment twice a month, to produce spring tides, they only come close to the three dimensional alignment that is required to produce a really big tide twice a year—in March and September. This produces even higher highs and lower lows, sometimes called *equinoctial springs*.

A less noticeable effect is caused by variations in the distance between the earth and the sun and moon, strengthening or reducing the effect of their gravity. On the very rare occasions when the sun, earth and moon are all perfectly lined up and at their closest points of approach to each other simultaneously, they are said to be "in syzygy." That word is more significant for Scrabble players than for navigators, but the event it describes is important because the associated low water is the lowest level to which the tide is ever predicted to fall, and is called the lowest astronomical tide (LAT).

Tide Levels and Datums

Like most complex phenomena, tides have given rise to a glut of technical terms. Some of these, like "high water full and change" have now become obsolete, but many others are still useful, and have survived with specific and distinct meanings (see Figure 5–4).

High Water The highest level reached by the sea during one tidal cycle.

Low Water The lowest level reached by the sea during one tidal cycle.

Chart Datum The level to which charted soundings and drying heights are referred. In the U.S. this is most often Mean Lower Low Water *(MLLW)*.

Mean Lower Low Water (MLLW) The average of the lower low water height of each tidal day observed over the National Tidal Datum Epoch—the specific 19-year period adopted by the National Ocean Service as the official time segment over which tide observations are taken and reduced to obtain mean values for tidal datums.

Mean High Water (MHW) The average of all the high water heights observed over the National Tidal Datum Epoch. This is the datum on which most U.S. charts base heights or elevations.

Mean Higher High Water (MHHW) The average of the higher high water height of each tidal day observed over the National Tidal Datum Epoch.

Lowest Astronomical Tide (LAT) The lowest level to which the tide is ever predicted to fall, without allowing for possible meteorological effects.

Highest Astronomical Tide The highest level to which the tide is ever expected to rise, without allowing for meteorological effects.

Height of Tide The actual level of the sea surface at any given moment measured from chart datum.

Range of Tide The height difference between low water and the following high water, or vice versa.

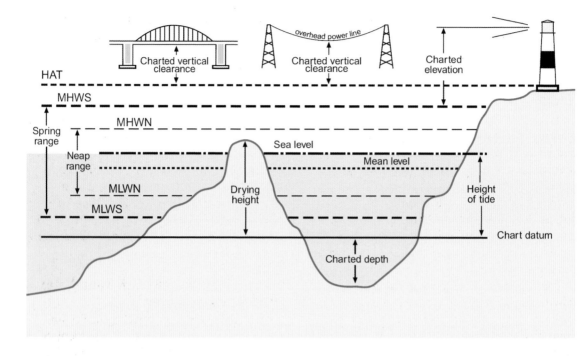

Fig 5–4 The rise and fall of the tide means that the marine navigator is concerned with several different sea levels, so it is important to know which is which. Charted depths and heights are generally based on the most pessimistic level!

Spring Tides Tides with the greatest range in each biweekly cycle.

Neap Tides Tides with the smallest range in each biweekly cycle.

Equinoctial Springs Spring tides with an unusually large range occurring at the time of the equinoxes (late March and late September).

Mean Low Water Springs (MLWS) The average height of low water during spring tides throughout the National Tidal Datum Epoch. This datum is used, to a considerable extent, for hydrographic work outside of the United States and is the level of reference for the Pacific approaches to the Panama Canal.

Sounding The depth of the sea bed below chart datum, shown on charts either as spot soundings or contours.

Drying Height The height of a feature such as a rock or shoal, which is sometimes covered by the tide, measured above chart datum.

Charted Height The height of a feature such as an island, which is rarely or never covered by the sea, usually measured from mean high water (MHW).

Elevation The height at which a light is displayed from a fixed structure measured above mean high water (MHW)—or above sea level in the case of a LNB.

Rise of Tide The height of sea level at any given moment, measured above the nearest low water.

Tide Tables

Although the factors governing the tides are complicated, they can be predicted, and those predictions are published in the form of tide tables. These range from wallet-sized cards, giving details of local tides, to the NOAA Tide Tables. The tide tables included in yachtsmen's almanacs are generally similar in content and layout to those produced by NOAA, and are usually generated from NOAA data.

The height of tide can vary minute by minute and from place to place, so it is quite impractical to publish full predictions for every point around the coast and for every hour of the year. Instead, detailed predictions are given for a selection of major locations, called primary stations. These give the time and height of high and low waters for each day.

Primary Station—High and Low Water

To find the time of high and low water at a primary location is a simple matter: find the page of the tables that relates to that particular place, and look through it to find the relevant day.

Times are given using the 24-hour clock, based on the standard time of the zone in which the place is located. When Daylight Saving Time is in effect (DST), an hour has to be added to the time shown in order to convert it to clock time.

Primary Stations—Intermediate Heights and Times

Unless you happen to be entering or leaving harbor at high or low water, you are likely to want to know the height of tide at some time other than those given in the tables, or to

Portland, Maine, 2009　43 39.6N 70 14W

Times and Heights of High and Low Waters

Daylight Savings Mar 8 2009 - Nov 1 2009 (ADD 1 HR)

	July			July			August			August			September			September		
	Time	ft	cm	Time	ft	cm	Time	ft	cm	Time	ft	cm	Time	ft	cm	Time	ft	cm
1 W / Th / Sa / Su / Tu / W	0610	8.8	268	**16** 0447	8.4	256	**1** 0133	0.9	27	**16** 0018	0.4	12	**1** 0244	1.0	30	**16** 0211	-0.3	-9
	1212	0.9	27	1051	1.0	30	0744	7.9	241	0631	8.3	253	0854	8.2	250	0826	9.5	290
	1834	9.8	299	1712	9.6	293	1336	1.7	52	1227	1.0	30	1448	1.5	46	1428	0.0	0
				2338	0.8	24	1955	9.3	283	1849	10.2	311	2103	9.3	283	2046	10.6	323
2 Th / F / Su / M / W / Th	0101	0.6	18	**17** 0547	8.3	253	**2** 0227	0.8	24	**17** 0125	0.1	3	**2** 0326	0.8	24	**17** 0306	-0.6	-18
	0712	8.5	259	1147	1.1	34	0839	8.0	244	0738	8.6	262	0935	8.5	259	0921	10.1	308
	1308	1.2	37	1808	9.9	302	1428	1.7	52	1333	0.7	21	1530	1.2	37	1525	-0.5	-15
	1930	9.7	296				2046	9.4	287	1954	10.5	320	2144	9.5	290	2142	10.9	332
3 F / Sa / M / Tu / Th / F	0159	0.6	18	**18** 0040	0.5	15	**3** 0316	0.7	21	**18** 0227	-0.4	-12	**3** 0403	0.6	18	**18** 0357	-0.9	-27
	0811	8.3	253	0650	8.4	256	0927	8.1	247	0841	9.1	277	1012	8.8	268	1011	10.5	320
	1403	1.4	43	1247	1.0	30	1516	1.6	49	1437	0.2	6	1609	0.9	27	1619	-0.9	-27
	2022	9.7	296	1908	10.3	314	2131	9.5	290	2056	10.9	332	2222	9.6	293	● 2234	10.9	332
4 Sa / Su / Tu / W / F / Sa	0252	0.5	15	**19** 0143	0.1	3	**4** 0359	0.6	18	**19** 0324	-0.8	-24	**4** 0436	0.5	15	**19** 0445	-0.9	-27
	0904	8.3	253	0754	8.6	262	1009	8.3	253	0938	9.7	296	1046	9.0	274	1058	10.8	329
	1453	1.5	46	1348	0.7	21	1558	1.4	43	1536	-0.3	-9	1645	0.7	21	1710	-1.1	-34
	2110	9.7	296	2009	10.7	326	2212	9.6	293	2154	11.3	344	2257	9.6	293	2324	10.7	326
5 Su / M / W / Th / Sa / Su	0340	0.4	12	**20** 0244	-0.4	-12	**5** 0437	0.5	15	**20** 0418	-1.2	-37	**5** 0508	0.4	12	**20** 0531	-0.7	-21
	0952	8.3	253	0856	9.0	274	1047	8.5	259	1031	10.2	311	1118	9.3	283	1144	10.9	332

Fig 5-5 Tide tables give the times and heights of high and low waters every day at a number of primary locations: this extract from *Reed's Nautical Almanac* is for Portland, Maine.

2009 REED's East Coast Edition

TABLE 3 – HEIGHT OF TIDE AT ANY TIME

Time from the nearest high water or low water

Duration of Rise or Fall

h.m.	h.m.	h.m.	h.m.	h.m.	h.m.	h.m.	h.m.	h.m.	h.m.	h.m.	h.m.	h.m.	h.m.	h.m.	h.m.
4 00	0 08	0 16	0 24	0 32	0 40	0 48	0 56	1 04	1 12	1 20	1 28	1 36	1 44	1 52	2 00
4 20	0 09	0 17	0 26	0 35	0 43	0 52	1 01	1 09	1 18	1 27	1 35	1 44	1 53	2 01	2 10
4 40	0 09	0 19	0 28	0 37	0 47	0 56	1 05	1 15	1 24	1 33	1 43	1 52	2 01	2 11	2 20
5 00	0 10	0 20	0 30	0 40	050	1 00	1 10	1 20	1 30	1 40	1 50	2 00	2 10	2 20	2 30
5 20	0 11	0 21	0 32	0 43	0 53	1 04	1 15	1 25	1 36	1 47	1 57	2 08	2 19	2 29	2 40
5 40	0 11	0 23	0 34	0 45	0 57	1 08	1 19	1 31	1 42	1 53	2 05	2 16	2 27	2 39	2 50
6 00	0 12	0 24	0 36	0 48	1 00	1 12	1 24	1 36	1 48	2 00	2 12	2 24	2 36	2 48	3 00
6 20	0 13	0 25	0 38	0 51	1 03	1 16	1 29	1 41	1 54	2 07	2 19	2 32	2 45	2 57	3 10
6 40	0 13	0 27	0 40	0 53	1 07	1 20	1 33	1 47	2 00	2 13	2 27	2 40	2 53	3 07	3 20
7 00	0 14	0 28	0 42	0 56	1 10	1 24	1 38	1 52	2 06	2 20	2 34	2 48	3 02	3 16	3 30
7 20	0 15	0 29	0 44	0 59	1 13	1 28	1 43	1 57	2 12	2 27	2 41	2 56	3 11	3 25	3 40
7 40	0 15	0 31	0 46	1 01	1 17	1 32	1 47	2 03	2 18	2 33	2 49	3 04	3 19	3 35	3 50
8 00	0 16	0 32	0 48	1 04	1 20	1 36	1 52	2 08	2 24	2 40	2 56	3 12	3 28	3 44	4 00
8 20	0 17	0 33	0 50	1 07	1 23	1 40	1 57	2 13	2 30	2 47	3 03	3 20	3 37	3 53	4 10
8 40	0 17	0 35	0 52	1 09	1 27	1 44	2 01	2 19	2 36	2 53	3 11	3 28	3 45	4 03	4 20
9 00	0 18	0 36	0 54	1 12	1 30	1 48	2 06	2 24	2 42	3 00	3 18	3 36	3 54	4 12	4 30
9 20	0 19	0 37	0 56	1 15	1 33	1 52	2 11	2 29	2 48	3 07	3 25	3 44	4 03	4 21	4 40
9 40	0 19	0 39	0 58	1 17	1 37	1 56	2 15	2 35	2 54	3 13	3 33	3 52	4 11	4 31	4 50
10 00	0 20	0 40	1 00	1 20	1 40	2 00	2 20	2 40	3 00	3 20	3 40	4 00	4 20	4 40	5 00
10 20	0 21	0 41	1 02	1 23	1 43	2 04	2 25	2 245	3 06	3 27	3 47	4 08	4 29	4 49	5 10
10 40	0 21	0 43	1 04	1 25	1 47	2 08	2 29	2 51	3 12	3 33	3 55	4 16	4 37	4 59	5 20

Correction to height

Range of Tide

Ft.	Ft.	Ft.	Ft.	Ft.	Ft.	Ft.	Ft.	Ft.	Ft.	Ft.	Ft.	Ft.	Ft.	Ft.	Ft.
0.5	0.0	0.0	0.0	0.0	0.0	0.0	0.1	0.1	0.1	0.1	0.1	0.2	0.2	0.2	0.2
1.0	0.0	0.0	0.0	0.0	0.1	0.1	0.1	0.2	0.2	0.2	0.3	0.3	0.4	0.4	0.5
1.5	0.0	0.0	0.0	0.1	0.1	0.1	0.2	0.2	0.3	0.4	0.4	0.5	0.6	0.7	0.8
2.0	0.0	0.0	0.0	0.1	0.1	0.2	0.3	0.3	0.4	0.5	0.6	0.7	0.8	0.9	1.0
2.5	0.0	0.0	0.1	0.1	0.2	0.2	0.3	0.4	0.5	0.6	0.7	0.9	1.0	1.1	1.2
3.0	0.0	0.0	0.1	0.1	0.2	0.3	0.4	0.5	0.6	0.8	0.9	1.0	1.2	1.3	1.5
3.5	0.0	0.0	0.1	0.2	0.2	0.3	0.4	0.6	0.7	0.9	1.0	1.2	1.4	1.6	1.8
4.0	0.0	0.0	0.1	0.2	0.3	0.4	0.5	0.7	0.8	1.0	1.2	1.4	1.6	1.8	2.0
4.5	0.0	0.0	0.1	0.2	0.3	0.4	0.6	0.7	0.9	1.1	1.3	1.6	1.8	2.0	2.2
5.0	0.0	0.1	0.1	0.2	0.3	0.5	0.6	0.8	1.0	1.2	1.5	1.7	2.0	2.2	2.5
5.5	0.0	0.1	0.1	0.2	0.4	0.5	0.7	0.9	1.1	1.4	1.6	1.9	2.2	2.5	2.8
6.0	0.0	0.1	0.1	0.3	0.4	0.6	0.8	1.0	1.2	1.5	1.8	2.1	2.4	2.7	3.0
6.5	0.0	0.1	0.2	0.3	0.4	0.6	0.8	1.1	1.3	1.6	1.9	2.2	2.6	2.9	3.2
7.0	0.0	0.1	0.2	0.3	0.5	0.7	0.9	1.2	1.4	1.8	2.1	2.4	2.8	3.1	3.5
7.5	0.0	0.1	0.2	0.3	0.5	0.7	1.0	1.2	1.5	1.9	2.2	2.6	3.0	3.4	3.8
8.0	0.0	0.1	0.2	0.3	0.5	0.8	1.0	1.3	1.6	2.0	2.4	2.8	3.2	3.6	4.0
8.5	0.0	0.1	0.2	0.4	0.6	0.8	1.1	1.4	1.8	2.1	2.5	2.9	3.4	3.8	4.2
9.0	0.0	0.1	0.2	0.4	0.6	0.9	1.2	1.5	1.9	2.2	2.7	3.1	3.6	4.0	4.5
9.5	0.0	0.1	0.2	0.4	0.6	0.9	1.2	1.6	2.0	2.4	2.8	3.3	3.8	4.3	4.8
10.0	0.0	0.1	0.2	0.4	0.7	1.0	1.3	1.7	2.1	2.5	3.0	3.5	4.0	4.5	5.0
10.5	0.0	0.1	0.3	0.5	0.7	1.0	1.3	1.7	2.2	2.6	3.1	3.6	4.2	4.7	5.2
11.0	0.0	0.1	0.3	0.5	0.7	1.1	1.4	1.8	2.3	2.8	3.3	3.8	4.4	4.9	5.5
11.5	0.0	0.1	0.3	0.5	0.8	1.1	1.5	1.9	2.4	2.9	3.4	4.0	4.6	5.1	5.8
12.0	0.0	0.1	0.3	0.5	0.8	1.1	1.5	2.0	2.5	3.0	3.6	4.1	4.8	5.4	6.0
12.5	0.0	0.1	0.3	0.5	0.8	1.2	1.6	2.1	2.6	3.1	3.7	4.3	5.0	5.6	6.2
13.0	0.0	0.1	0.3	0.6	0.9	1.2	1.7	2.2	2.7	3.2	3.9	4.5	5.1	5.8	6.5
13.5	0.0	0.1	0.3	0.6	0.9	1.3	1.7	2.2	2.8	3.4	4.0	4.7	5.3	6.0	6.8
14.0	0.0	0.2	0.3	0.6	0.9	1.3	1.8	2.3	2.9	3.5	4.2	4.8	5.5	6.3	7.0
14.5	0.0	0.2	0.4	0.6	1.0	1.4	1.9	2.4	3.0	3.6	4.3	5.0	5.7	6.5	7.2
15.0	0.0	0.2	0.4	0.6	1.0	1.4	1.9	2.5	3.1	3.8	4.4	5.2	5.9	6.7	7.5
15.5	0.0	0.2	0.4	0.7	1.0	1.5	2.0	2.6	3.2	3.9	4.6	5.4	6.1	6.9	7.8
16.0	0.0	0.2	0.4	0.7	1.1	1.5	2.1	2.6	3.3	4.0	4.7	5.5	6.3	7.2	8.0
16.5	0.0	0.2	0.4	0.7	1.1	1.6	2.1	2.7	3.4	4.1	4.9	5.7	6.5	7.4	8.2
17.0	0.0	0.2	0.4	0.7	1.1	1.6	2.2	2.8	3.5	4.2	5.0	5.9	6.7	7.6	8.5
17.5	0.0	0.2	0.4	0.8	1.2	1.7	2.2	2.9	3.6	4.4	5.2	6.0	6.9	7.8	8.8
18.0	0.0	0.2	0.4	0.8	1.2	1.7	2.3	3.0	3.7	4.5	5.3	6.2	7.1	8.1	9.0
18.5	0.1	0.2	0.5	0.8	1.2	1.8	2.4	3.1	3.8	4.6	5.5	6.4	7.3	8.3	9.2
19.0	0.1	0.2	0.5	0.8	1.3	1.8	2.4	3.1	3.9	4.8	5.6	6.6	7.5	8.5	9.5
19.5	0.1	0.2	0.5	0.8	1.3	1.9	2.5	3.2	4.0	4.9	5.8	6.7	7.7	8.7	9.8
20.0	0.1	0.2	0.5	0.9	1.3	1.9	2.6	3.3	4.1	5.0	5.9	6.9	7.9	9.0	10.0

Before using this table, get the times and heights of the two tide events that your desired time of height falls between. Calculate the duration of time and the range of heights between the two events, and the time difference between your desired time and the nearest high or low.

Enter the table with the Duration of Rise or Fall boldfaced in the upper left column that is closest to your calculation. Scan that row to find the Time from Nearest High or Low closest to your difference. Use that column to enter the bottom section of the table. Find the row whose boldfaced value Range of Tide is closest to yours, and get your correction value where the row and column cross.

When the nearest tide is high water, subtract the correction; and vice versa.

Fig 5–6 "Table 3" can be used to calculate the height of tide at a specific time, or the time at which the tide will reach a specific height (see text). (Source: *Reeds Nautical Almanac*)

know the time at which the tide will reach some predetermined height in order to get out over a bar. Even in areas of great tidal range and ample deep water where getting over a bar is of no concern, it's often valuable to

know the earliest (after a low) and/or latest (after the high) that the deck level will be close enough to pier level to make it convenient for getting things (or people!) on or off the boat.

To find height at a given time
1. From the Tide Table, get the times of the tides immediately before and after your desired time.
2. Get the respective heights of each tide and subtract to determine the total range of this particular tidal change.
3. Determine the total duration of the tidal change by subtracting the earlier time from the later.
4. Determine the interval between your desired time and the nearest tide
5. Enter Table 3 on the line whose "Duration of Rise or Fall" is closest to the interval you determined from Step 3.
6. Go across that line to find the closest figure to the interval you determined in Step 4
7. Read down that column to the line whose "Range of Tide" number (bold figures on extreme left) is closest to the figure you determined in Step 2.
8. The number you arrive at will be the correction to the nearest tide: subtracted from a high; added to a low.

To find the time for a required height
This is effectively the same problem in reverse, so the preparation—steps 1, 2 & 3—is exactly the same.
4. Using the row for the range of tide you determined in Step 2, enter the Correction to Height (lower) table, reading across to find the required adjustment. NOTE: this table only has figures to half tide; when determining a needed height, add the correction to the height of a low, subtract it from the height of a high, using the figures you extracted for Step 2 as the basis for adjustment.
5. When you find the figure closest to your needed height, go up the column to the Duration of Rise or Fall (upper) table until you get to the row whose Duration of Rise or Fall (bold numbers on the left) is closest to the interval you determined in Step 3.
6. The number in the column you determined from Step 4 and the row you got from Step 5 will be the time difference to work with in Step 7.
7. To learn the time of your required height, add this interval to the time of a nearest low; subtract it from the time of a nearest high, making sure you apply the adjustment to the same tidal level (low or high) you used in Step 4.

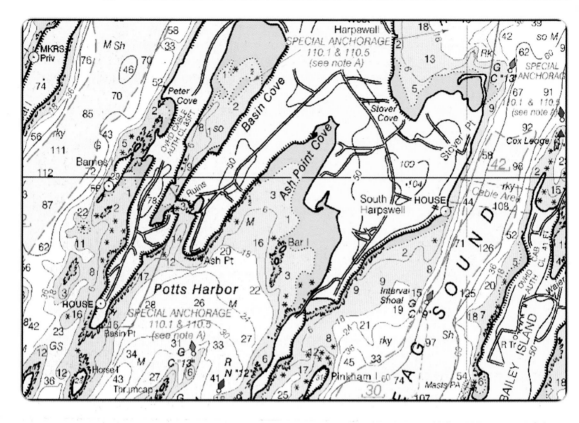

Fig 5–7 Extract from NOS Chart 13290 *Casco Bay*, showing Potts Harbor and Basin Cove.

Tidal Heights—Example 1: Height at a Given Time

You are cruising Downeast and have planned a stop in Portland, Maine to pick up some needed supplies that you've arranged to be delivered to the Public Landing at State Pier. The water depth, per se, is no problem; Portland is a deep-water port. But with a range of tide on the order of 10 feet, you want to be loading supplies closer to high tide than low. Even with the floating pier at the public landing, too steep a ramp would only complicate the process. Your ETA is 0930 on August 17. Will this be a good time or should you change your plans?

Checking the Tide Table (Figure 5–5) you see that the high tide at 0738 (EST) will be 8.6 feet above charted datum and the low at 1333 plus 0.7. Adding the hour for DST you have 0838 for the high and 1433 for the low with a total range of 7.9 feet and a Duration of Fall amounting to 5h 55m. If you arrive at 0930, this will be 52 minutes after high.

While you guestimate that this should be okay, you decide you'd better actually calculate the height of tide at 0930 *and* at 1015 to be certain you'll have easy going throughout the entire loading process, so you add the

45 minutes to the initial 52 for another Time From Nearest High of 1 hr 37 minutes. Now let's calculate the heights. (The numbers we'll work with are outlined in blue for 0930, green for 1015 on Figure 5–6: Table 3.)

1. Enter the Duration of Rise or Fall (top) portion of Table 3 on the line for 6h 00m (the closest to 5h 55m) and read across to the column with 36 m for time from nearest high (the closest to the 37 min you calculated for 0930).
2. Look down this column to the line in the lower table (Range of Tide) for 8-ft (closest to 7.9 ft) where you'll find 0.2.

3. Subtract this from the high tide level of 8.6 and you'll see that there will still be a height of 8.4 feet when you arrive at 0930.
4. Recalculating for 1015 you again enter the top table on the 6h 00m line, this time going across to the column for 1h 36m, the closest to your calculated 1h 37m.
5. Go down this column to the 8.0 line in the Range of Tide table and you arrive at 1.3.
6. Subtract 1.3 from 8.6 for a height of tide at 1015 of 7.3, which should still be adequate for carrying supplies down the ramp. You don't have to change your plans!

Tidal Heights—Example 2: Time of a Required Height

While taking on supplies in Portland, you learn that a severe tropical storm that was initially thought to be heading way out to sea is now predicted to approach the Maine coast more closely—and within the next 36 hours! The people from the chandlery who delivered your supplies tell you about a nearly land-locked cove not too far from Portland that offers ideal shelter from winds of just about any force and definitely from any direction. It's called "Basin Cove" (See Figure 5–7). With 7-to 9-foot depths at low tide, good holding ground and protective land nearly all around it, Basin Cove is the perfect place to ride out any storm. The only drawback is that when you consult the chart, you see that the entrance is narrow and shallow with but 3 feet just outside it and the remnants of an old dam (ruins) across the entrance itself. This combination of less-than-desirable attributes means that you'll want to enter the cove on a rising tide, just as soon as you have sufficient depth for your 6-foot draft, yet delayed by enough to allow a margin of error. Considering the narrowness of the entrance and other factors, you definitely want to get in there and be anchored securely before dark. Will all this work for you? Let's figure it out. (Pertinent numbers are outlined in red on Figure 5–6.)

First, again consider what you know. From the Tide Tables, still using Portland because your printed tables don't have a subordinate station for this part of Casco Bay (NOAA's on-line site does, but the difference is only 2 minutes—not enough to create a problem) you determine that there will be a low (0.7 feet) at 1333 EST and a high (10.5 feet) at 1954. Adding the hour for DST you get low at 1433, high at 2054. This gives a total range of 9.8 feet over a Duration of Rise of 6 hours 21 minutes. Your boat draws 6 feet, so you increase this by 2 feet to play it safe and thus determine you need to add 5 feet to the 3-foot charted depth to have minimum safe clearance of 8 feet.

1. Enter the lower portion of Table 3 on the line for 10.0 Range of Tide (the closest to 9.8), going all the way to the far right column for a 5-foot correction to height.
2. Then go up this column to the upper table and the line with a 6h 20m Duration of Rise. Here you'll see a Time from the Nearest Tide of 3h 10m.

3. Add the 3 hours 10 minutes to the low tide time of 1433 to get 1743 as the earliest you can enter Basin Cove. Since this is about two hours before sunset—which is around 1940 according to the tables (see page 140) and NOAA weather radio—you can even wait a bit before entering; certainly until well after 1800, just to add a greater margin of safety.

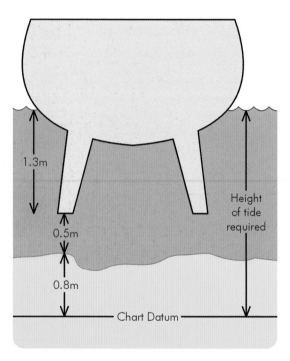

Fig 5-8 A simple sketch, like this, makes it easy to work out your under-keel clearance from the information given on the chart and in tide tables, and reduces the risk of making a mistake.

Subordinate Stations

Many small-craft harbors and anchorages, particularly the smaller, more attractive places, are classed as subordinate stations. They are generally of less commercial or military interest than primary stations, so they have not justified the long-term sequence of tidal observations required to produce full tide tables, nor would they justify the space required to publish a full set of predictions. Instead, it is up to the individual navigator to prepare his own tide tables, by applying published differences to the data which is given for a nearby primary station.

In *Reeds Nautical Almanac*, for instance, the entry for Whale Harbor, in the Florida Keys (Figure 5–9), shows that it is referred to the primary station of Miami, Government Cut. Start by writing down the relevant data for Miami, exactly as it appears in the tide tables—do not add the hour for DST at this stage. The extract from the Miami tide tables (Figure 5–10) shows that on May 16th, low water was at 0705, 0.5 feet, and high water was at 1324, 1.9 feet.

The difference tables look complicated, but it will help to think of them divided into two halves—one dealing with times, and the other with height—and to sub-divide each half: one column for high tide; the other for low. The first time column tells us that high water at Whale Harbor is only 7 minutes after high at Miami (+0h 07m), a seemingly insignificant difference. The second column reveals that low tide is nearly an hour later than Miami's (+0h 51m), which could be significant. Perhaps even more important are columns 3 and 4, which

PLACE	POSITION		DIFFERENCES				RANGE
			Time		Height		
	north latitude	west longitude	high h m	low h m	high ft	low ft	spring ft
Snake Creek, Windley Key 24 57.1		80 35.3	+0 49	+0 56	*0.46	*0.50	1.28
Snake Creek, Plantation Key 24 57.2		80 35.2	+1 08	+1 56	*0.36	*0.50	0.98
Whale Harbor, Hawk Channel.........24 56.4		80 36.5	+0 07	+0 51	*0.65	*0.36	1.87
Upper Matecumbe, Hawk Channel..24 54.9		80 37.9	+0 34	+0 49	*0.87	*1.21	2.38
Alligator Reef, Hawk Channel.........24 51.0		80 37.1	+0 08	+0 24	*0.86	*1.36	2.37
on Key West, p.495							
Flamingo, Florida Bay 25 08.5		80 55.4	+5 28	+7 20	*1.47	*1.08	2.52
Upper Matecumbe, W end, ...24 53.8		80 39.5	-1 00	+0 14	*0.98	*0.33	1.80
Indian Key, Hawk Channel................24 52.6		80 40.6	-0 58	-0 35	*1.30	*0.71	2.30
Shell Key Channel, Florida Bay 24 54.8		80 39.6	-0 20	+0 45	*0.78	*0.78	1.28
Lignumvitae Key NE side, Florida Bay 24 54.2		80 41.7	+0 00	+1 21	*0.53	*0.53	0.85

Fig 5–9 An excerpt from Tidal Difference Tables, which give the difference between the tide at a subordinate station compared with the tide at a nearby primary station. (Source: *Reeds Nautical Almanac*)

Miami, Government Cut, Florida, 2009   25 45.8N   80 07W

Times and Heights of High and Low Waters

Daylight Savings Mar 8 2009 - Nov 1 2009 (ADD 1 HR)

	April						May						June					
	Time	Height		Time	Height		Time	Height		Time	Height		Time	Height		Time	Height	
	h m	ft	cm	h m	ft	cm	h m	ft	cm	h m	ft	cm	h m	ft	cm	h m	ft	cm
1 W	0040 0620 1247 1848	2.4 0.3 2.2 -0.1	73 9 67 -3	**16** Th	0052 0648 1259 1909	2.0 0.6 1.9 0.4	61 18 58 12	**1** F ◐	0127 0719 1349 1947	2.5 0.2 2.3 0.0	76 6 70 0	**16** Sa	0105 0705 1324 1921	2.1 0.5 1.9 0.5	64 15 58 15	**1** M	0259 0905 1543 2134	2.3 -0.1 2.3 0.2	70 -3 70 6	**16** Tu	0156 0802 1442 2029	2.0 0.2 2.0 0.4	61 6 61 12
2 Th ◐	0142 0727 1355 1959	2.3 0.3 2.2 0.0	70 9 67 0	**17** F ◑	0145 0748 1358 2011	2.0 0.7 1.9 0.5	61 21 58 15	**2** Sa ◑	0228 0826 1458 2055	2.4 0.2 2.3 0.1	73 6 70 3	**17** Su ◑	0154 0759 1422 2019	2.0 0.5 1.9 0.5	61 15 58 15	**2** Tu	0356 1000 1643 2230	2.3 -0.1 2.4 0.3	70 -3 73 9	**17** W	0247 0857 1542 2128	2.0 0.1 2.1 0.4	61 3 64 12
3 F	0249 0839 1508	2.3 0.3 2.2	70 9 67	**18** Sa	0242 0849 1502	1.9 0.6 1.9	58 18 58	**3** Su	0330 0929 1605	2.4 0.1 2.4	73 3 73	**18** M	0245 0853 1522	2.0 0.4 2.0	61 12 61	**3** W	0451 1052 1739	2.2 -0.2 2.4	67 -6 73	**18** Th	0343 0953 1643	2.1 -0.1 2.2	64 -3 67

Fig 5–10 The difference tables for Whale Harbor refer to these tide tables for Miami Harbor Entrance (Government Cut).

give us the difference in tidal range at the secondary station as compared to the range at the reference station. These are sometimes pure numbers with a + or − to indicate whether they are to be added to or subtracted from the primary station's stated heights. But more often the number will be preceded by an asterisk, which means the stated high or low is a ratio, a number by which the primary station's height of tide is multiplied. There's also a "Range" column, which shows us the average range of spring tides at this location. Since most of the time the range will be less, the 1.87 shown, when coupled with the area's relatively shoal waters to begin with, makes that 7 minute difference at high tide more important than it first appeared to be—when you need every inch of rising tide to clear, you can't miss high tide by much or you could miss out completely.

May - Whale Harbor, Windley Key, Hawk Channel

Date	Day	Time		Height	Time		Height	Time		Height	Time		Height
05/01/2009	Fri	02:34AM LDT	1.6	H	09:10AM LDT	0.1	L	02:56PM LDT	1.5	H	09:38PM LDT	0.0	L
05/02/2009	Sat	03:35AM LDT	1.6	H	10:17AM LDT	0.1	L	04:05PM LDT	1.5	H	10:46PM LDT	0.0	L
05/03/2009	Sun	04:37AM LDT	1.6	H	11:20AM LDT	0.0	L	05:12PM LDT	1.6	H	11:49PM LDT	0.0	L
05/04/2009	Mon	05:36AM LDT	1.6	H	12:17PM LDT	-0.0	L	06:14PM LDT	1.6	H			
05/05/2009	Tue	12:46AM LDT	0.0	L	06:30AM LDT	1.6	H	01:09PM LDT	-0.1	L	07:09PM LDT	1.7	H
05/06/2009	Wed	01:38AM LDT	0.0	L	07:20AM LDT	1.6	H	01:57PM LDT	-0.1	L	07:59PM LDT	1.7	H
05/07/2009	Thu	02:25AM LDT	0.0	L	08:06AM LDT	1.6	H	02:41PM LDT	-0.1	L	08:44PM LDT	1.7	H
05/08/2009	Fri	03:10AM LDT	0.0	L	08:49AM LDT	1.6	H	03:24PM LDT	-0.1	L	09:26PM LDT	1.7	H
05/09/2009	Sat	03:52AM LDT	0.1	L	09:29AM LDT	1.6	H	04:05PM LDT	-0.1	L	10:06PM LDT	1.7	H
05/10/2009	Sun	04:32AM LDT	0.1	L	10:08AM LDT	1.5	H	04:45PM LDT	-0.1	L	10:45PM LDT	1.6	H
05/11/2009	Mon	05:12AM LDT	0.1	L	10:47AM LDT	1.5	H	05:24PM LDT	-0.0	L	11:24PM LDT	1.6	H
05/12/2009	Tue	05:52AM LDT	0.1	L	11:26AM LDT	1.4	H	06:04PM LDT	0.0	L			
05/13/2009	Wed	12:03AM LDT	1.5	H	06:33AM LDT	0.1	L	12:06PM LDT	1.4	H	06:45PM LDT	0.1	L
05/14/2009	Thu	12:44AM LDT	1.4	H	07:17AM LDT	0.2	L	12:50PM LDT	1.3	H	07:29PM LDT	0.1	L
05/15/2009	Fri	01:27AM LDT	1.4	H	08:04AM LDT	0.2	L	01:38PM LDT	1.3	H	08:18PM LDT	0.1	L
05/16/2009	Sat	02:12AM LDT	1.4	H	08:56AM LDT	0.2	L	02:31PM LDT	1.2	H	09:12PM LDT	0.2	L
05/17/2009	Sun	03:01AM LDT	1.3	H	09:50AM LDT	0.2	L	03:29PM LDT	1.2	H	10:10PM LDT	0.2	L
05/18/2009	Mon	03:52AM LDT	1.3	H	10:44AM LDT	0.1	L	04:29PM LDT	1.3	H	11:08PM LDT	0.2	L
05/19/2009	Tue	04:45AM LDT	1.3	H	11:35AM LDT	0.1	L	05:29PM LDT	1.4	H			

Fig 5-11 An excerpt from NOAA's online tide tables for Whale Harbor. Note that Subordinate Station tables are usually not available in printed form. Note also that unlike printed tables, which almost always show standard time in 24 hour terms, the online version has been corrected for DST and uses the 12-hour clock, showing times as AM or PM. (Source: NOAA)

In this particular instance, high water at Miami is 1324 EST. The difference at Whale Harbor, +0h 07m, means high tide at Whale Harbor will be at 1331 EST or 1431 DST, the time basis on May 16. The height of tide should be 1.2 feet above charted depth, determined by multiplying 1.9 (the stated height at Miami) by 0.65 (the Whale Harbor correction factor).

There is also a "lazy" way to gather tidal data for secondary stations: Use NOAA's website (http://tidesandcurrents.noaa.gov/), where the details for secondary stations are also spelled out as fully as for the primary. Figure 5–10 shows the same info we had to develop mathematically when working from printed tables.

Subordinate Stations— Intermediate Times and Heights

The procedure for calculating the height of tide at secondary ports for times between high and low waters is exactly the same as for primary stations, except that the basic high and low water data first have to be derived from the primary tables on which they are based before you can apply the differences in the subordinate station tables. Once you have calculated the basic high and low data for the subordinate station, you then can determine the intermediate times and heights.

Tides, Tables, and Times

It's important to remember that the tide tables NOAA provides to publishers for printing, whether as dedicated tables or as portions of almanacs or cruising guides, list standard time only for the entire year. During the period of Daylight Saving Time (DST) you must add an hour to the listed times to convert them to local time.

Most on-line tide tables, however, including NOAA's, have made the conversion for you showing the tides in DST rather than standard time when it is appropriate. Most computer software, either for PCs or dedicated chart plotters that include tidal information (see chapter 3) will also display tides in the time basis that should apply on the date concerned.

Since failing to convert standard time to daylight time will make all of your tidal calculations one hour early and yet converting times from tables using DST will make them an hour late, it is imperative that you take the time to note the basis of the tables you are working with. They all state it quite clearly but not always prominently. Be sure to look closely and then add the hour or not as the situation demands.

The Effect of Weather

Tidal calculations, giving answers with a precision of minutes and tenths of a meter (or foot), *look* very accurate. Indeed, the astronomical data on which the predictions are based is as reliable as sunrise and sunset, and the calculations that convert these into tide tables are the result of decades of painstaking observations. So, barring mishaps in the production of the tables themselves, tidal predictions are inherently reliable. What cannot be planned on in advance, however, is the effect of weather.

Prolonged high barometric pressure over a large area can depress the sea level, or winds blowing the sea on to the coast can raise it, so tide tables have to be based on the assumption of average weather conditions. Every 11 millibars of pressure difference can make a change of close to 1/3 of a foot to the predicted height, and a prolonged force 5 blowing onshore can raise the sea level by 8 inches or more.

The combined effect of wind and barometric pressure typically produces variations of about ± 8 inches in height and ±10 minutes in time, but in extreme conditions the differences can be very much greater. Easterly winds blowing into New York Harbor, for instance, have been known to raise the sea level at the Battery by 2 meters (6.5 feet) or more. On the upper Chesapeake, a strong wind (particularly from the North or South) can completely negate the tide. A winter gale from the North will hold the "tide" out when it should be coming in according to the tables. It's wind-driven rather than gravity-induced tide. More local effects can be caused by the passage of an intense, fast-moving depression, causing relatively rapid changes in sea level lasting for an hour or so, and usually of a few tenths of a meter.

The cumulative effect of meteorological factors on tidal heights and times is very difficult to predict with any accuracy, so although tidal calculations should usually be carried out as precisely as possible, their accuracy should not be relied on as absolute.

For some purposes, only an approximate calculation is all that is required, and the use of full tables and mathematical calculations is not warranted. One cannot, however, assume that the tide rises and falls at a constant rate. The bell-shaped graph in Figure 5–12 is typical. From low water the tide rises slowly at first, then increasingly quickly, before slowing down again toward high water and then reversing the slow-fast-slow pattern as it falls toward low water again.

RULE OF TWELFTHS

A good approximation to this typical curve is given by a simple arithmetical process called "the Rule of Twelfths," which states that:

in the first hour the tide rises one twelfth of its range.

in the second hour it rises two twelfths of its range.

in the third hour it rises three twelfths of its range.

in the fourth hour it rises three twelfths of its range.

in the fifth hour it rises two twelfths of its range.

in the sixth hour it rises one twelfth of its range.

Notice that this calculation is based on the range of the tide, so the result will be the rise of tide not the height of tide. Low water must be added to the rise of tide in order to get the height above chart datum.

Tidal Anomalies

The Rule of Twelfths is a good approximation to the typical tidal curve of places such as Baltimore, Maryland, which, though a considerable distance up Chesapeake Bay is nonetheless exposed almost directly to the Atlantic tide. There are many places, however, where the presence of shallow water or islands close offshore or other influences cause distortions in the shape of the tidal wave, in much the same way as a shelving beach distorts incoming swell into surf.

The Florida Keys provide a perfect example. Most of the oceanside harbors are quite predictable with "normal" Atlantic tides. Many are even listed as subordinate stations based on either Miami or Key West tides. The Bay side is quite different, however, the result of numerous, often conflicting influences

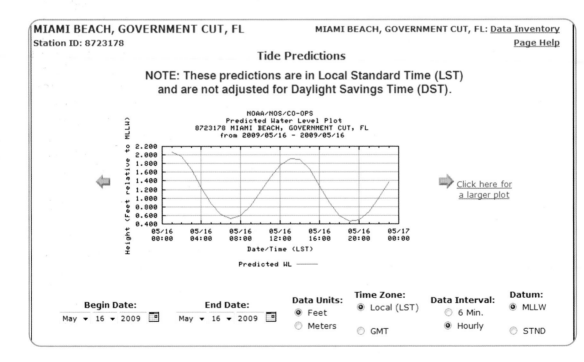

Fig 5–12 Many local sources of tidal information, such as waterfront newspapers, as well as some computer programs and even NOAA itself, present tidal data in graphical form, at least for primary stations (click on "Graphical Predictions" at http://tidesandcurrents.noaa.gov/). This page from NOAA's Web site has the same data shown in tabular form in Figure 5–9. Note the choice of time reference: GMT (UTC) or local standard time. (Source: NOAA)

ranging from the ocean tidal wave flowing around the islands to the Gulf of Mexico tidal flow adding its aspects and yet further influences coming from the water flow in Florida Bay, which is not purely tidal in nature. This combination of factors can create situations that virtually defy rational prediction.

Farther up the Atlantic coast, there are also places where the tide seems to "stand" at high for longer than the Rule of Twelfths would suggest. One example is seen in the Cape Cod canal, where anomalies are caused by the extreme difference in tidal influences at each end of the canal. Cape Cod Bay on the eastern end has an average 9-foot-plus range, largely influenced by the vast North Atlantic tidal wave, while the Buzzard's Bay end has tides of a considerably lesser range (3.5 to 4 feet), that ebb and flow on a different schedule. This can create standing waves within the canal that raise havoc with accurate predictions and a neat sinusoidal curve of rise and fall. Fortunately, the entire canal has a low-tide-depth sufficient for ships, so the stage of tide at any time is rarely of great importance to yachtsmen. What *is* important, however, is the current created by these tidal differences, which can easily run at more than 4 knots and sometimes even reach 7 knots. The need to pay attention to this aspect leads us to . . .

Tidal Currents

Raising sea level by several meters across a huge area takes an enormous volume of water. That water obviously has to come from somewhere, so one side effect of tides—vertical movements of the sea's surface—is the horizontal movement of large quantities of water from place to place. These horizontal movements are called tidal currents.

Tidal currents can be subdivided into two main groups: "rectilinear" and "rotary." Rectilinear tidal currents are found in reasonably well-defined channels, where the water can only flow in two main directions. In the case of a river estuary, a tidal current can quite clearly be seen to be moving "in" or "out." These two directions are often referred to as "flood" and "ebb": The flood tide corresponds to the rising sea level and the ebb to the falling sea level.

Where the water movement is not constrained by a definite channel, the tidal currents are continually changing in direction, and turn through 360° in each tidal cycle. This gives rise to the name "rotary" tidal currents—even though the flow is considerably stronger in approximately opposite directions than in any others.

Tidal Current Information

The waters adjacent to North America include some very strong tidal currents, though they are often localized. Interestingly enough, the strongest currents are not necessarily found where the tidal range is greatest. In southeast Florida for example, where the range of tide is but 3 feet or less, currents in inlets and bays can easily exceed 2.5 knots. Of course, at the other end of the Atlantic coast in Downeast Maine, where the tidal range can be greater than 10 feet, such currents (and even stronger ones) are to be expected, especially near the mouths of rivers and entrances to bays or sounds. Rates of 2.5 to 3 knots or more (8 knots or more in some narrow passages) are not at all unusual along many parts of our coastline, so a sailing yacht's speed over the ground can easily be halved or doubled by the tidal current. Their effect on motor boats may be less obvious, but strong currents can have a definite effect on the sea state, so for any cruising yachtsman, tidal currents are a force to be reckoned with.

Current Tables, which are still generated (but also no longer published) by NOAA, have a similar format to the Tide Tables (see Figure 5–13). While they have fewer reference stations, both primary and secondary, the information is presented in similar fashion with full details for primary stations and "corrections" for the secondary that are based on a nearby primary. Most Current Tables also include a table for determining the current at times between maximum and slack, and though NOS no longer publishes current data in graphical form, many private publications, such as *Reed's Nautical Almanac*, still contain current diagrams—at least for the locations for which they have "always" existed, such as Nantucket Sound and Buzzard's Bay, Narragansett Bay, Long Island Sound, New York Harbor, Delaware Bay, and Chesapeake Bay.

Using the Tables

In many cases, such as when transiting turbulent trouble-spots, your only concern is the time of slack water. Trying to get through any of these maelstroms at any other time can be problematic at best, and often downright impossible for a low-powered boat. But much of the time your main concern will be trying to benefit from a fair current and avoid running into the fowl. It's also nice to know in advance what sort of current will be facing you when you reach your destination as this knowledge can help you in planning your approach. Times of slack are obvious and straightforward—you can read them straight from a table. The times of maximum current, both flood and ebb, are also listed and are totally clear as well. It's the "in between" aspects that require some interpretation.

Interpolating for Time

The flow of current accelerates and decelerates along curves that are quite similar to those involved in the rise and fall of the tide, though the change in horizontal flow is rarely in phase with the rise and fall but more often lags it—sometimes by several hours. From slack water, which is usually rather brief, the flow steadily increases in velocity until it reaches the maximum (either flood or ebb), which is also

Baltimore Harbor Approach (off Sandy Pt.), Maryland, 2009

F–Flood, Dir. 025° True   E–Ebb, Dir. 190° True

Daylight Savings Mar 8 2009 - Nov 1 2009 (ADD 1 HR)

July

Day	Slack (h m)	Max (h m)	knots	Day	Slack (h m)	Max (h m)	knots
1 W	0339	0644	0.8E	16 Th	0313	0619	0.7E
	1021	1233	0.3F			1158	*
	1447	1809	0.7E			1724	0.6E
	2103				2017		
2 Th		0052	1.1F	17 F		0016	1.0F
	0434	0746	0.9E		0407	0719	0.8E
	1134	1338	0.3F			1302	*
	1548	1904	0.6E			1817	0.6E
	2151				2104		
3 F		0144	1.1F	18 Sa		0108	1.1F
	0526	0842	0.9E		0458	0815	0.9E
	1236	1440	0.3F			1404	*
	1651	1959	0.6E			1914	0.6E
	2239				2157		
4 Sa		0234	1.2F	19 Su		0201	1.2F
	0613	0933	1.0E		0547	0906	0.9E
	1328	1535	0.3F		1308	1501	0.3F
	1752	2051	0.5E		1700	2014	0.6E
	2326				2254		

August

Day	Slack (h m)	Max (h m)	knots	Day	Slack (h m)	Max (h m)	knots
1 Sa		0117	1.0F	16 Su		0041	1.1F
	0458	0815	0.9E		0428	0745	0.8E
	1208	1417	0.3F		1143	1340	0.3F
	1634	1937	0.5E		1544	1900	0.6E
	2216				2144		
2 Su		0210	1.0F	17 M		0140	1.1F
	0546	0906	0.9E		0521	0837	0.9E
	1256	1511	0.4F		1223	1437	0.4F
	1737	2033	0.5E		1658	2006	0.6E
	2309				2251		
3 M		0259	1.0F	18 Tu		0237	1.1F
	0630	0951	1.0E		0610	0924	1.0E
	1336	1559	0.4F		1258	1528	0.5F
	1833	2125	0.5E		1804	2108	0.7E
					2357		
4 Tu	0000	0345	1.0F	19 W		0332	1.1F
	0711	1031	1.0E		0656	1008	1.0E
	1412	1642	0.5F		1333	1616	0.7F
	1923	2213	0.6E		1904	2207	0.8E

September

Day	Slack (h m)	Max (h m)	knots	Day	Slack (h m)	Max (h m)	knots
1 Tu		0234	0.9F	16 W		0223	0.9F
	0556	0914	0.9E		0541	0850	0.9E
	1245	1525	0.5F		1206	1501	0.7F
	1814	2108	0.6E		1800	2105	0.8E
	2352						
2 W		0321	0.9F	17 Th	0006	0319	0.9F
	0639	0954	0.9E		0628	0935	0.9E
	1319	1605	0.6F		1243	1548	0.9F
	1900	2155	0.6E		1855	2201	0.9E
3 Th	0043	0405	0.9F	18 F	0109	0411	0.9F
	0718	1031	0.9E		0714	1019	0.9E
	1350	1642	0.7F		1320	1634	1.0F
	1942	2239	0.7E	●	1946	2254	1.0E
4 F	0133	0447	0.9F	19 Sa	0208	0501	0.8F
	0756	1105	0.9E		0757	1101	0.9E
	1418	1718	0.8F		1358	1719	1.1F
O	2022	2322	0.8E	O	2036	2345	1.0E

Fig 5-13 An excerpt from the Current Table for Baltimore Harbor Approach. Note that while Ebb and Flood flow in essentially opposite directions, they are not always exactly 180° opposite. (Source: *Reeds Nautical Almanac*)

Speed of Current At Any Time

NOTE: *Use table A for all places except those listed below for table B. Use Table B for Cape Cod Canal, Hell Gate, Chesapeake and Delaware Canal, and all stations in table 2 which are referred to them.*

TABLE A
Interval between slack and maximum current

h:m	1:20	1:40	2:00	2:20	2:40	3:00	3:20	3:40	4:00	4:20	4:40	5:00	5:20	5:40
0:20	0.5	0.4	0.4	0.3	0.3	0.3	0.3	0.3	0.2	0.2	0.2	0.2	0.2	0.2
0:40	0.8	0.7	0.6	0.5	0.5	0.5	0.4	0.4	0.4	0.4	0.3	0.3	0.3	0.3
1:00	0.9	0.8	0.8	0.7	0.7	0.6	0.6	0.5	0.5	0.5	0.4	0.4	0.4	0.4
1:20	1.0	1.0	0.9	0.8	0.8	0.7	0.7	0.6	0.6	0.6	0.5	0.5	0.5	0.5
1:40	-	1.0	1.0	0.9	0.9	0.8	0.8	0.7	0.7	0.7	0.6	0.6	0.6	0.6
2:00	-	-	1.0	1.0	0.9	0.9	0.9	0.8	0.8	0.7	0.7	0.7	0.7	0.6
2:20	-	-	-	1.0	1.0	1.0	0.9	0.9	0.8	0.8	0.8	0.7	0.7	0.7
2:40	-	-	-	-	1.0	1.0	1.0	0.9	0.9	0.9	0.8	0.8	0.8	0.7
3:00	-	-	-	-	-	1.0	1.0	1.0	0.9	0.9	0.9	0.9	0.8	0.8
3:20	-	-	-	-	-	-	1.0	1.0	1.0	1.0	0.9	0.9	0.9	0.9
3:40	-	-	-	-	-	-	-	1.0	1.0	1.0	1.0	0.9	0.9	0.9
4:00	-	-	-	-	-	-	-	-	1.0	1.0	1.0	1.0	0.9	0.9
4:20	-	-	-	-	-	-	-	-	-	1.0	1.0	1.0	1.0	0.9
4:40	-	-	-	-	-	-	-	-	-	-	1.0	1.0	1.0	1.0
5:00	-	-	-	-	-	-	-	-	-	-	-	1.0	1.0	1.0
5:20	-	-	-	-	-	-	-	-	-	-	-	-	1.0	1.0
5:40	-	-	-	-	-	-	-	-	-	-	-	-	-	1.0

Interval between slack and desired time (left axis label)

TABLE B
Interval between slack and maximum current

h:m	1:20	1:40	2:00	2:20	2:40	3:00	3:20	3:40	4:00	4:20	4:40	5:00	5:20	5:40
0:20	0.4	0.3	0.3	0.2	0.2	0.2	0.2	0.1	0.1	0.1	0.1	0.1	0.1	0.1
0:40	0.7	0.6	0.5	0.4	0.4	0.3	0.3	0.3	0.3	0.2	0.2	0.2	0.2	0.2
1:00	0.9	0.8	0.7	0.6	0.6	0.5	0.5	0.4	0.4	0.4	0.3	0.3	0.3	0.3
1:20	1.0	1.0	0.9	0.8	0.7	0.6	0.6	0.5	0.5	0.5	0.4	0.4	0.4	0.4
1:40	-	1.0	1.0	0.9	0.8	0.8	0.7	0.7	0.6	0.6	0.5	0.5	0.5	0.4
2:00	-	-	1.0	1.0	0.9	0.9	0.8	0.8	0.7	0.7	0.6	0.6	0.6	0.5
2:20	-	-	-	1.0	1.0	0.9	0.9	0.8	0.8	0.7	0.7	0.7	0.6	0.6
2:40	-	-	-	-	-1.0	1.0	1.0	0.9	0.9	0.8	0.8	0.7	0.7	0.7
3:00	-	-	-	-	-	1.0	1.0	1.0	0.9	0.9	0.8	0.8	0.8	0.7
3:20	-	-	-	-	-	-	1.0	1.0	1.0	0.9	0.9	0.9	0.8	0.8
3:40	-	-	-	-	-	-	-	1.0	1.0	1.0	0.9	0.9	0.9	0.9
4:00	-	-	-	-	-	-	-	-	1.0	1.0	1.0	1.0	0.9	0.9
4:20	-	-	-	-	-	-	-	-	-	1.0	1.0	1.0	1.0	0.9
4:40	-	-	-	-	-	-	-	-	-	-	1.0	1.0	1.0	1.0
5:00	-	-	-	-	-	-	-	-	-	-	-	1.0	1.0	1.0
5:20	-	-	-	-	-	-	-	-	-	-	-	-	1.0	1.0
5:40	-	-	-	-	-	-	-	-	-	-	-	-	-	1.0

Interval between slack and desired time (left axis label)

INSTRUCTIONS

1. From predictions find the time of slack water and the time and velocity of maximum current (flood or ebb), one of which is immediately before and the other after the time for which the velocity is desired.

2. Find the interval of time between the above slack and maximum current, and enter the top of table A or B with the interval which most nearly agrees with this value.

3. Find the interval of time between the above slack and the time desired, and enter the side of table A or B with the interval which most nearly agrees with this value.

4. Find, in the table, the factor corresponding to the above two intervals, and multiply the maximum velocity by this factor. The result will be the approximate velocity at the time desired.

Fig 5–14 "Table 3" from the current tables allows mariners to determine the speed of current at any time (see text). Note there are TWO tables: A for most places, B for canals and other constricted areas in which current patterns are somewhat different from more open waters. (Source: *Reeds Nautical Almanac*)

The Race, Long Island Sound, 2009

F–Flood, Dir. 302° True   E–Ebb, Dir. 112° True

Daylight Savings Mar 8 2009 - Nov 1 2009 (ADD 1 HR)

	July Slack h m	Maximum h m	knots		Slack h m	Maximum h m	knots
1 F	0036	0325	2.5F			0219	3.3F
10 F	0045	0356	3.0E	25 Sa	0119	0423	3.9E
	0712	1000	2.5F		0737	1032	3.6F
	1319	1618	2.6F		1351	1652	3.7F
	1923	2213	2.4F		2007	2256	3.2F
11 Sa	0122	0435	2.9E	26 Su	0211	0513	3.6E
	0747	1039	2.5F		0826	1121	3.3F

	August Slack h m	Maximum h m	knots		Slack h m	Maximum h m	knots
1	0205	0503	1.9F		0117	0400	2.3F
10 M	0131	0444	2.8E	25 Tu	0237	0535	3.0E
	0746	1045	2.7F		0844	1138	2.9F
	1355	1709	2.9E		1500	1805	3.1E
	2017	2309	2.4F		2129		
11 Tu	0212	0526	2.6E	26 W		0011	2.4F
	0825	1128	2.6F		0331	0627	2.6E

	September Slack h m	Maximum h m	knots		Slack h m	Maximum h m	knots
1	2039	2331	2.4F			2151	
10 Th	0236	0547	2.5E	25 F		0031	1.9F
	0842	1149	2.6F		0356	0649	2.1E
	1456	1820	2.9E		0959	1249	2.0F
	2135			◐	1614	1922	2.3E
					2252		
11 F		0026	2.2F	26 Sa		0131	1.7F
	0334	0644	2.3E		0458	0749	1.9E

Fig 5–15 Excerpt from Current Tables for "The Race, Long Island Sound" (Source: *Reeds Nautical Almanac*)

brief, but generally longer then the period of slack. Then the current gradually slows down until it once again becomes briefly slack before it starts to flow back in the opposite direction. Finding the anticipated current velocity at any time is quite simple. The tables have two axes: columns for the interval between slack and maximum current; rows for the interval between slack and the time in question. Where the two values intersect there's a figure. Just multiply the maximum velocity (stated in the basic tables) by this value to determine the expected velocity at the time in question—whether it is flood or ebb is determined by the base flow to which it is applied. Just remember that tidal currents, like the tides themselves, are also greatly influenced by atmospheric conditions. Predictions and calculations of currents will be reasonably accurate, but not precisely so. Determining currents always requires some interpretation based on observation and experience. Navigation is still a bit of an art!

Estimating Tidal Currents

Tidal currents are nothing more than moving water—something with which we all have everyday experience. If you watch rainwater flowing down a gutter, it is obvious from the leaves and twigs on its surface that the water in the deepest part of the gutter is flowing faster than the water in the shallower parts. It is the same with tidal currents: they are generally strongest in deep water and weaker in the shallows, where they are slowed down by contact with the seabed. It is the depth of water that is important—not the proximity of the shore.

Tidal currents flow faster around headlands, or where a channel narrows, than they do in bays or wider sections of the channel. This could be compared to water flowing through a funnel: The water flows faster through the narrow section than it does through the less constricted part immediately upstream. If you stir a pan of water, swirling eddies develop around the back of the spoon. The same thing would happen if you held the spoon stationary and the water flowed round it, and—on a much larger scale—where a prominent headland juts out into a strong tidal current. This can set up quite strong "back eddies" or "counter-currents." A good example of this is seen off Sandy Hook, New Jersey when there's a strong ebbing current flowing out of New York Harbor.

The presence of eddies can sometimes be seen either by turbulence where opposing tidal currents meet, such as in Hell Gate, where

Tidal Currents—Example

On Monday, August 10, you plan to sail east out of Long Island Sound, heading to Block Island. Knowing that The Race, the narrows at the eastern end of the sound, can have some strong currents, you consult the Current Tables to determine what awaits you. Ideally, you'd sail through The Race on the ebb—to have the current behind you—but closer to slack than maximum ebb so as to have better control. You definitely don't want to try going though The Race against the current.

After adding the hour for Daylight Saving Time, you see that slack before ebb won't be until 1455, with maximum ebb of 2.9 knots at 1809. Maximum flood of 2.7 knots will be at 1145. Because you will be sailing into the current all morning (flood currents run west in the Sound), you estimate that your chances of getting to The Race by 1455 are slim to none. By all calculations you'll probably arrive there about 1630. What will the current be?

1. Subtract the Time of Slack (1455) from the Time of Maximum Ebb (1809) for an interval of 3 hours 14 minutes.
2. Subtract the Time of Slack (1455) from your ETA (1630) for an interval of 1 hour 35 minutes after Slack.
3. Enter Table A in the column for 3:20, the closest to the 3h14m you calculated for the interval between Slack and Max.
4. Come down to the row for 1:40, the closest to your 1h 35m interval between Slack and ETA.
5. Multiply the Maximum Ebb (2.9) by the resulting 0.8 for an expected current at 1630 of 2.3 knots.

Deciding this is still a bit more than you want to deal with, you plan your departure time for 45 minutes earlier so the current in The Race will be under 2 knots when you arrive less than an hour after slack.

water flowing out of Long Island Sound collides with the junction of the East and Harlem Rivers producing serious swirls at any time except during slack water. In some places the eddy itself is less visible than the scum and debris that collects and rotates slowly in the "dead" area in the middle of it.

Direct personal observation of the effects of tidal currents can also provide useful information to supplement or confirm the data given in almanacs and tidal current tables or charts. Moored boats, or the "wake" that develops when the current flows past navigation marks or crab pot buoys, give a good indication of the direction of the tidal current, and an impression of its strength. Over a period of time, the boat's movement over the ground, derived from a succession of fixes, can be compared with its course and distance traveled; any discrepancy may be due to the tidal current, though it can be difficult to separate this from other factors such as compass or helmsman error and leeway.

Tidal Currents and Sea State

Tidal currents can have a marked effect on the sea state—which can be especially significant for high-speed motorboats.

Overfalls, sometimes called tide rips, are relatively localized effects, caused where a strong tidal current is deflected upwards or broken into turbulence by obstructions on the sea bed, producing particularly steep and irregular waves close down-current of the obstruction. Although overfalls are made worse by strong winds, the fact that they are not created by the wind means that they can produce rough water even in otherwise calm conditions. On the other hand, this makes them easily predictable, so areas prone to overfalls are often marked on the chart.

Most of the waves one encounters at sea are generated by the wind, but their size and shape can be modified by the current. If the current is flowing in the same direction as the wind that created the waves, the relative wind speed over the surface of the moving water is reduced, so the waves it creates are smaller. As well as this, the current has the effect of "stretching" the length of each wave, reducing its slope and making its crest less likely to break. When the wind and current are in opposition, the opposite happens; the wind speed relative to the surface of the water is increased, making the waves larger while, at the same time, the current shortens their wavelength to produce higher and steeper waves that are more likely to have breaking crests.

This can mean that a passage that would be uncomfortable in wind against current conditions becomes pleasant when wind and current are together, or that a passage that seemed perfectly reasonable when wind and current were together becomes unpleasant or even dangerous when the tide, and thus, tidal current turns.

It can also have a major effect on passage planning strategy. Sailboat navigators, whose boat speed may be little more than that of the tidal current, will usually plan a passage so that the current is in their favor—so they are likely to choose wind-against-current conditions to make progress upwind.

A planing motor cruiser, on the other hand, can easily overcome a contrary current—even one of five knots or more—but might be forced to throttle back to displacement speeds by wind-against-current sea conditions. Its navigator might well accept a foul current, in order to make progress upwind in flatter water.

6 | Lights, Buoys and Fog Signals

Lighthouses have been used to guide—and sometimes mislead—navigators, for centuries. The Pharos of Alexandria was built over 2,250 years ago and was regarded as one of the seven wonders of the ancient world, with a wood burning fire that could be seen over 20 miles away. Within two millennia, of course, lighthouses have become considerably more sophisticated, and even in an age increasingly dependent on electronic navigation aids, they are still of major importance in coastal navigation.

Their range has not increased dramatically: The big developments—apart from improving reliability—have been to give them distinctive characteristics that make it possible to distinguish one light from another. These characteristics can be divided into three groups: rhythm, period and color.

Rhythm

The simplest possible rhythm for a light is "fixed"—showing continuously and steadily. Unfortunately, a great many lights that have nothing to do with marine navigation also show continuously and steadily, so fixed lights are mostly used in minor roles, such as marking the ends of jetties. More important lights usually have more sophisticated rhythms.

A flashing light, in everyday language, simply means one that is going on and off, but its navigational meaning is more specific: It means that the total duration of light is shorter than the total duration of darkness.

If this situation is reversed so that the light is visible for longer than the intervals of darkness, it is described as an occulting light. A fourth possibility is for the duration of light and darkness to be equal, in which case the light is described as isophase. There is nothing that can be done to vary the rhythm of a fixed or isophase light, but flashing or occulting rhythms are open to many variations.

A straightforward flashing light involves a regular flash and an occulting light involves a regular eclipse ("flash of darkness"). The flashes can, however, come in groups, with each group separated from the next by a longer interval of darkness, to produce a group flashing light. As a further, but rarely used, variation, one group may be different from the next, such as the famous "I Love You" signal from Minot's Ledge Light off the coast of Massachusetts: a single flash followed by a group of four flashes, followed by a group of three before the pattern repeats itself—in a rhythm known as composite group flashing. Flashing, group flashing and composite group flashing all have their occulting equivalents.

For a flashing light, another possibility is to extend the flash by as much as two seconds to produce a long flashing (LFl) light. Alternatively, if the flashes are speeded up to between 50 and 80 per minute (about the same rate as a car's direction indicators) the light moves into a different classification known as quick (Q), while if they are faster still—100–120 per minute—the light is classed as very quick (VQ). These, too, lend themselves to variations such as group quick in which a group of a specified number of quick flashes is regularly repeated.

Period

The "period" of a light refers to how often its rhythm is repeated. For a flashing light, it

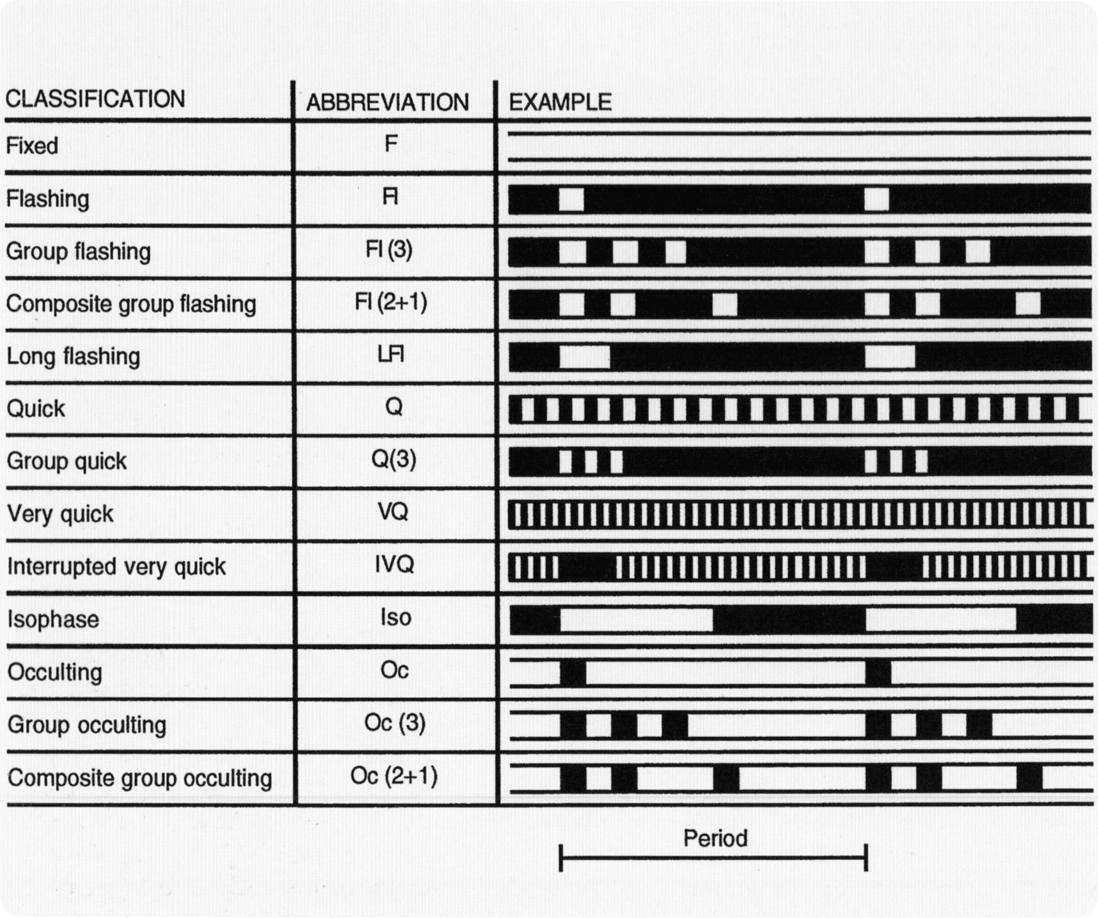

CLASSIFICATION	ABBREVIATION	EXAMPLE
Fixed	F	
Flashing	Fl	
Group flashing	Fl (3)	
Composite group flashing	Fl (2+1)	
Long flashing	LFl	
Quick	Q	
Group quick	Q(3)	
Very quick	VQ	
Interrupted very quick	IVQ	
Isophase	Iso	
Occulting	Oc	
Group occulting	Oc (3)	
Composite group occulting	Oc (2+1)	

Period

Fig 6–1 The rhythm of a light can be classified into one of four main groups, but the variations are almost infinite. This chart gives examples of some of the most common variations.

simply means the time between the start of one flash and the start of the next, while for a composite group flashing light, it means the time from the start of the first flash of one group to the start of the first flash when that group is repeated.

Color

Color is one of the most obvious of all light characteristics—except perhaps to those who are red-green color blind—but it is seldom used to distinguish major lighthouses for the simple reason that a colored light is not visible over as great a range as a white light.

It really comes into its own for the short and mid-range lights set up in the approaches to harbors, where there may be large numbers of lights that the navigator has to identify quickly but positively. White, red and green are the most common colors, but yellow is used occasionally.

Sectored Lights

Another possible use of color is of enormous value in night piloting. A light can be arranged so that it shows a different color when seen from one direction than from another. A common application of this is to indicate the

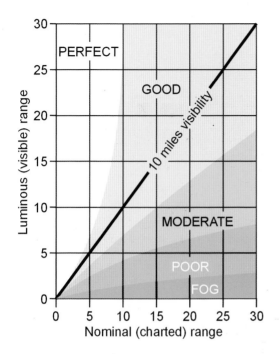

Fig 6–2 The range at which a light can be seen depends on atmospheric conditions, as well as on its brightness. In fog, a 20-mile light may be only visible for 2 miles. In very good visibility it might be visible for 30 miles or more.

line of a deep channel flanked by shallower water, where a light at one end of the channel is often arranged to show a white light over the deep water, a red light over the shallows on the port side, and a green light over the shallows on the starboard side.

On harbor and approach charts the sectors are clearly shown, but they are often omitted from coastal charts. This makes it easy to forget that you will see only one color at a time—depending on which sector you happen to be in—rather than all the colors alternately. The key difference is that the abbreviation for an alternating light is preceded by the letters *Al*.

The Range of a Light

The distance at which a light can be seen depends on a number of factors, quite apart from the observer's eyesight. Its height above

sea level and the observer's height of eye determine its geographical range—whether or not it can be seen above the horizon. The intensity of the light and the prevailing atmospheric conditions determine its luminous range—how far it could be seen if there were no horizon in the way.

The ranges quoted on charts and in lists of lights cannot possibly take account of all these variables; they have to cater for the officer of the watch on a container ship 80 feet above the sea on a crisp, clear winter's night, as well as for a yachtsman in the small hours of a misty spring morning, so they quote nominal ranges, which assume an atmospheric visibility of ten miles and an observer's height of eye sufficient to ensure that the light is above the horizon. The practical effect of this is that you cannot necessarily expect to see a light at the nominal range given on the chart: it will appear at whichever is the lesser of the geographical and luminous ranges.

Coast Pilots usually include a table for finding the geographical range, based on the elevation of the light and the height of eye of the observer (see Figure 4–9 page 62). This table is not included as such in yachtsmen's almanacs; it is unnecessary because it is exactly the same as the rising and dipping distance table mentioned in Chapter 4.

The Light Lists used to routinely include a chart for estimating luminous range from the nominal range and prevailing visibility, but latest editions seem to have omitted it. This is usually omitted from yachtsmen's almanacs, also, but a simplified version of it is given in Figure 6–2.

Buoys and Beacons

Major lighthouses are vastly outnumbered by a huge array of more minor visual aids to navigation—buoys and beacons—used to mark channels or specific hazards. They come in a wide range of shapes and sizes: Buoys can be no bigger than a football, or they can be substantial metal structures bigger and considerably heavier than most boats. Beacons range from tree branches stuck into the bed of little-used creeks (and placed there by local fishermen), to large stone towers that may be bigger than some lighthouses. Most large buoys and beacons have lights, but many smaller ones do not.

The IALA System

Until the early 1970s, each country had its own "convention of buoyage"—the code by which the shape and color of a mark conveyed information about what it was marking and where the best water was to be found.

Different codes for different countries was obviously a potential source of confusion, so over the following ten years most countries adopted a standardized system which brought together the best features of all those in use. It was known as the IALA system, named after the International Association of Lighthouse Authorities.

One irreconcilable difference was between the British and American systems, in which a red buoy meant opposite things on opposite sides of the Atlantic. That could only be resolved by having two IALA systems designated "A" and "B."

IALA B is used around the USA and Pacific Rim. IALA A is used throughout Europe and Scandinavia, and much of the rest of the world. Most Americans will only encounter IALA A system buoyage if they happen to cruise to Bermuda.

The IALA systems include three main groups of buoys and beacons:

n cardinal marks used mainly to mark hazards;
n lateral marks used to mark the sides of a clearly-defined channel;
n a miscellaneous group.

Cardinal Marks

Cardinal marks are named after the four cardinal points of the compass. A north cardinal lies to the north of a hazard with clear water to the north of it; a south cardinal marks the southern edge and so on, although in practice very few hazards are marked on all four sides. Fortunately, you can file this information in the "nice to know" category as Cardinal marks are no longer used in the United States (though they are in Canada); you'll probably never see even one of them.

IALA B Lateral Marks

Lateral marks are used to mark the sides of a channel. Going into a river estuary, for example, you would expect to find green, can-shaped (flat topped) buoys—logically called "cans," and/or square green dayboards, on your port side, and red conical-topped buoys (called "nuns"), and/or triangular red dayboards, on your starboard side. It helps to use the old mnemonic: "Red Right Returning." Leaving the river, of course, you would be heading in the opposite direction, so the green can-shaped marks would be on your starboard side and the red conical marks would be on your port side. This means that it is vitally important to know the direction of buoyage for the area in which you are operating. In rivers and estuaries, the direction of buoyage is always "inward," and in open water it is clockwise around continents. Consequently, "Red Right" applies: When going southward along the entire east coast of North America, when going northward along the west coast of Florida, when going westward along the remainder of the Gulf coast, and when going northward along our Pacific coast.

In some places even these rules can lead to ambiguity. When there are several buoys or markers involved, it helps to look at the numbers (which will always be even on red marks and odd on green). If the numbers are in increasing order, it means you are "inward" bound and should keep red marks on your starboard. If the numbers are decreasing, you are "outward" bound and should keep green marks to starboard. If the marks are isolated and you can't discern a numerical progression, the channel often lies between the green and red. But this isn't sufficiently true to make it a hard-and-fast rule. In fact, the red and green can often mark the opposite ends of a single danger, in which case going between them could prove to be disastrous! It's best to remember that the direction of buoyage is always indicated on the chart and a quick glance can eliminate all confusion. Lateral buoys and beacons may or may not be lit. Those that are usually show a light of the same color as the buoy or beacon itself.

Preferred Channel Marks

Preferred channel marks are a variation on the normal lateral marks, used where a channel divides. If the preferred channel is to starboard, the mark where the channel forks could be seen as the first port-hand mark of the main channel, so its predominant characteristics are those of a port-hand buoy: it is can-shaped (or square), and green. It could also be seen as the first starboard-hand buoy of the minor channel, so it also has some of the characteristics of a starboard-hand buoy, in the form of a red band. Its light is green, composite group flashing "2+1."

If the preferred channel is to port, the opposite applies: The mark at the fork has characteristics that are predominantly those of a starboard-hand buoy: red, conical, but with a green band, and, if lit, a red composite group flashing 2+1 light.

Preferred channel marks are never numbered but may be lettered for positive identification.

Miscellaneous Marks

Safe water marks might seem a strange concept, at odds with the idea of marking specific hazards or the sides of a channel, but they are useful as "landfall" buoys, marking the seaward end of a long harbor approach channel. Less common than lateral marks, their role means that they are usually quite large, and often, though not invariably, with lights. They may be spherical, or of the pillar shape associated with cardinal buoys, but their top mark is always a red sphere, and their color scheme a distinctive pattern of vertical red and white stripes. Their lights are equally distinctive, being white, and most often, Morse "A"—a short flash followed by a long one.

Isolated danger marks are used to draw attention to hazards that are entirely surrounded by navigable water and are sufficiently small in extent that they do not warrant two or more cardinal marks. Their color scheme is a pattern of black and red horizontal bands, and their top marks consist of two black spheres. This could be taken as a reminder that those fitted with lights show white flashes in groups of two.

Special marks can be used for all sorts of other purposes, such as anchorage areas. Large inflatable ones are often laid as the turning marks for yacht racing. All special marks are yellow. They may show a yellow light and can be of any shape.

Intracoastal Waterway Marks

Aids to navigation marking the Intracoastal Waterway (ICW) display unique yellow symbols to distinguish them from aids marking other waters. Yellow triangles should be considered "red" and passed by keeping them on the starboard hand of the vessel. Yellow squares should be considered "green" and passed by keeping them on the port. Of course, in both cases these directions apply when heading "inward," or clockwise around the U.S. Most of the time, the yellow triangles will be on red marks and the yellow squares on green. But not always! Whenever the ICW happens to share a portion of another marked channel, it is entirely possible that "inward progress" along the ICW is running counter to the "inward" travel of the other waterway. In these cases, if you are following the ICW, always be guided by the shape of the yellow symbols rather than to the base color and shape of the aids they happen to be placed on. When transiting areas with such buoyage, it helps to circle the area on the chart and boldly mark it, "marks reversed," just to remind yourself.

The United States Aids to Navigation System (IALA B) is shown in detail in the Appendix on page 168.

Western River Marks

Note: The Western Rivers Marking System is merging with the U.S. Aids to Navigation System and was to have been discontinued completely on December 31, 2003. Vessel operators may yet encounter both systems, however, during a still-ongoing transitional period. The Western Rivers Marking System is a variation of the standard U.S. Aids to Navigation System and is found on the Mississippi River and tributaries above Baton Rouge, LA and on certain other rivers that flow toward the Gulf of Mexico. Red daybeacons, lights, and buoys mark the starboard banks and limits of channels as vessels "return from sea" or proceed upstream. Green daybeacons, lights, and buoys mark the port banks and limits of navigable channels while going upstream. The Western River System varies of the standard U.S. system as follows:

1. Buoys are not numbered.
2. Daybeacons are not numbered but normally have an attached "Mile Marker" board that indicates the distance in statute miles from a fixed point (normally the river mouth).
3. Lights on green buoys and beacons with green daymarks show a single flash, which may be green or white.
4. Lights on red buoys and beacons with red daymarks show a double flash [Group Flashing (2)], which may be red or white.
5. Isolated Danger marks and Safe Water marks are not used.

Mile Markers

These markers are some of the most useful aids on a river. They are attached to daybeacons or displayed in other easily seen places. Since the U.S. Corps of Engineers erects them, they show distance in statute miles rather than nautical

miles. With the exception of the Ohio River, mile markers indicate the distance upstream from the mouth of a river. Ohio River markers start at its headwaters and indicate the distance downstream. Mile Markers also help a vessel operator locate his/her position on a river chart.

River Buoys

Changes in river channels caused by fluctuations in water level, current speed and shifting shoals make buoys maintenance a continuous task for the Coast Guard. In wintertime where rivers freeze, buoys are lost or moved from position. Because of their somewhat temporary nature, river buoys do not have letters or numbers and are not usually shown on river charts.

Sources of Information

The chart is the most immediate source of information about lighthouses, buoys and the various other kinds of lit navigation aids, and large-scale charts can be expected to provide almost everything you might need to know.

Small-scale "Sailing" charts cannot provide as much information or they would be impossibly cluttered, so minor lights and buoys are omitted and the amount of detail given of those that remain is reduced. How much is left depends on the scale of the chart and the importance of the light, but in general, elevation is the first detail to be edited out, followed by period, and finally range. The light's color and rhythm are usually retained.

The Coast Guard's Light Lists include considerably more detail (see Figure 6–3, an excerpt from Light List Volume 2), including a much fuller specification of the light's rhythm, a description of the light structure itself, and its height above the surrounding ground. This is particularly useful by day, when it can be handy to know whether you are looking for a high tower or a relatively squat building on top of a cliff. Yachtsmen's almanacs generally provide a little more information than can be found on a chart, but usually go into less detail than the Coast Guard's *Light Lists*.

FOG SIGNALS

Most lighthouses, and some major buoys and beacons, are fitted with fog signals, making a noise that can be used to identify them, and as a rough guide to their direction, in fog. The most powerful—now being phased out since most lighthouses have become unattended—is a **diaphone** (noted as "Dia" on charts), which uses compressed air to produce a long, low note (*BEEEEEOH*) that finishes with a distinct *grunt*.

Horns (Horn) can be of various types, using air or electricity to vibrate a diaphragm—as in a car's horn, but much more powerful. Just as with car horns, fog horns are often installed in groups, sounding a chord rather than a single note. They can be at any pitch, or even vary in pitch, but they never have the diaphone's grunt.

Sirens (Siren) are generally higher in pitch than horns or diaphones, but are very variable in tone and power. **Reeds** (Reed) are weak, high-pitched fog signals, often used at harbor entrances, and **Explosive** (Explos) signals are self-explanatory.

Bells, gongs, and whistles are used mainly on buoys, where they may be operated either by the rocking or heaving motion of the sea, or by machinery. Bells and gongs are self-explanatory, but whistles are often much lower in pitch than one might expect if you have not heard one before.

Mechanically operated fog signals can have distinctive characteristics, much as lights do: England's famous Fastnet Rock lighthouse, for instance, is "Horn (4) 60s"—meaning that it sounds four blasts on its horn in quick succession, repeated at 60-second intervals.

It is important to appreciate, though, that the way sound travels through waterlogged air can be erratic—it can seem to be reflected by some patches of fog, or be absorbed or muffled by others. This means that bearings of fog signals should be used with extreme caution, and with no attempt at any greater precision than "ahead," "astern" or "to port" or "starboard." The distance at which a fog signal can be heard is equally erratic, so "audible distances" are never quoted.

(1) No.	(2) Name and Location	(3) Position	(4) Characteristic	(5) Height	(6) Range	(7) Structure	(8) Remarks
			SEACOAST (New Jersey) - Fifth District				
	CAPE MAY TO FENWICK ISLAND (Chart 12214)						
90	**Hereford Inlet Light**	39 00 24 N 74 47 28 W	Fl W 10s	57	24	White square tower with cupola on white dwelling.	
95	*Hereford Inlet Lighted Whistle Buoy H*	38 58 59 N 74 46 11 W	Mo (A) W		5	Red and white stripes with red spherical topmark.	
100	*Five Fathom Bank Northeast Lighted Bell Buoy 2FB*	38 58 12 N 74 31 35 W	Fl R 4s		4	Red.	
105	*Five Fathom Bank Northwest Lighted Gong Buoy 3FB*	38 57 28 N 74 42 36 W	Fl G 4s		5	Green.	

Fig 6–3 The Light Lists provide detailed information on every U.S. Aid to Navigation extant. The number shown in column (1) is the ATON's specific "Light List Number." (Source: U.S. Coast Guard)

7 Estimating Position and Shaping a Course

It is always nice to know where you are, but there may be times when fixing is impossible—such as on a boat without electronic position fixing devices and with no land or sea marks in sight. Even in these situations all is not lost, as long as you know the direction you have been steering (from a compass) and the distance you have traveled (from the log). If there were no wind or current it is easy to see how these two could be used to deduce a position:

1. Starting from your last known position, draw a line on the chart representing your course steered.
2. Find the distance you have traveled from your last known position by subtracting your log reading at the time from your log reading now or by calculating the distance from speed and time.
3. Again starting from your last known position, measure that distance along the line representing your course. A position derived only from the course steered and distance traveled, like this, is called a Ded (from deduced) Reckoning position, though it is more often spelled "dead." We commonly refer to it as a "DR" position.

The time interval between successive DRs can be anything from a few minutes to several hours: The only requirement is that you have to know how far you have traveled and on what course. As long as your speed and course are reasonably constant, a DR can even be plotted in advance to give a rough idea of how the navigational situation is likely to develop. It is wise to plot a DR at least every hour and a more cautious

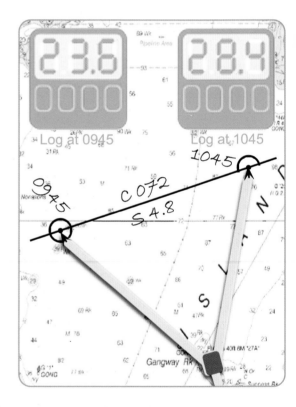

Fig 7–1 A dead reckoning position is based solely on the course steered and distance traveled: it takes no account of leeway or current. In this example, the log reading at the time of the 0945 fix was 23.6, and an hour later it was 28.4, so the distance covered was 4.8 miles. The boat had been steering 072°, so the 1045 DR is found by measuring 4.8 miles from the 0945 position, along the line representing the course steered.

navigator will increase the frequency to every half-hour. You should also plot a DR: after every change of course or speed, after every fix or running fix, and any time you plot even a single position line.

Chartwork—Example 1

At 1540, a yacht passes very close to the Port Everglades sea buoy, and immediately alters course to 065° (Magnetic). Variation is 6° West. Her log, at that time, reads 74.3. At 1640, her log reads 80.1. What is her 1640 DR position?

Passing close to the PE sea buoy gives a good fix, so it is marked on the chart by a circle, and labeled with the time (see Figure 7–2). The course steered is 065° (M). The "Cadet" rule says that when converting from compass to true, easterly variation and deviation must be added, but in this case the variation is westerly, so it must be subtracted:

065° (M) – 6°(W) = 059° (T).

The course, 059° (T), is drawn on to the chart, from the fix, and labeled. It is a matter of personal preference whether to use True or Magnetic for labels, but it must be specified! Standard practice is to work in True, which requires no designation. If you prefer to work in magnetic, however, always label courses with an M, as a reminder. From 1540 to 1640, the log reading has advanced from 74.3 to 80.1, indicating that the yacht has traveled 5.8 miles through the water. Using the latitude scale on the side of the chart (one minute of latitude = one nautical mile), the dividers are set to 5.8 miles, and used to measure 5.8 miles along the course line, from the 1640 fix. This point represents the 1640 DR position, so it is marked with a semi-circle and labeled with the time.

At 1640, the skipper also takes a visual bearing of the prominent white and black steel skeleton tower of the Hillsboro Inlet lighthouse. He plots the bearing on the chart and faces a dilemma: The position line is nowhere near his DR. Where is the yacht's estimated position?

It would be tempting to choose the point at which the position line crosses the course line. But even considering possible log error, the yacht shouldn't be this far from the DR just one hour after a very reliable fix. So where to place it?

Given that even with the inherent errors in visual bearings, odds are greater that the boat is on the position line than the course line, he should place the EP somewhere on it also. But where? Draw a perpendicular from the DR through the LOP. Where it crosses the position line is the EP, which should be marked with a square and also labeled with the time.

If a latitude and longitude of the EP are required, they can be read from the scales on the side and top of the chart respectively: in this case 25° 12.0'N, 079° 58.1'W.

If you are curious as to the cause of the discrepancy between DR and EP, it is current. In this case, the Gulf Stream, which races northward in this area at up to 4 knots. When the effects of current are known, they can be accounted for, and this discrepancy thus eliminated, by "Shaping a Course." We'll see how to do this later in the chapter.

Because it ignores the ongoing effects of wind and tide, the accuracy of a DR deteriorates with the passage of time: A DR based on an hour-old fix will be much less accurate than one originating from a fix taken in the past six minutes. So whether it is wise to depend on a DR for very long depends on how quickly you are approaching a potential hazard, and on how much your boat is affected by external factors such as wind and current.

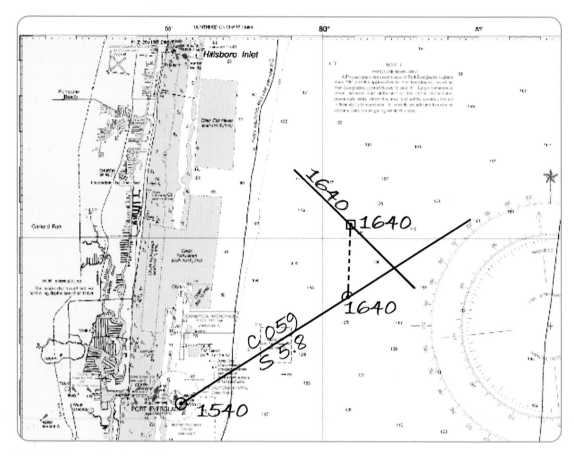

Fig 7–2 Chartwork—Example 1

Allowing for Wind

As well as providing the motive power for
sailing yachts, the wind can make all boats—
sail or power—slide sideways, so that they are
not actually moving through the water in the
direction they are pointing. This effect is called
leeway.

A boat's propensity for making leeway
depends on the balance between the windage
offered by its rig, superstructure and topsides,
and the lateral resistance offered by the
underwater parts of the hull, keel, running gear
and rudder. This means that the amount of
leeway made by a sailboat is to some extent
determined by its design: A boat with a high-
windage rig and shoal draft is likely to make

more leeway than one with a low-resistance rig
and deep keel. Design is not the whole story,
however; the skipper and crew play their part
too. Reefing or bad sail shape increase the
amount of windage compared with the
forward drive developed by the sails, so they
tend to increase leeway. Excessive heeling also
tends to increase leeway by reducing the lateral
resistance of the keel.

Leeway is generally greatest when close
hauled, and reduces to nothing on a dead
run—when, of course, it is in the same
direction as the boat's forward movement
anyway. "Pinching" when close-hauled tends
to increase leeway even more.

Many helmsmen luff up in gusts, either
because they have a background in dinghy

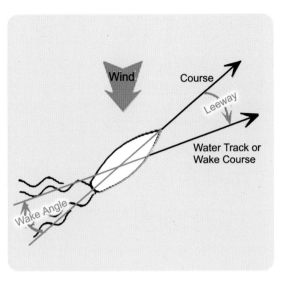

Fig 7-3 Leeway is caused by wind pushing the boat sideways, so that it follows a track through the water that is slightly downwind of the course steered. Sometimes called the "wake course," the water track makes the same angle to the boat's heading as the wake makes to dead astern—which is how the wake would flow were there no leeway.

racing or because the "weather helm" of many cruising boats increases the load on the steering in gusts. It is an efficient way of sailing, because it takes advantage of the shift in the apparent wind that occurs as a gust strikes.

Navigationally, however, the effect is that the average heading may be several degrees closer to the wind than the course the helmsman thinks he is steering. This is often enough to cancel out leeway altogether, or even to produce "apparent leeway" upwind.

Motorboats may make more leeway than a modern sailboat because they often have high topsides and superstructures, without the advantage of a deep keel to increase their lateral resistance. They also have a tendency to heel to windward when underway in a fresh breeze, which can be counteracted by the helmsman steering downwind. This means that helmsman's errors are more likely to add to a motorboat's leeway than to reduce it. Leeway

Fig 7-4 A more accurate and useful position takes account of leeway. The procedure is essentially the same as that used to find a DR in Figure 7-1, except that the water track is plotted as well as the course steered. In this case, with a northerly wind and leeway estimated at 10°, the wake course is 082°. The result is an estimated position (EP), which has a higher probability of being where you actually are than does the DR, which ignores the forces of nature.

is difficult to measure with any accuracy, particularly in the rough conditions in which it is likely to be greatest. When there is no current, it can be measured by passing close to a mark such as a buoy, and then—after several minutes—comparing the bearing of the buoy with the course steered. Add or subtract 180° from the bearing of the buoy to find the direction actually traveled. The difference between this and the course steered is the leeway in degrees. In tidal waters much the same can be achieved by taking bearings of a free-floating mark such as a dan buoy.

97

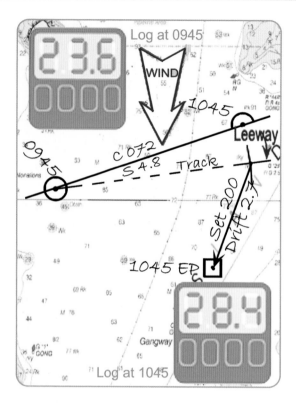

Fig 7–5 An even better EP can be derived by also allowing for the effect of current. In this case, the current is setting approximately 200° at 2.7 knots. From the EP found in Figure 7–4, (allowing for leeway) a line drawn in a 200° direction (the current's "set") for 2.7 miles (its "drift") represents the current's effect between 0945 and 1045.

Fig 7–6 An EP does not have to be run over a full hour, but make sure you use the current that would be experienced in the same time, not a full hour's worth. Compare this with Figure 7–5: Here, in the half hour from 0945 to 1015, the log reading has increased from 23.6 to 26.0, indicating a distance run of 2.4 miles. This has been used to work up the 1015 DR. In half an hour, the 2.7 knot tidal current will have made the boat drift 1.35 miles, so the EP is 1.35 miles from the EP determined by leeway alone.

A third option is to estimate leeway, based on experience after a number of longish passages. If there is a consistent error between your estimated position and your fix, which cannot be ascribed to tide, deviation or anything else, this may well be taken as an indication of your leeway.

Having measured or estimated your leeway, it can be allowed for when plotting on the chart by adding or subtracting the angle of leeway to or from the course before drawing the track line on to the chart. To differentiate this "course adjusted for leeway" from the course actually steered, it is often called the water track or wake course (Figure 7–4) and labeled "track."

Whether leeway should be added or subtracted depends on the relative wind direction: If you are on starboard tack (i.e., with the wind blowing from the starboard side) it should be subtracted. One simple way to make sure you apply leeway in the right direction is to pencil a large arrow onto the chart representing the wind direction, and then make sure that the water track drawn on the chart is downwind of the course (Figure 7–4). As an alternative, it may help to remember that "subtract" and "starboard" both begin

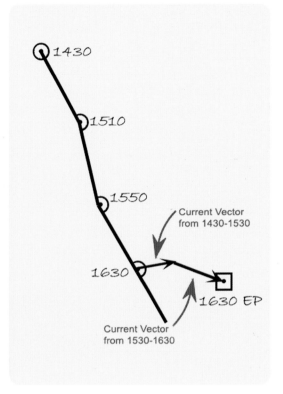

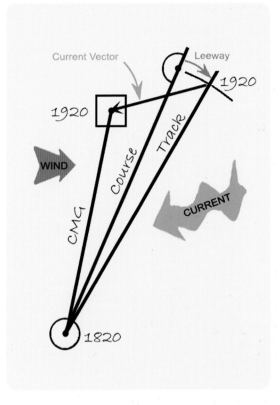

Fig 7-7 The same principle can be used to work up an EP over several hours. Again, it is important to use the right amount of tidal current, by drawing in each hour's current vector, nose to tail from the latest DR. Here, a fix was taken at 1430, and DRs plotted at 1510 and 1550 (when the boat altered course) and again at 1630. The DRs took no account of tidal currents, so converting the 1630 DR into an EP requires two hours' worth of current to be applied.

Fig 7-8 The direction and distance between two successive positions can be used to work out the boat's ground track and ground speed (course and speed made good—CMG & SMG).

with an S, and "port" and "plus" both begin with a P.

Allowing for Current

The effect of current can be considerably greater than leeway. This is particularly true for sailboats, whose speed through the water may be little more—or even possibly less—than the speed of the current, but even planing motorboats can seldom ignore it altogether.

The principle of accounting for the effect of current can be explained by a simple, if rather far-fetched, example:

Imagine two boats starting off from the same place and both heading eastward. One is capable of infinite speed, so it covers six miles in no time at all, then stops and drifts while it waits for the other to catch up. The other boat, meanwhile, is making six knots through the water, so after one hour, the two are together again. During that hour, both have been affected by a current setting southward at a rate of one knot, so in the one hour that it was waiting, the first boat has drifted one mile south. Its actual movement could be plotted on a chart as a DR based on an easterly course

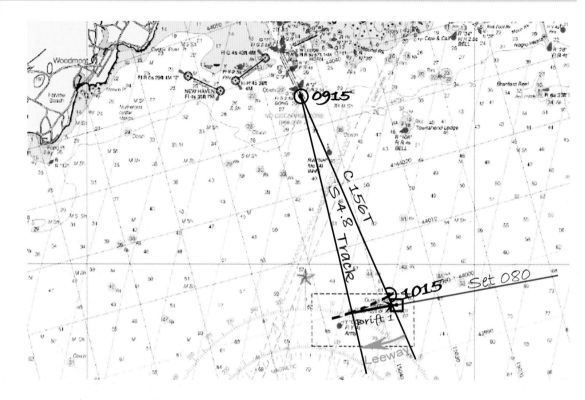

Fig 7-9 Chartwork—Example 2

and a distance run of six miles, followed by a southerly "course" for a distance of one mile, to give an estimated position that takes account of the current.

The other boat has covered the same distance on the same course, and has been affected by the same current to end up in the same place, so the chartwork required to find its position is exactly the same, even though the route it took to reach that position was different. This means that in order to find an estimated position you should:

1. Draw a line on the chart representing the boat's movement through the water (its water track).
2. Measure along the water track a distance corresponding to the distance covered through the water, to give a position allowing for leeway.

3. From this position draw a line corresponding to the direction of the current.
4. Measure along this line a distance corresponding to the distance you would have drifted in the same time.
5. Mark this position—your estimated position—with a square and the time.

On a longish passage it is usually convenient to work out an estimated position at hourly intervals, because this is an easily-remembered routine. This is not, however, essential, and an EP can be run over any convenient time interval. The important thing to remember is that the allowance made for current must always cover the same time interval as the distance run (see Figures 7–5, 7–6 and 7–7).

Chartwork—Example 2

A yacht leaves New Haven, CT, clearing the outer channel buoys at 0915, and steers 170° (Magnetic). Variation is 14° West. Her log, at that time, reads 0.6. At 1015, it reads 5.4. Her skipper estimates that in the northwesterly wind, she is making 10° of leeway, and from the current tables and the Long Island Sound Current diagrams in Reed's Nautical Almanac assesses the current to be 080° (True) at 1 knot. What is her estimated position at 1015?

Passing close to gong #1 gives a good fix, so the 0915 position can be marked on the chart with a circle (to signify a fix) and labeled with the time (see Figure 7–9). The course steered is 170° (Magnetic).

Using the "Cadet" rule (from Compass to True add east, subtract west), this corresponds to 156° (T). As the wind is on the port side, leeway has to be added (port=plus), giving a water track of 166° (T). The track will always be downwind of the course.

Comparing the two log readings shows that at 1015, the yacht has traveled 4.8 miles through the water. The latitude scale on the side of the chart is used as a scale of distance, and dividers are used to mark off a distance of 4.8 miles from the 0915 fix, on both the course line and track, to produce the 1015 DR and a position corrected for leeway.

From this position, the direction (set) of the current is drawn on to the chart in an 080° (T) direction. The boat has been subject to a current of 1.0 knot for one hour, so the latitude scale is used to set the dividers to 1 mile, in order to mark off an hour's worth of drift along the current vector.

This mark represents the boat's 1015 EP, so it is identified by a square and labeled with the time. Interestingly, the current has more than offset the leeway, so the 1015 EP is not only very close to, but actually slightly ahead of, the 1015 DR!

Course and Speed Over the Ground

Once you have two positions that relate to different times, it is possible to work out your course and speed over the ground. The ground track—sometimes known as the course over the ground (COG) or course made good (CMG)—is the direction from the earlier position to the later one, and the distance made good is the distance between the two. From the distance made good, the speed made good can be found by dividing by the time taken.

The course and speed calculated by this method are only as accurate and reliable as the positions on which they are based, so if either of the positions is estimated, then the course and speed will also be estimates.

Shaping a Course

The process of estimating a position allows you to work out the direction and distance you have actually traveled—variously known as ground track, course made good or course over the ground—but it is a retrospective view, based on events that have already happened.

If you have set off by simply pointing the boat toward where you want to go, the effects of wind and current mean that the chances of your ground track actually heading straight to your destination are slim. There are obvious advantages in being able to calculate a course to steer that will give you the ground track you really want. This is known as shaping a course: a forward-looking process

Chartwork—Example 3

At 2010, a yacht obtains a fix by visual bearing and radar range of Horton Point Light, 125° (M), 2.2 miles. The log reading is 103.2. She steers 351° (M) until 2205 she alters course to 031° (M) to avoid a fishing boat: the log reading is 110.7. At 2225, with the log reading 112.1, she alters course to 351° (M) once more, and stays on that course until 2310, when the log reads 115.4.

She makes negligible leeway, but the tidal current data is:

2040 082° (T) 2.1 knots
2140 074° (T) 1.5 knots
2240 066° (T) 0.8 knots

Variation is 14° W

What is her estimated position at 2310?

There is no leeway to contend with, so once the fix has been plotted, finding the 2205 DR position is a matter of drawing in the course of 351° (M) = 337° (T) and measuring off the distance run: 110.7 − 103.2 = 7.5 miles (see Figure 7–10).

The 2225 DR is again based on the course steered and the distance run from the 2205 DR: 017°(T) for 1.4 miles. The 2310 DR is plotted in the same way: 337°(T) for 3.3 miles.

The last known position was at 2010, so the DR has been running for three hours so three hours' worth of current has to be applied to it to convert it to an EP. The current data for 2040 can be assumed to be valid from 2010 to 2110, and so on, so there is no interpolation required, and the three current vectors can be applied—tail to nose—starting from the 2310 DR, to produce the EP for 2310.

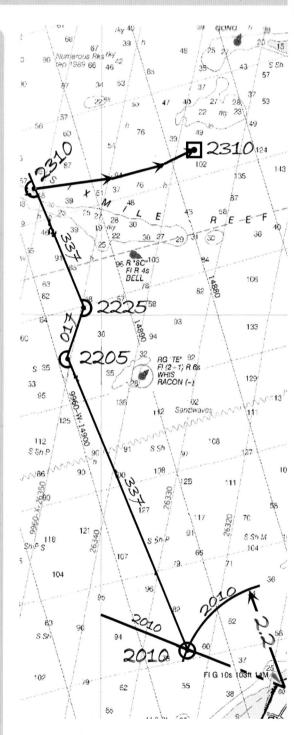

Fig 7–10 Chartwork—Example 3

that in some ways can be seen as an EP worked out in reverse.

1. Draw your intended track onto the chart as a straight line, from where you are, and passing through your destination.
2. Estimate your likely speed, and from this, work out roughly how long the passage is likely to take.
3. From tidal current tables or other sources, such as Coast Pilots or almanacs, find the tidal current you expect to experience.
4. From your starting point draw in the current vector, to represent the direction and distance the boat would move if it were stationary in the water and drifting with the current.

5. Use your estimated speed to work out how far you would expect to travel through the water in the time interval covered by your tidal current prediction.
6. Set a drawing compass or dividers to this distance, and with one point at the end of the current vector, use the other to make a mark on your intended track (drawn in step 1).
7. Join the end of the current vector to the mark made in step 6. This represents the water track that is required in order to achieve your intended ground track. In other words, it is the course to steer with no allowance for leeway.
8. Add or subtract the expected angle of leeway to or from the direction of the water

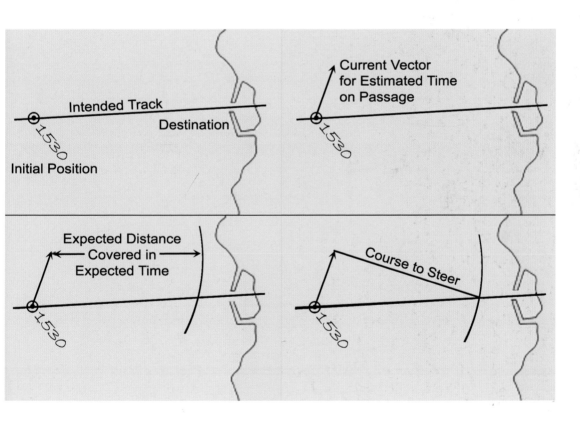

Fig 7–11 Allowing for the effect of the current in advance allows you to "shape a course" so that your ground track (course over ground) corresponds with the direction you want to go. The intended track is drawn in first, from the present position to the intended destination, then the current from the present position. Then, from the end of the current vector, the expected distance run in the same time is marked off with dividers or a drawing compass. A line joining the end of the current vector to where the distances arc cuts the intended track indicates the course to steer.

track to give a course to steer which is slightly more upwind.

Do not be concerned if some of the chart work in this process passes very close to (or even over) potential hazards—it often happens that shaping a course involves drawing on the yellow (land) part of the chart! Shaping a course is a purely geometric process that could be carried out almost as effectively on a blank sheet of paper because none of the lines drawn for course correction required on the chart has any direct relationship to the boat's actual progress over the ground.

Shaping a Course for Several Hours

Much the same process can be used for passages likely to take several hours, though it

requires a slight modification to take account of the fact that the tidal current varies from time to time and from place to place.

At stage three of the process, use a tidal current table or other source to estimate the tidal current, both direction and velocity, for each hour of the intended passage.

Remember that the tidal current that is relevant to the end of your passage may not be the same as the one that relates to its start. Then, from your starting point draw in these current vectors tail-to-nose, to represent the cumulative effect of current over the whole passage—the direction and distance the boat would move if it were stationary in the water and drifting with the current. From this point, mark off the distance you will travel, to cut the required track line to give the course to steer.

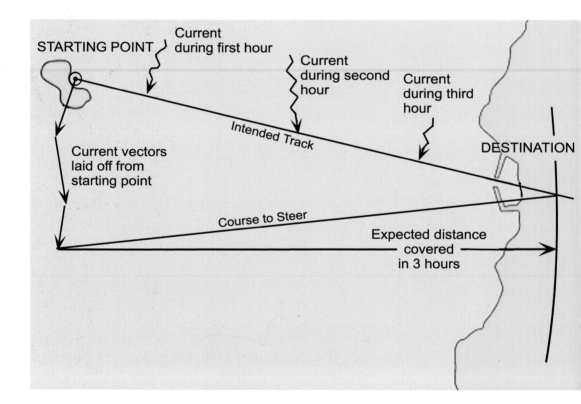

Fig 7-12 A course can be shaped for several hours. As with an EP run over several hours, it is important to allow for the same number of hours' worth of current as the time taken to travel the distance, adding the current vectors together.

Is It Worth It?

The process of shaping a course may seem long-winded, particularly for a passage that is expected to last several hours, so it may be tempting to ask whether it is really worth the effort. For boats whose speed is low compared to that of the tidal current, the answer is almost invariably "Yes."

If you take the extreme—but not impossible—situation of a boat whose speed is less than the speed of the tidal current then it is only by shaping a course that it can hope to reach its destination at all. For slightly faster boats, course shaping shortens passage times, and can often do away with an up-current slog at the end of a passage.

In general, the benefits of course shaping diminish as the boat's speed increases. Whether the benefits are worth the time involved is a decision entirely up to the skipper/navigator, but as a very rough guide it is a decision worth thinking about if the tidal current setting across your intended track is more than about 5% of your boat's speed.

The classic geometrical method of working out a course to steer can be very accurate, but for many purposes, a method based on mental arithmetic is just as good. It is called the "one in sixty rule," because it relies on the fact that if you are one degree off course for 60 miles, then you will end up one mile off track. It is only an approximation, but it is surprisingly accurate, and holds true for angles very much larger than 1°. If, for instance, you are 10° off course, then you will be 10 miles off track after 60 miles or one mile off course after six. The converse also holds true: If you are experiencing a current that would push you one mile off track in an hour, then in a six-knot boat you would have to steer 10° up-current to counteract it. In more general terms:

$$\frac{\text{current speed} \times 60}{\text{boat speed}} =$$

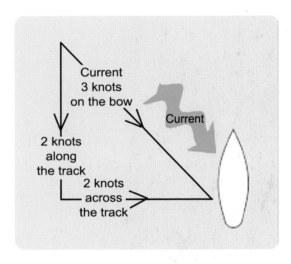

Fig 7–13 A rough estimate of the effect of a tidal current at an angle to the boat's course can be made by thinking of it acting two-thirds along the track, and two-thirds across the track.

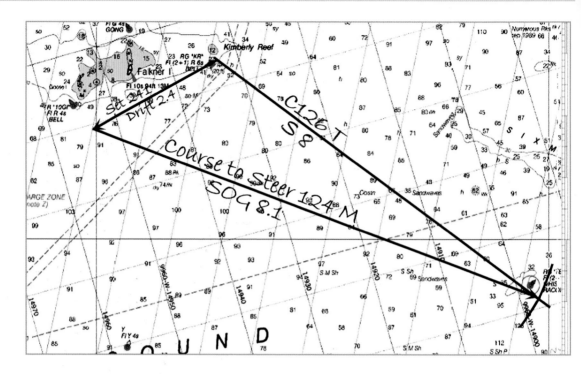

Fig 7-14 Chartwork—Example 4

Chartwork—Example 4

From Kimberly Reef buoy ("KR") what is the most direct course to steer for "TE" buoy? The boat speed is estimated to be 8 knots, with negligible leeway, but there is a current of 2.4 knots, setting in a 241° (T) direction. Variation is 14°W.

From the KR buoy, draw in the intended ground track—a straight line passing through the destination. In practice, it is often useful to continue this line well beyond the intended destination (see Figure 7–14).

The distance to be covered is approximately 6 miles, so at 8 knots it should take less

than an hour, so it is sufficient to consider one hour's worth of current. This is drawn in, from the starting point, as a vector with a 241° (T) direction, and length of 2.4 miles.

Having allowed a full hour's worth of current, it is important to allow an hour's worth of boat-speed, so the dividers or drawing compass must be set to 8 miles. Then, with one point of the dividers at the end of the current vector, the other point is used to draw an arc across the intended track. Joining the end of the current vector to the spot where the arc cuts the intended track gives the course to steer (in this case, 110° (T) or 124° (M)).

Chartwork—Example 5

At 0815 a racing yacht's position is fixed by GPS at 41° 01.45¢ N 072° 50.01¢ W. Find the optimum course to steer to reach the temporary yellow racing buoy just west of New Haven's main channel, if the boat's speed is expected to be 4 knots, and the currents are:

0845 263° 0.8
0945 266° 1.3
1045 254° 2.0

Leeway is negligible, and variation is 14° W.

From the fix, draw in the intended ground track as a straight line passing through the destination, and continuing beyond it (see Figure 7–15). In this case, the distance to be covered is just over 11 miles, so at 4 knots it can be expected to take about three hours. The three hours of current is plotted on the chart as a series of three vectors—as though plotting the boat's position if she drifted with the current.

In the same three hours, the boat will cover 12 miles through the water, so set the dividers or drawing compass to 12 miles. With one point of the dividers at the end of the cumulative current vector, the other point is used to draw an arc across the intended track.

The line joining the end of the current vector to the spot where the arc cuts the intended track gives the course to steer—in this case, 358° (T) or 012° (M).

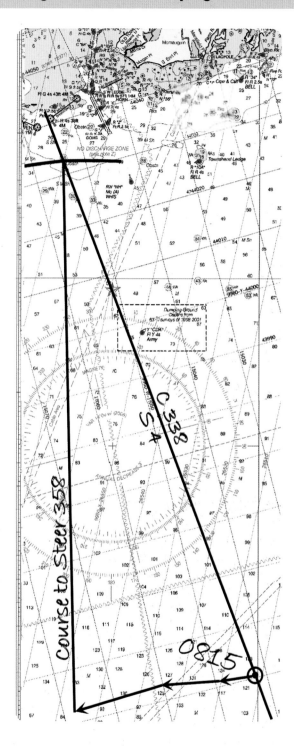

Fig 7–15 Chartwork—Example 5

107

8 Radar

Radar is quite unlike any of the other electronic navigation aids covered so far in this book. Not only is it more expensive to buy and more demanding of electrical power, but it also requires more skill on the part of the operator to set it up and adjust it to suit prevailing conditions and to interpret the picture on its screen. In return it is the most versatile of all electronic aids.

How Radar Works

The basic principle of radar is similar to that of an echo sounder: it transmits pulses of energy and measures the time that elapses before the echo of each one returns. One major difference is that instead of using ultrasonic sound, radar uses extremely high frequency radio waves, called microwaves—in the order of 9.5 GHz (9500 MHz) and with a wavelength of about 3 cm. The other big difference is that instead of being transmitted downward, like the ultrasonic clicks of an echo sounder, a radar's microwave pulses are focused into a beam by a rotating antenna (also called the scanner) and transmitted horizontally through 360° around the boat.

So a radar is able to measure the range of a target from the time it takes a microwave pulse to make the out and back trip, and measures

Fig 8-1 A flush-mounted multi-function display in radar mode, at the helm position of a new motor cruiser

the target's bearing from the direction that the scanner is pointing. This information is used to build up a picture on the display—sometimes called a PPI or "plan position indicator," because the overall effect is like a plan, or bird's-eye view, of the boat's surroundings.

Basic Operation

All radars have seven main controls, though these may be combined with each other, automated, or buried in a system of menus or soft keys along with other controls.

On/Standby/Transmit

The on/standby/transmit control is used to turn the set on. It will have to be left in its standby mode for at least a minute or two while the magnetron—the component that actually generates the microwaves—warms up, so on most modern sets this warm-up period is indicated by a count-down timer on the screen. Once the warm-up is completed, switching to transmit mode turns the transmitter on. This should produce a picture on the screen, though it may leave room for considerable improvement by means of the other controls.

Brilliance

The brilliance control determines the brightness of the picture exactly like the corresponding control on a television set, and should be adjusted to give a clear but not dazzling image. On radars with a liquid crystal display, the brilliance control may have to be used in conjunction with the contrast setting; the two are interdependent, and their adjustment depends on the angle from which you are looking at the screen.

Gain

Gain refers to the amount of amplification applied to the returning echo. In some ways it is easy to confuse the effect of the gain control with that of brilliance, because turning it up makes weak contacts look bigger, brighter, and more consistent. The two are not interchangeable, however. Brilliance is adjusted to make the picture clearer or more comfortable to look at, whereas the setting of the gain control can determine whether some contacts appear at all. As a rule, the gain should be turned up until the screen is filled with a background speckle, and then turned down until the speckle just disappears, but it may need to be readjusted each time the radar's operating range is changed. Most modern radars have the option of having the gain set itself automatically by choosing "Auto" on the gain control.

Range

The range control, as its name suggests, is used to adjust the operating range of the set, typically in about eight steps from one eighth or one quarter of a mile, to between 16 and 48 (or maybe even 72) miles. The range to use depends on the job in hand: Short ranges (between half a mile and 4 miles) are generally of most use for piloting; medium ranges (4, 6 or 8 miles) for collision avoidance and long ranges (8 to 24 miles) for coastal and offshore navigation. Ranges in excess of 24 miles are of very little practical use for small boat radars other than for using the longest range possible to view surrounding weather—airborne precipitation can be seen at greater distances than surface objects, even from a relatively low-mounted scanner.

Tuning

The tuning control, like its counterpart on a domestic radio, is used to adjust the receiver to give the best possible reception of incoming signals. As the radar is listening for echoes of its own transmissions, it may come as a surprise to find that any adjustment is required, but it should be borne in mind the returning echoes are very weak indeed, so a precise match between the transmitter and receiver is of paramount importance. The radar's tuning

Fig 8-2 Small, lightweight scanners and compact liquid crystal displays have brought radar within reach of all but the smallest cruising boats.

the picture, by removing unwanted contacts or clutter.

Sea Clutter Control

This is sometimes called STC or swept gain, and is used to remove the clutter caused by echoes from waves, that can otherwise form a bright circle or starburst pattern in the center of the screen. Under normal conditions—with the sea clutter control turned way down—the radar may be receiving echoes from targets at a variety of different ranges, but with much weaker echoes from very distant targets than from targets close at hand. This means that the echoes that return very soon after each pulse has been transmitted, need much less amplification than those received later. The sea clutter control works by reducing the amplification of early returns even more, while leaving the later levels of amplification intact. On the screen, this has the effect of obliterating weak contacts close to the boat, allowing stronger contacts to show up more clearly. If it is overdone, however, the sea clutter control is quite capable of suppressing the amplification to such an extent that even the strongest contacts—such as land—are obliterated at ranges up to several miles from the boat, so it should be used with considerable caution and always as little as is necessary.

Rain Clutter

This control is sometimes known as FTC or differentiation and, as its name suggests, is used to remove the clutter caused by meteorological effects such as rain, snow, or hail. A heavy rain shower can be quite an effective reflector of radar pulses, but it does not reflect them in the same way as a solid object. Instead of returning an echo which is a crisp copy of the transmitted pulse, rain echoes are weaker but more drawn out. On the screen, this produces a large but relatively diffuse contact, often described as looking like a smudge or cotton wool. The rain clutter control acts by ignoring all but the leading

control offers very fine adjustment, to allow for small variations in the transmitting frequency caused mainly by variations of temperature. To tune a radar, start by setting the brilliance to a comfortable level, adjusting the gain until the background speckle just disappears, and selecting a medium range. Choose a weak contact somewhere near the edge of the screen and concentrate on that, while adjusting the gain control in small steps—allowing at least two seconds between each step—until the chosen contact is as big, bright, and consistent as possible. Tuning can also often be set to automatic.

The adjustment of these first five controls is aimed at giving "targets" (the physical objects that reflect radar waves) the best possible chance of appearing on the screen as "contacts." Two more controls are used to refine or clarify

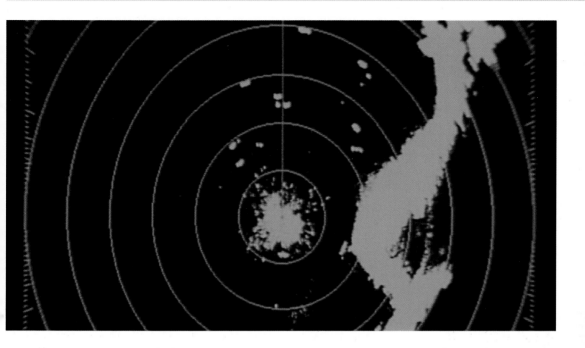

Fig 8-3 Sea clutter forms a bright "sunburst" effect around the center of the radar display, which can obscure important contacts.

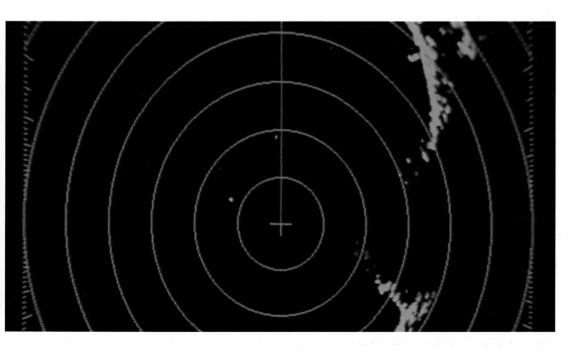

Fig 8-4 Sea clutter can be reduced with the sea clutter control, but it must be used with care. Notice how excessive use of the sea clutter control has removed several genuine contacts that appeared in the previous picture, and is starting to make even the land disappear!

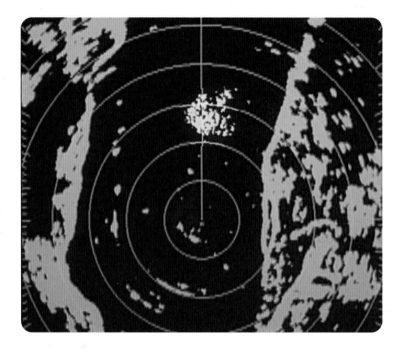

Fig 8–5 Rain clutter (the speckled patch just above the center of this radar picture) can obscure contacts.

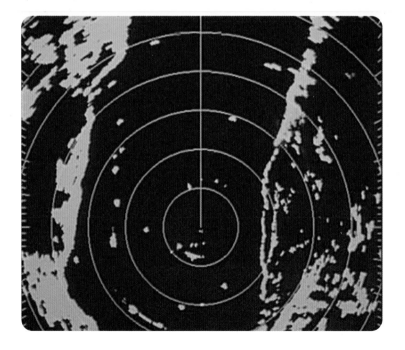

Fig 8–6 The rain clutter controls reduce rain clutter, but can weaken other contacts. Notice how the coastline to starboard appears to be breaking up.

edge of each returning echo. This effectively reduces the energy received from rain echoes to such an extent that they do not appear as a contact at all. Almost inevitably though, it reduces the energy received from real targets. The drawn out echoes produced by gently sloping coastlines such as beaches or mudflats are particularly badly affected, so the rain clutter control, like the sea clutter control, should only be used when necessary.

Interpreting the Picture

The first time one looks at a radar screen, it often comes as something of a disappointment: The picture may look crude and blobby, and bits of the coastline may be missing, making it difficult to relate what appears on the screen to the chart of the same area. A radar is definitely not "an all-seeing eye," and interpreting the picture calls for practice and a slightly deeper understanding of how the radar works. To begin with, it may help to visualize the stream of microwave pulses leaving the radar scanner as being like the beam of a searchlight. In order to produce an echo, a target has to be "illuminated" by the radar beam. Some materials, such as fiberglass, which are opaque to light are transparent to radar waves. But something such as a steel funnel in the way of the radar beam can block radar waves just as effectively as it blocks light, to cause a shadow zone that can never be illuminated.

The obvious solution to this problem is to make sure that the radar scanner is mounted higher than any large metal objects on the boat. Land has a very similar effect, though without the easy cure. Bays or river entrances will be hidden from the radar by surrounding

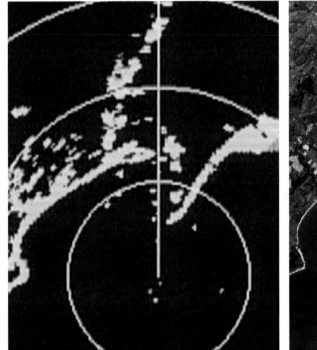 

Fig 8-7 Comparing the radar picture (left) with a satellite photograph shows that radar is not an all-seeing eye; in particular, its view can be blocked by headlands and islands, creating gaps in its picture of a coastline.

headlands just as they are hidden from the naked eye. This is the main reason why there are gaps in the radar picture of the coastline. The biggest obstruction of all is the earth itself. There is nothing unfamiliar about the idea of things being invisible because they are "below the horizon," nor that hills can be seen at longer ranges than low-lying ground or the shoreline itself because they are tall enough to be "above the horizon." The same effect appears on radar: At long ranges, hills may appear to be isolated islands and the true coastline may not show up at all. Microwaves bend very slightly to follow the curvature of the earth, so the radar horizon is about 5% more distant than the visual one. Its distance can be found with the formula:

$$R = 2.2 \times \sqrt{H_a}$$

where R is the horizon range, and Ha is the antenna height in meters.

So for an antenna nine meters (30 feet) above sea level, the radar horizon would be about six and a half miles away. Once a target has been illuminated by the radar beam, its ability to produce an echo depends on its material, size, shape, and to some extent, on its surface texture. Some materials (such as fiberglass) are almost transparent to the microwaves. Others (such as wood) absorb microwaves. This is why yachtsmen should never assume that their fiberglass or wooden vessels will be "seen" by a ship's radar. Some materials, most significantly metal, rock, and water, are good reflectors of microwaves. The effect of size is fairly obvious: In general, a large target can reflect more of the radar energy than a small one, so it stands a better chance of appearing as a contact on the radar screen. The effect of size, however, is masked to some extent by the effect of shape. Spherical or cylindrical objects are poor reflectors because they scatter radar energy, instead of reflecting it back the way it came. Flat surfaces, on the other hand, can be very good

reflectors indeed, because if they happen to be positioned exactly at right angles to the approaching radar beam the effect is very much like a mirror, directing the radar energy straight back to the antenna. At any other angle, however, a flat surface is likely to send the echo off in the wrong direction. The most reliable all-around reflectors tend to be those with uneven surfaces, because although some of the radar energy may be scattered, the rough surface almost guarantees that at least some of it will be returned.

Pulse Length and Beam Width

A radar scanner does not produce a perfectly parallel-sided beam, nor are its pulses of

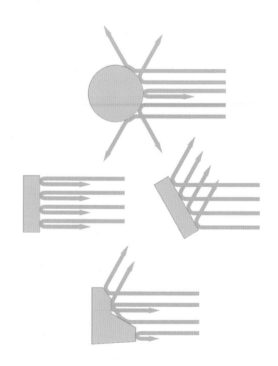

Fig 8-8 The strength of a radar echo is partly determined by the shape of the target. Round objects scatter radar waves, while flat ones reflect them but possibly in the wrong direction.

microwave energy instantaneous. The beam width of a radar set is expressed as an angle—implying that the edges of the beam diverge as the distance from the scanner increases. For most small-boat radars, the horizontal beam width is between 2° and 6°—the larger the scanner, the narrower the beam width.

The vertical beam width is invariably much greater, usually in the order of 25–30°. This is a good thing as it ensures that at least some part of the radar beam will be pointing horizontally even when the boat pitches and rolls.

A large horizontal beam width, by contrast, is a disadvantage because a good reflector will go on producing an echo for as long as it is "illuminated" by the radar beam, so on a radar set with a 6° beam width even a small target such as a buoy can be expected to produce a contact 6° across. If you have two targets less than 6° apart, and both are expanded in this way, then they will merge together to form a single large contact; the radar will be unable to discriminate between them. The effect of poor bearing discrimination is most obvious when you are looking for a narrow harbor entrance, because until you are close enough for the entrance to be wider than the radar beam, the gap will not show up on the screen.

The pulse length is specified in microseconds (μs) and is usually somewhere between 0.05 μs and 1 μs. This means that the end of the pulse may be leaving the scanner when the start of the pulse has already been traveling for one millionth of a second—enough, at a speed of 162 000 nautical miles per second, for it to have covered some 300 meters (328 yards). Just as horizontal beam width has the effect of making targets look wider than they really are, pulse length makes them look longer. This in turn affects the radar's ability to discriminate between two targets that are on the same bearing but at different ranges: if the two targets are less than half the pulse length apart they will appear on the screen as a single contact.

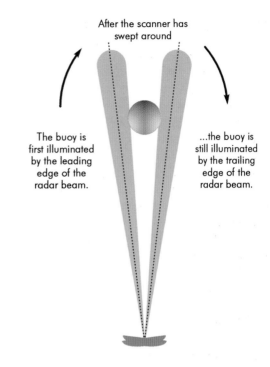

After the scanner has swept around

The buoy is first illuminated by the leading edge of the radar beam.

...the buoy is still illuminated by the trailing edge of the radar beam.

Fig 8–9 A small target may produce an echo whenever it is in the radar beam, so a large beam width makes small targets look much bigger than they really are.

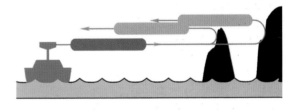

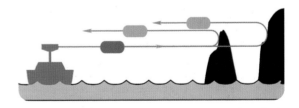

Fig 8–10 If a long pulse length is used, the echoes from two closely-spaced objects merge together, so the two objects appear as a single contact on the screen.

Most radars are capable of operating with two or three different pulse lengths. In general, long pulse lengths are used for long ranges, because by transmitting for longer, the radar is able to pack more energy into each pulse so it stands a better chance of receiving a discernible echo over great distances. Short pulse lengths are usually associated with short-range operation where the need for particularly strong echoes is less and the need for good range discrimination is likely to be greater.

On small-boat radars, the pulse length is one of many internal settings that are altered by the range control, though some offer a manual override.

Display Modes

On the most basic radar display your own position is always at the center of the picture with a bright line stretching upward from it representing the boat's heading. For this reason it is known as a relative motion head-up display: "relative motion" because the boat appears to be stationary at the center of the picture while fixed objects, such as land, move past it; and "head-up" because the boat's heading is always straight up the screen. The head-up display is good because it is relatively easy to relate the radar picture with what you see by looking around the boat, especially if the radar display is mounted so that you face forward when looking at it, but it also has its drawbacks. The orientation of the picture depends on the boat's heading at that particular moment so, as the boat yaws, the entire picture, with the exception of the heading mark, rotates around the center of the screen. This can make it very difficult to measure bearings as accurately as might otherwise be possible.

A more noticeable, but generally less significant, characteristic of a head-up display is that the orientation of the picture will only correspond with the north-up orientation of the chart when the boat is steering north: on southerly headings the radar picture will look upside down when compared with the chart.

Most of the current generation of small-boat radars can be connected to an electronic compass, using the heading information it provides to rotate the entire picture into a north-up mode. This goes a long way toward solving both problems: The radar picture is stabilized, and it should conform with the chart. This makes north-up presentation particularly useful for navigation but at the same time makes it more difficult to relate the screen image to the real world outside the boat. On southerly headings, for instance, an object on the starboard beam will appear as a contact on the left hand side of the display.

An alternative presentation is known as course-up. As the name suggests, this means that the boat's "course"—usually whatever the heading happened to be at the moment "course up" was selected—is toward the top of the screen. The general effect is very much like a head-up display in that objects ahead of the boat appear at the top of the screen and objects astern appear at the bottom. The big difference is that the heading marker is no longer fixed: As the boat yaws, the heading marker yaws with it but the rest of the picture remains stable. Having a stable picture that is easy to relate to the real world makes the course-up mode particularly useful for collision avoidance.

A fourth display mode—called true motion— is now offered on some of the most up-market small-boat radars. A true motion radar uses speed and course inputs from either a log and compass or an electronic position fixer to move the center of the radar picture (the boat) across the display screen. This more accurately reflects the real-world situation by making fixed objects such as land and buoys appear to be stationary. This, however, is not quite such a big advantage as it seems, and can even be counterproductive because it makes assessing collision risks considerably more difficult.

Measuring Bearings

The radar set that could provide only a picture of its surroundings might be of casual interest but it would be of little practical use: it is radar's ability to measure ranges and bearings that makes it a valuable tool for navigation and collision avoidance.

On all modern radars, bearing is measured by means of an electronic bearing line (EBL)— a straight line similar to the heading marker, that is anchored to the center of the picture but can be swept around the screen like the second hand of a clock. Controls on the front panel of the set allow the radar operator to position the EBL so it points straight at any contact on the screen, while the bearing of the EBL is displayed in a data window— usually in one corner of the main display.

Radars that are interfaced to a corrected electronic compass usually offer the option of having the bearing displayed in either true or compass, but for head-up radars the indicated bearing is relative to the boat's heading, measured clockwise: a bearing of 010° (R) means "10° off the starboard bow," while a bearing of 330° (R) means "30° off the port bow." To convert a relative bearing to a compass bearing, add the ship's heading to the relative bearing and subtract 360° if necessary, for example:

Relative bearing	120° (R)
Heading	315° (C)
	435° (C)
	−360°
Compass bearing	075° (C)

When taking bearings by radar, especially when using a set with a small scanner, it is important to remember the effect of beam width, which enlarges both sides of every contact by approximately half the beam width. For small contacts such as ships and buoys, this means the EBL should be positioned so that it cuts through the center of the contact.

When taking the bearing of islands or headlands, the EBL should be positioned just

inland of the edge of the contact by an amount equal to half the beam width. Even this is only an approximation, and if one takes into account the difficulty of getting the EBL accurately lined up with a contact on an unstabilized head-up picture, of noting the boat's heading at precisely the right moment, and the risk of arithmetical errors in converting from relative to compass, it is clear that radar bearings are unlikely to be as accurate or as reliable as those taken visually with a hand-bearing compass. This means radar bearings should be used only when absolutely necessary, and even then only with some caution.

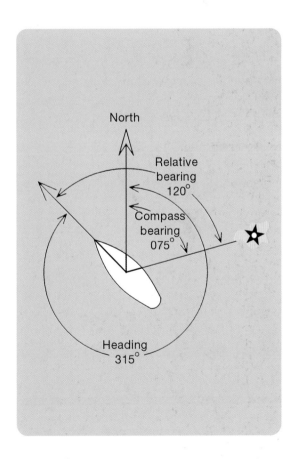

Fig 8-11 A head-up radar measures bearings relative to the boat's heading. To convert relative bearings to true bearings, the heading must be added to the relative bearing.

Measuring Ranges

The standard display of a marine radar includes a pattern of concentric rings, equally spaced at predetermined ranges from the center. Their spacing depends on the operating range of the radar. On a 3-mile scale, for instance, the rings are typically ½ mile apart, increasing to 4 miles when the radar is set to a 24-mile range. These fixed range rings are very useful for making a quick estimate of the range of a contact, but on the long range settings in particular they are not precise enough for accurate navigation. For this reason, almost all radars have at least one variable range marker (VRM)—an extra range ring whose radius can be varied by the operator. The setting of the VRM is usually shown in one corner of the display.

Measuring the range of a contact is a simple matter of expanding or contracting the VRM, by means of controls on the radar's front panel, until it just touches the nearest part of the contact, and reading off the indicated range. Radar is much better at measuring range than bearing; range measurements are not affected by the yawing of the boat, by compass errors or by the radar's beam width, and on a properly set up and well-maintained radar should be accurate to about 1% of the range scale in use.

The Cursor

As small-boat radars become generally more sophisticated, most are now equipped with a feature called a cursor, which effectively combines the functions of the VRM and EBL. The details of its use vary from set to set, but the cursor usually appears on the screen as a small cross that can be moved around either by means of a track-ball, a touch-sensitive pad, or by up/down/left/right arrow keys. Like the VRM and EBL, the cursor's range and bearing from the center are shown on the display, so a target's range and bearing can be measured simultaneously by placing the cursor on the contact.

Navigating by Radar

The fact that the EBL can be used for measuring bearings suggests that radar could be used as an alternative to a hand-bearing compass for taking fixes based on the bearings of two or three conspicuous objects. Measuring bearings, however, is not radar's strong point, so although a position line based on a radar bearing is better than nothing, it is generally much better to make use of radar's ability to measure range. Range measurements of two or three landmarks can be combined to produce a fix, or a single range measurement can be crossed with a visual position line of the same object.

The criteria for choosing landmarks for a range-based radar fix are much the same as those relating to a visual fix: Landmarks should be distinct and easily identified on the chart and on the radar screen; they should be well spaced around the boat; near objects are preferable to more distant ones—in this case because radar is inherently more accurate over short ranges than long ones, and because it is easier to take precise range measurements on the shorter range settings. Steeply-sloping objects, such as cliffs or harbor walls, are preferable to gently-sloping beaches because—just as when taking visual bearings—it is difficult to be sure exactly which part of the radar contact corresponds with which part of the chart.

Radar range measurements can usually be taken more quickly than visual bearings, so the order in which measurements are taken is less important. Ideally, however, ranges should be measured in the opposite sequence to visual bearings: Start with landmarks that are almost abeam and finish with those that are directly ahead or astern.

Radar for Collision Avoidance

What sets radar apart from other electronic navigation aids is its unique role in collision avoidance. It is capable of far more than merely detecting the presence of other vessels, and is so important that it receives special mention in the International Regulations for the Prevention of Collisions at Sea (COLREGS): *"every vessel shall use all available means . . . to determine if risk of collision exists"* and *"proper use shall be made of radar equipment if fitted and operational."* It is a well-known principle of collision avoidance that *"there is a risk of collision if the compass bearing of an approaching vessel does not appreciably change."* Notice that the rule refers to "compass bearing" not to "relative bearing." This is to remove the possibility of confusion that might arise if the boat was yawing, or slowly but progressively altering course.

In practice, however, if the boat is on a steady course and the relative bearing is steady, then the compass bearing must also be steady, so many experienced skippers back up bearings taken with a hand-bearing compass by lining up an approaching vessel with some fixed part of the boat's structure—to give a rough check of its relative bearing. A similar rough check can be carried out with a head-up radar by putting the EBL (electronic bearing line) on the approaching contact. If the contact subsequently appears to slide along the EBL toward the center of the display, then its relative bearing is not changing. Doing the same thing with a stabilized (course-up or north-up) display is even better; compass stabilization means that the EBL represents a compass bearing rather than a relative one, so in this case a contact sliding along the EBL is almost certainly confirmation that there is a risk of collision.

The radar makes it particularly obvious why the steady bearing rule is such a surefire way of assessing the risk of collision, because if a contact has been heading straight for the center

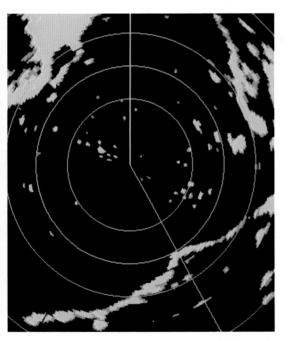

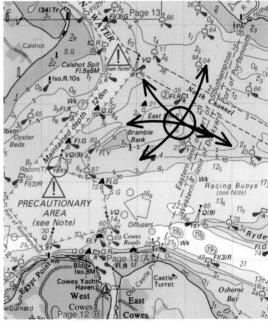

Fig 8–12 The radar picture was taken on a yacht heading south-westward, so the distinctive yellow land mass in the top left hand corner corresponds to the land shown in the bottom of the chart. The green ring is the variable range marker, being used to measure the distance to the headland in the bottom right hand corner of the screen (top right of the chart). The ranges of three features can be plotted on the chart to produce a fix (see text).

of the screen for several minutes, and neither of the vessels involved alters course or speed then it is clear that the contact will continue to move in the same direction and sooner or later will arrive at the center of the screen. This, of course, represents your own boat, so the implication is that sooner or later you and the other vessel will be sharing the same piece of water.

If the approaching contact is not sliding directly along the EBL, then it is not heading for the center of the screen and there is therefore no immediate risk of collision, but it could still pass uncomfortably close. Measurements of bearing alone are not enough to predict how close such a near miss is likely to be, but with radar it is possible to work out the other vessel's closest

point of approach (CPA). The principle is similar to that used in assessing the risk of collision: if neither vessel alters course or speed then the contact will continue to move across the radar screen in the same direction and at the same speed. One practical difference is that because the contact is not heading straight for the center of the screen the EBL alone cannot be used to show its direction of movement. Instead its position on the screen must be systematically recorded—plotted—either with a whiteboard marker or china-marking pencil on the radar screen itself or on a paper representation of it, called a plotting sheet.

Ideally, successive plots should be made at regular intervals of three, six, or twelve

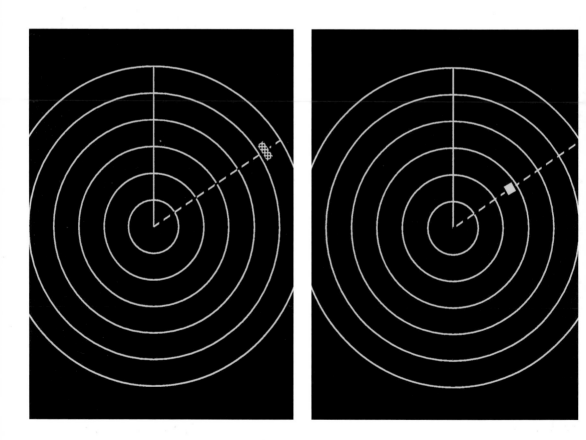

Fig 8–13 If a target appears to be sliding straight down the electronic bearing line toward the center of the display, there is a risk of collision.

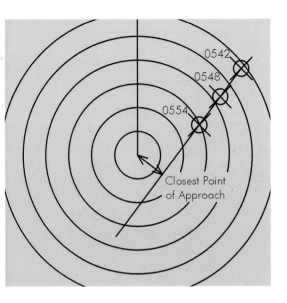

Fig 8-14 Recording the past movement of a contact allows its future movement to be predicted, to find its closest point of approach.

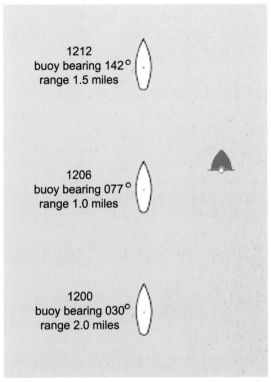

Fig 8-15 The contact representing a stationary target moves down the radar screen, parallel to the heading marker but in the opposite direction, and at the same speed as the boat.

minutes, but when using an unstabilized (head-up) set, being on course is more important than precise timing. After the first few plots a trend should become clear. If neither vessel has altered course or speed the contact will appear to be moving in a straight line. If both vessels continue to maintain their courses and speeds, it is reasonable to assume that the contact will continue to move along the same straight line, so projecting it on past the center of the screen gives a forecast of the contact's future movement. The point at which the line passes closest to the center of the screen represents the closest point of approach.

If the initial plots were made at regular intervals it is possible to evaluate the contact's speed of movement, and to mark off equal distances along the projected line to give a good idea of when the target is likely to reach its CPA.

Assessing a Target's Course and Speed

The normal steering and sailing rules of the COLREGS do not apply until vessels are within sight of one another so, strictly speaking, you should not have to use radar information alone to make decisions about collision avoidance. Many large ships, however, routinely travel at 20 knots or more, so in poor visibility the time between first sighting and a possible collision may be less than five minutes. Valuable time can be gained if you can assess the other vessel's course and speed before it becomes visible. Doing so is a matter of systematic plotting and some straightforward geometry, but understanding the principles demands a good appreciation of relative motion.

It may help to think of the very simple situation of a boat in still water passing a stationary object (Figure 8–15). The drawing

121

represents a boat traveling at 15 knots, with the buoy first appearing on its radar screen at a range of 2 miles, 30° off its starboard bow. After six minutes the boat has moved on 1½ miles, so the buoy is almost abeam and its range has reduced to one mile, and after another six minutes the buoy is over 1½ miles away on the starboard quarter. Translated onto a radar screen, the buoy appears to have moved parallel to the boat's course, but in the opposite direction. Its apparent speed is the same as the boat's true speed. Now imagine the same situation, except that this time another vessel has just passed the buoy at the same moment as the first plot (Figure 8–16). Six minutes later it is slightly closer and dead ahead. On the radar screen it appears to be moving from right to left, almost at right

angles to our own boat's course, and to have covered one mile in six minutes. But we know that six minutes ago it was at the buoy—and the buoy is now a mile away on our starboard beam—so the target's true movement through the water is not represented by its movement across the radar screen, but by a line from the buoy to its present position. This shows that the target is actually on a converging course and it has travelled 1.6 miles in 6 minutes, so its speed must be 16 knots. Of course, one cannot rely on approaching ships passing close to convenient buoys just when we want them to! But knowing that stationary objects always appear to move parallel to the boat's course but in the opposite direction and at the same speed, it is always possible to combine a plot of a real target with that of an imaginary buoy.

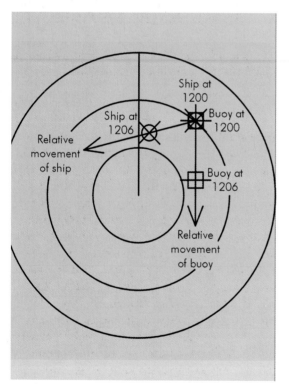

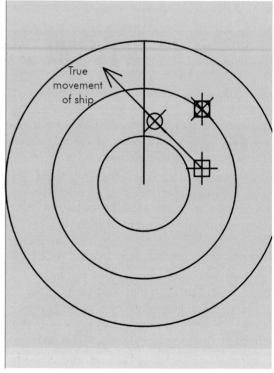

Fig 8–16 If a ship passes a buoy at 1200, then the difference between their 1206 positions represents the movement of the ship.

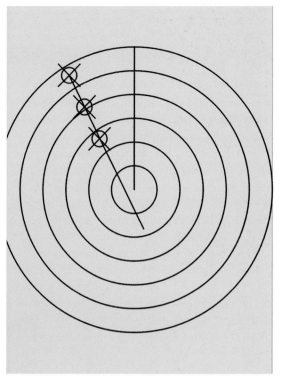 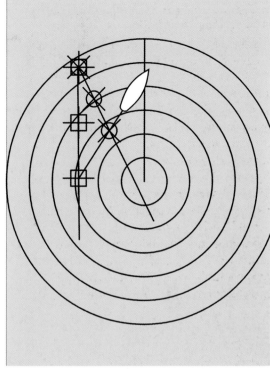

Fig 8–17 Knowing how the contact representing a stationary target would move on the radar screen means that a ship does not have to pass a real buoy for you to be able to work out its course and speed; you can plot the movement of an imaginary buoy instead.

Figure 8–17 shows a developing near-miss situation. The contact first appeared 50° off the port bow at a range of six miles and after 18 minutes has closed to two miles, with less than 10° change of bearing. At first sight this might appear to be a vessel crossing from left to right. If it had dropped a drifting marker buoy at the precise moment of the first plot, the buoy contact would have moved parallel to the heading marker but in the opposite direction and at the same speed as our own—in this case 20 knots. Joining the plot of the imaginary marker buoy to the corresponding plot of the real contact shows that the other vessel is on a converging course, at a speed of about 14 knots: so it is not a give-way crossing vessel, but one that we are overtaking—placing the onus on us to keep clear.

A Caveat

This should in no way be construed as legal advice, but one does not need to be an attorney to see the wisdom in paying attention to the decisions rendered in important court cases. If you recall the statement made earlier in this chapter, "*every vessel shall use all available means . . . to determine if risk of collision exists*" and "*proper use shall be made of radar equipment if fitted and operational*" you will easily understand why so many operators of radar-equipped vessels that were involved in collisions have been found guilty of negligence for not posting a proper lookout, when hearings revealed that they were *not* using their radar at the time of the collision. Since many courts have also ruled that operators of radar-equipped vessels who didn't

123

know how to properly employ the radar were also guilty of negligence, it behooves every skipper of every radar-equipped vessel to: 1) have it on at all times when underway; and 2) to learn how to use it properly. Of course, having the set on at all times can be a great help in learning to interpret the picture, as you can relate what you see around you to what is shown on the display.

Automatic Identification System (AIS)

This fairly new system is not exactly necessary for navigation, nor is it an integral part of radar. But since we're on the subject of collision avoidance, it is pertinent to this discussion. One of the problems with a standard radar display is that even when you accurately plot the course and speed of a contact, you have absolutely no idea of what it represents. And you can't always rely on the size and strength of the "blip" to guide you; a small sailboat with a good radar reflector can produce a larger, more brilliant radar image than a much larger but older commercial fishing boat that is built of wood.

Now picture a radar display, with overlaid electronic chart data, that includes a mark for every significant vessel within radio range. By "clicking" on a mark, you could learn the vessel's name, course and speed, classification (size and type), radio call sign, registration number, and other essential information. You could also gather maneuvering data, closest point of approach, time to closest point of approach and other navigation information,

more accurate and more timely than information available from radar plotting, either manual or automatic (ARPA). Display information previously available only to modern Vessel Traffic Service operations centers can now be available to every AIS-equipped vessel.

With this information, you could call any vessel over VHF radio by name, rather than by "ship off my port bow" or some other imprecise means. Or you could dial it up directly using GMDSS equipment as its MMSI number (the marine equivalent of a unique phone number for VHF) will also be displayed.

AIS is an on-board broadcast system: a transponder that operates on the VHF maritime band. It is capable of handling well over 4,500 reports per minute and updates as often as every two seconds. All large ships are currently required to be AIS-equipped (with Class A systems) and smaller commercial vessels, such as tugs and ferries, will soon face this requirement also. Class B AIS systems are now available for pleasure craft for well under $1,000, which will allow recreational boaters to take advantage of the system on a voluntary basis, as well. Since these units are true transponders, transmitting vital information about your craft in addition to receiving and displaying data on the others around you (although there are Class C units that only receive), they can only contribute to greater safety afloat as they become more common. And of course, as they do, their prices should fall even further, making them more affordable for all.

9 | Piloting

On passage in open water, navigation is mainly concerned with reaching your intended destination. Fixing or estimating your position and shaping a course are simply means to this end, and hazards are avoided by taking care to pass well clear of them.

There are times, however—particularly when entering and leaving harbor—when it may be necessary to venture into more confined waters. Here, the main concern is likely to be hazard avoidance, yet the hazards may well be so close and so numerous that the methods used for offshore and coastal navigation are too slow and too inaccurate. Situations like these call for a different range of skills and techniques, together known as piloting.

Piloting is seldom concerned with knowing exactly where you are. More often it involves following a clearly defined track—you should know that you are "on track," without necessarily knowing exactly how far you have progressed along it.

Buoy Hopping

One of the most obvious ways of marking a channel is by means of buoys or beacons. In narrow rivers and estuaries, where the marks are closely-spaced and positioned very close to the edge of the channel, they give an immediate visual indication of the line to be followed, so steering along the channel is simply a matter of passing each mark on its correct side. It is important to be aware, however, that the presence of buoys or beacons does not necessarily indicate that there is enough water

in the channel at any particular time; some well-marked channels are only passable for a short period around high water.

In more major channels, where the marks have been laid mainly for the benefit of ships, the buoys or beacons are likely to be larger but farther apart, and there may be quite large areas of water outside the marked channel that are still quite deep enough for small craft. In this situation, there is a lot to be said in favor of passing on the "wrong" side of buoys, in order to keep out of the way of larger vessels using the main channel. This calls for a slightly different, more carefully-planned technique— often known as buoy hopping—which involves steering from one buoy to the next, then on to the next, and so on—in other words, treating each buoy as a waypoint.

It sounds simple, and usually is, but there are a couple of pitfalls to avoid. One of these is the risk of missing a buoy—thereby cutting a corner, and possibly going aground on the very hazard the missed buoy was intended to mark. The first line of defense against this is to plan ahead, noting the bearing and approximate distance of each buoy from the one before. This ensures that by the time you have reached one buoy, you know where to look for the next. At night, especially, it is important to know what you are looking for: the apparent brightness of a light is a very poor indication of its range, so it is possible to be seduced into going for a large, brightly-lit mark if the one you really want is relatively small and weak.

In long or intricate buoyed channels it can be very easy to lose track of which buoys have

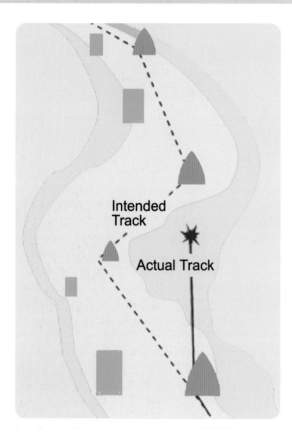

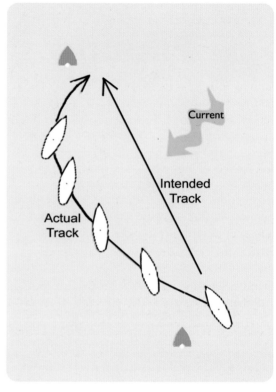

Fig 9–1 Be careful not to cut corners when buoy hopping: Make sure you know the bearing and distance of each buoy from the one before.

Fig 9–2 If there is a strong wind or tidal current setting across your intended track, it is not enough just to aim at the next buoy; the wind or current will push you sideways on to a curving track.

already been passed, and to either skip one or two or believe yourself to be farther back than you really are. The defense against this is to record the fact that you have passed each mark as you do so, either with a note of the time on the chart—as a fix—or by crossing off the buoy on the chart, or by ticking it off on a pre-prepared list. Be strict with yourself: Don't let enthusiasm push you into ticking off a buoy until you really have passed it, nor let activities associated with arrival or departure distract you from the job in hand.

The other pitfall to watch out for is the effect of wind and current. Although, in clearly defined channels, the tidal or river currents usually set along the line of the channel, this is not always the case. A winding channel may

have been carved by river water on the ebb tide, but once the sandbanks have been covered by a rising tide, the flood current may go straight over them—possibly flowing quite strongly, almost straight across the channel.

In this case it is not enough simply to "aim at the next buoy," because the current will push the boat sideways, forcing the helmsman to alter course slightly to keep the buoy ahead. Unless he aims up current of the mark, however, he will never make up the ground already lost, and as the process repeats itself, the boat's actual track will be a curve, bulging down-current of the intended straight line. This curving track could come to an abrupt halt on the hazard the buoys were intended to mark!

Alternatively, it could be disorienting to find yourself arriving at a buoy from the "wrong" direction.

The best way to prevent this from happening is to look beyond the buoy for some kind of landmark—any kind of fixed and recognizable object. It does not have to appear on the chart: anything will do, ranging from houses or beach huts to a distinctive bush or even a parked car. In Chapter 4, it was pointed out that two objects that appear to be in line form a particularly useful position line. In this instance the buoy and landmark also form a range, which—even if it cannot be plotted on a chart—coincides with the intended track. If the buoy and landmark appear to drift apart, then the boat must have moved off the range, and therefore off the intended track. It is a

reasonably simple matter to alter course to keep the two in line: If the buoy appears to be drifting left of the landmark, alter course to port; and if it appears to be drifting to the right, alter course to starboard.

Leading Lines

The use of an impromptu range in buoy hopping suggests that long straight channels could be very effectively marked without using buoys at all, by setting up range marks especially for the purpose. Such marks are called leading marks, or leading lights. As with most navigation aids, however, they should only be used in conjunction with a chart, partly because the presence of leading marks is not in

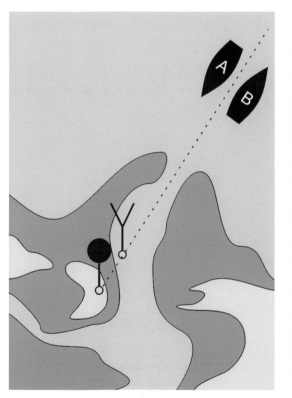

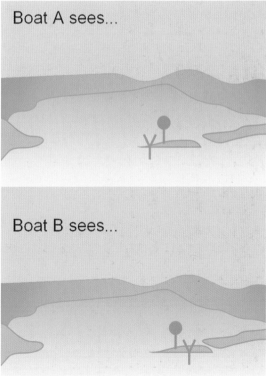

Fig 9-3 Boat A—inbound—sees the front marker to the left, so she should alter course to port to get back on the leading line. Boat B—outbound—sees the back marker to the left, so she should also alter course to port.

itself a guarantee that the channel is of any specific depth. Remember, too, that ranges are usually good only for a certain distance, at which point you must turn to follow either another charted range or just different channel markers as the channel heads in another direction. The turning point may not be obvious, so if you don't consult the chart you could find yourself following a range straight onto the shoals it was meant to help you avoid.

If, as is often the case, leading marks are set up on shore, then yachts heading into the harbor will be steering toward them, so the same rule applies as for the impromptu range used in buoy-hopping: If the nearer (front) mark appears to be drifting left, steer more to port, and vice versa. Craft leaving harbor will, of course, have the leading marks astern. Now the rule has to be reversed: If the further (rear) mark appears to be drifting left, steer more to port.

"Open" Ranges

A variation on the range theme is known as an "open" range. This is most often used in relation to natural landmarks that are nearly—but not quite—in the right place, because a range is described as being "open" when the marks are not quite in line with each other.

Compass Bearings

A leading line is essentially just a position line that coincides with the intended track. In theory, any kind of position line would do as long as it is sufficiently accurate and reliable, and in practice it is quite common to come across circumstances in which a compass bearing will serve the purpose, because there is a suitable landmark right on the intended track.

Having found such a landmark on the chart, and noted what its bearing should be, the easiest way to use a compass bearing as a leading mark is either to use the hand-bearing compass to look along the intended bearing, or to turn the boat briefly on to that heading. If the mark is then to the left of your line of sight you need to come to port to get back on track, and vice versa.

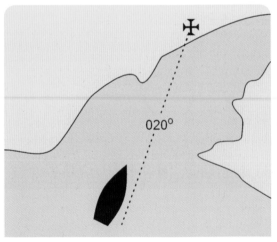

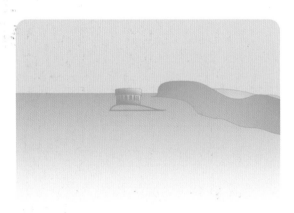

Fig 9–4 An "open" range is one where the two marks are not quite in line with each other. Here, the fort would be described as "just open to the left of the headland."

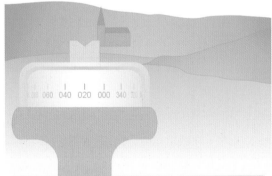

Fig 9–5 A compass bearing can be used as a leading line, as long as absolute accuracy is not essential.

Clearing Lines

Leading lines, especially those marked by ranges, are generally extremely precise; it is easy to see at once if you have strayed off the line. That, however, is not always a good thing. Sailing yachts cannot beat to windward in a straight line, and if inbound and outbound vessels meet on a range line, both are likely to stay as close to it as possible, thereby reducing the gap between them as they pass.

In many cases, the width of the channel is such that a high degree of precision is unnecessary—the channel is not like a single, narrow tightrope with dangers on each side, but a wide corridor. Clearing lines are position lines that have been planned in advance to make the edges of the safe corridor visible.

A typical situation is illustrated in Figure 9–6, in which a wide bay is bordered by underwater hazards. Lines drawn from the church at the head of the bay divide it into three areas—a safe, funnel-shaped corridor with hazardous areas on each side.

As long as the navigator of the approaching yacht sees the church on a bearing that is between 010° and 040°, then the boat must be somewhere within the safe sector bounded by the 010° and 040° lines of bearing.

Although visual bearings are probably the commonest type of clearing line, they are not the only possibility: any type of position line can be used as long as it can be plotted on the chart in advance. In some places, for instance, ranges have been set up specifically to mark the edges of hazards. Nor do clearing bearings have to be used in pairs. If the only hazard is on one side of the intended track, then a single position line is all that is required to avoid it.

A single clearing line can be particularly useful in the early stages of piloting, between making a landfall and entering harbor, when the navigator is faced with the conflicting needs of going close enough to the coast to be able to identify the inshore marks, while staying far enough offshore to be safe until the

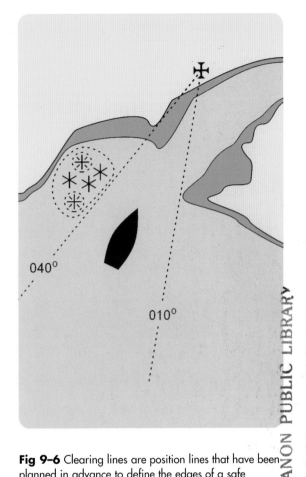

Fig 9–6 Clearing lines are position lines that have been planned in advance to define the edges of a safe approach corridor. In this case, the bearing of the church must be not more than 040° and not less than 010°.

way in has been positively identified. In this situation, a clearing bearing on a single major landmark is enough to set a definite limit to how close it is safe to go without having found the inshore marks.

Sectored Lights

Sectored lights are a relatively high-tech variation on the idea of clearing lines that use directional lights to make the edges of the safe corridor visible without even a hand-bearing compass. A typical example is shown in Figure 9–7.

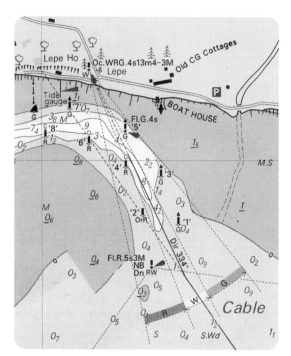

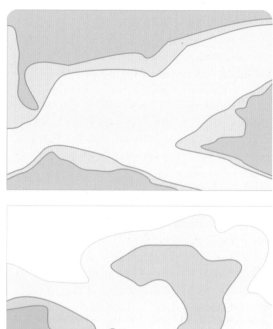

Fig 9–7 A sectored light shows different colors over different arcs. Usually (but not always) a vessel in the deepest channel will see a white light, and one outside the channel will see a red or green light.

Fig 9–8 An echo sounder can be used to follow depth contours, but beware of forked channels (top) and hooked contours (bottom).

Even more sophisticated versions have five sectors, rather than three, with a white light showing over the main channel, alternating green and white and red and white showing along its edges, and plain green and red outside the channel.

Sectored lights make piloting so easy that their main disadvantage is that they are—with a very few exceptions—useless by day. Using sectored lights still calls for some care, though, as the fact that the color of a directional light varies depending on where it is being seen from means that you need to be careful in identifying it.

Soundings

No matter where one goes, it is almost inevitable that until you are secured to an

alongside berth, the closest solid ground will be the seabed, directly below. This too can be used to provide a position line, and can, therefore, be used as a clearing line—simply by deciding, for instance, that "I will not go into water less than five meters (16 feet) deep."

The snag with using depth contours in this way is that they are not straight lines, so when the echo sounder reading reduces to the chosen limit, it may not be obvious which way to turn in order to get back into deeper water. It is important to plan piloting by contour as carefully as piloting by any other method, to avoid traps such as the hook-shaped contour and the forked channel shown in Figure 9–8. Once planned, however, contour piloting lends itself to short-handed operation, because the echo sounder's deep and shallow alarms can be set to give an automatic audible warning of when to alter course.

Head-up Radar

At its most basic, a head-up radar can be treated somewhat like a video game: You pick a feature to head for, such as a buoy or a gap between two islands, and alter course until the heading mark is pointing straight at it. The principle can be modified slightly, in order to pass a set distance off a headland, for instance, by using a china-marking pencil or a whiteboard marker to draw a line on the screen parallel to the heading marker and the appropriate distance from it. Then it is simply a matter of steering the boat so as to keep the headland sliding along the marked line.

These techniques, though, are no more than the radar equivalent of aiming for the next buoy by eye, and suffer the same drawbacks if there is any wind or current setting across your intended track.

Unfortunately, radar's poor bearing discrimination and its inability to pick out specific landmarks ashore mean that the problem cannot be overcome by using clearing bearings.

The principle of clearing lines can still be used with radar, in the form of clearing ranges. Figure 9–9 shows a harbor entrance encumbered by shallow patches. The gap between the shoals is just under 100 meters (328 feet) wide, and lies between 0.29 and 0.33 miles off the shore. In other words, a boat would be in danger of grounding if it is not closer than 0.29 miles to the shore or more than 0.33 miles from it. By setting VRMs or guard zones, or by drawing circles on the screen at the appropriate distance from the center, it's possible to see at a glance if the boat strays outside these limits.

In this case, another clearing range could be used to decide when to make the bold turn to port toward the harbor entrance. The shoal patches are no closer than 0.13 miles from the eastern side of this funnel-shaped entrance, so once the boat is within 0.13 miles of the coastline ahead, her navigator knows he must be clear of the shallows and that it is safe to alter course.

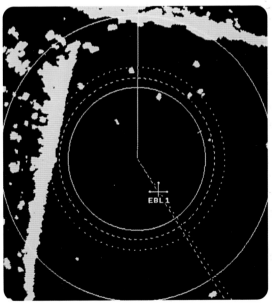

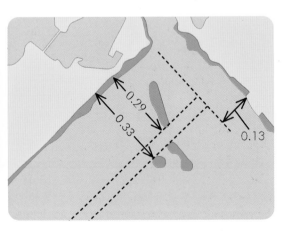

Fig 9–9 Clearing ranges can be used to find a safe passage between shallows, and to show when to turn.

Fig 9–10 Here is the radar picture of the same situation with guard zones (shown by dotted lines) used to mark the relevant ranges.

North-up Radar

North-up radar is an even more powerful piloting tool, particularly because of a technique known as parallel indexing. This is based on the fact that on a stabilized radar it is possible to predict how the contact representing a stationary object will appear to move across the screen, assuming that the boat follows a predetermined track.

Figure 9–11(a) shows a yacht's planned track past a small island. Its track is 110°(M) and it passes 1 mile from the island. Figure 9–11(b) shows how the same situation appears on radar: The contact representing the island moves across the screen on a reciprocal (opposite) track of 290°(M), passing a mile from the center of the screen. If the contact fails to behave as predicted, then the assumption must be that the yacht is not on her planned track; if the island is too far from the center, for instance, then the yacht needs to alter course toward the island, in order to reduce the range, and vice versa.

As with traditional piloting, one of the main keys to success is preparation:

1. Choose a suitable target (the "index target") that will be within range when the radar is set to a range scale that gives sufficient accuracy, that will show up on radar, and that can be positively identified. Large shore-based structures such as jetties are better than buoys, which can easily be confused with other boats.
2. Measure the range and bearing from any point on the planned track to the index target.
3. Set the VRM and EBL (or the cursor) to this range and bearing, and mark this point on screen with a china-marking pencil.
4. Set the EBL to the direction of the intended track, and draw a straight line parallel to the EBL, passing through the mark made in step 3.
5. Write the range scale used in the planning on the screen in china-marking pencil, and

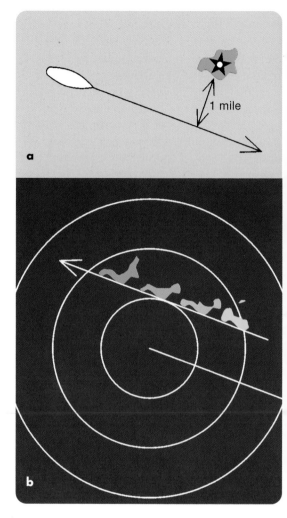

Fig 9–11 Parallel indexing is a powerful piloting technique, but can only be applied on a north-up radar display. It involves plotting the intended movement of a fixed reference target in advance.

onto the chart, to reduce the risk of using a different scale when you put the plan into effect!

The parallel indexing technique can be taken a stage further, by repeating the process for each leg of the intended track. The end result should be a pattern of lines on the radar screen that copy the intended track drawn on the chart, but inverted. This means, incidentally, that a quick and effective check against major blunders is to turn the chart south-up, and compare it with the lines you drew on the screen!

Blind piloting by radar is not easy; it requires great care in the planning stage, a well set-up radar, and an operator who is thoroughly familiar with it, so it is well worth practicing in good conditions.

Eyeballing

These precise, formal piloting techniques will cover most situations, but there may still be occasions when there are simply no marks available. Even this does not necessarily make piloting impossible—it just calls for more inventiveness, flexibility and intuition. One might, for instance, be faced with a gap between an island and the shore, with an underwater rock in the middle (Figure 9–13). Even with no other marks available, it is clear that the rock can be avoided by sticking closer to one side of the channel than the other. Similarly, if there were shoals on each side but a deeper channel through the center, the channel could be found simply by steering for the middle of the gap.

Planning for Piloting

The whole point of piloting is that it enables a boat to be navigated accurately but quickly, without spending time on chartwork, so it defeats the object if the skipper or navigator tries to carry out piloting "on the fly"—searching the chart and pilot books for information when the boat is already moving through confined waters.

Planning is essential, but there are no hard and fast rules; every harbor is different, and the plan for each one may well vary depending on the size of the boat, the state of the tide, the weather and visibility, and whether it is day or

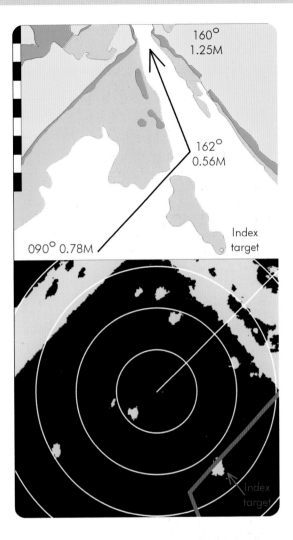

Fig 9–12 Parallel indexing can be applied to more complicated piloting situations. Notice that the reference line drawn on the screen is the same shape as the intended track on the chart, rotated through 180°.

night. The first stage of the process is likely to be gathering information, in particular from the pilot book, cruising guides and tide tables. Knowing the height of tide is almost always important, because it enables you to take a more intelligent look at the large-scale chart of the area. What appears to be a winding channel between rocks and sandbanks may turn out to be a straightforward approach across open water if the tide is high enough to

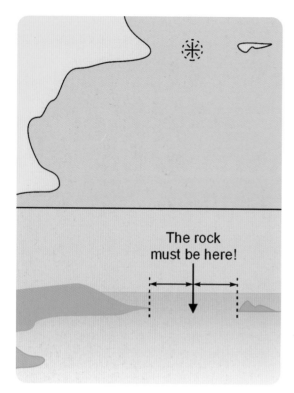

The rock
must be here!

Fig 9–13 In simple situations, it may be possible to steer by eye, relying on an informed guess about the position of hidden hazards.

cover the hazards; conversely, half tide or low water may reveal enough of the sandbanks to make a channel obvious, or make useful landmarks out of rocks that would be hidden hazards at high water.

At a fairly early stage in the planning process, it is best to establish any constraints that are likely to affect your freedom of movement—things such as locks or bridges that open only at certain times, sand bars that can only be crossed with a given rise of tide, and any harbor regulations that prevent you from entering certain areas.

Having established a "feel" for the area, the chances are that one or more routes will present themselves as possible ways in (or out). In some of the most complicated situations, it may be difficult to decide which to choose, but pilot

books often give useful advice, such as: *"Muskeget Channel is an opening 6 miles wide on the south side of Nantucket Sound between Muskeget and Chappaquiddick Islands. The opening is full of shifting shoals. The best water is found close to the eastward of Wasque Shoal and about 1.5 miles eastward of the eastern shore of Chappaquiddick Island. Although this channel is partly buoyed, strangers should never attempt it as tidal currents with velocities of 2 to 5 knots make navigation dangerous. The currents through the channel are strong, having a velocity of 3.8 knots on the flood and 3.3 knots on the ebb about 1.5 miles east of Wasque Point. The flood sets north-northeastward and ebbs south-south-westward."*

Having chosen a channel—or at least narrowed down the choice—it is possible to start making a more definite plan. Assess the hazards, and the marks that are available to help avoid them. Here, too, pilot books, cruising guides and almanacs can be a great help, sometimes offering "canned" piloting plans that may include almost everything you need. Even so, it is a mistake to rely entirely on the pilot book alone—at the very least, its suggestions should be checked against the chart.

Without such a "canned" plan you will need to devise your own strategy from scratch, based on the various techniques described earlier in this chapter. If possible, try to avoid depending entirely on a single technique: a crucial buoy may have broken adrift, or a leading mark may be obscured by trees, so it is always useful to have a back-up method in reserve, even if it is only a compass course and an idea of the distance to go.

Having decided on your strategy, write it down, either on the chart or on a notepad, or both. This written plan is not intended to be a reproduction of the pilot book or a record for posterity: it should consist of working notes sufficient to stop you having to refer to the chart at every alteration of course. It will almost

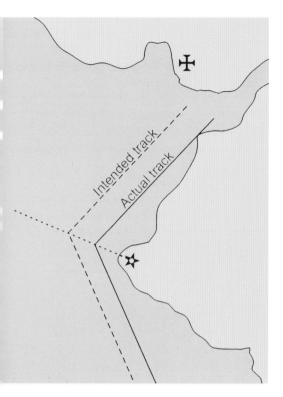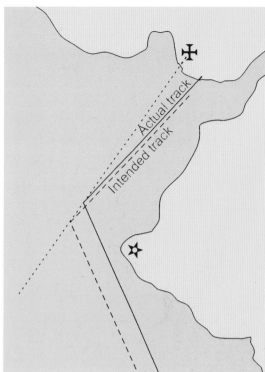

Fig 9–14 When using a compass bearing to decide when to alter course, it is better to use a landmark that will be directly ahead or astern on the new course than one which is abeam.

certainly include the expected height of tide, and the range and bearing of each landmark from the one before, together with a description of it.

"From green can No 43 315° 400 m to green can No 45—LEAVE TO PORT" for instance, is far more useful than "LEAVE No 43 and 45 to port," because it tells you what to look for and where to look for it, as well as what to do when you've found it. A common difficulty is deciding where to start and stop the piloting plan, and the common mistake is to start too late and finish too early. It is important to be certain that the first mark, or starting point, of the plan can safely be located by conventional navigation, and to end the plan at your intended berth or mooring.

Turning Marks

The essence of piloting is that it involves sticking to a pre-planned track, so it is often important to make an alteration of course at a specific point. It is very tempting to use a bearing of something abeam for the purpose— "we'll turn when the beacon tower is abeam." Although this may seem very precise, because the bearing of objects abeam changes relatively quickly, it does not actually serve the purpose: as Figure 9–15 shows, if you are already off track, then using a mark that is abeam virtually guarantees that you will still be off track after you have altered course. It is far better to use a mark that will be directly ahead or astern on the new course.

Transferred Turning Marks

A transferred position line, like that used to produce a running fix, can be used in much the same way, though with less accuracy. It is particularly useful when trying to find an inconspicuous harbor, when the only obvious

135

landmark is on a headland a few miles along the coast.

Again, the key to success is to make sure that the transferred position line is on a bearing that is the same as (or the reciprocal of) the new course. Draw in the required line of bearing to cut through the charted landmark, and measure along the initial track to find the distance you will have to travel from the bearing line to your intended turning point. Note the log reading when the landmark is on the pre-drawn bearing and—allowing for current—make the turn when you have run the required distance.

Piloting in Practice

Having devoted time and effort to planning, good piloting should mean no more than

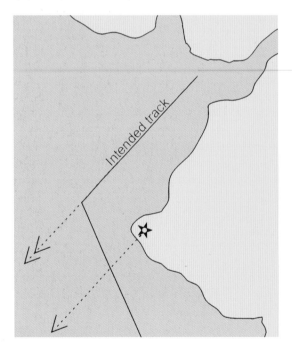

Intended track

Fig 9–15 A transferred position line can be used to determine when to turn—to find an inconspicuous harbor entrance, for instance—but for greatest accuracy, it is important that the bearing used is parallel to the boat's new course.

sticking to the plan. This, however, is itself a two-stage process, involving identifying the marks for each leg, and guiding the boat accurately along the intended track. This, ideally, calls for good teamwork between the helmsman and navigator, rather than one person trying to do it all.

The navigator should be looking at least one step ahead, locating and identifying the marks for the next leg, while the helmsman concentrates on steering the boat. Then, as they approach a turning point—a buoy, or a change from one range to another—the navigator should point out the new marks to the helmsman.

As the helmsman turns the boat on to the new course, the navigator should first check that the new heading corresponds with the plan, and that the helmsman is, indeed, steering by the correct marks, before setting about the job of finding the next set of marks. One exception to this principle of being one step ahead is when using clearing lines. It is difficult, if not impossible, to take bearings at the same time as steering, so the navigator may well have to involve himself with the current leg, as well as looking for the marks for the next leg.

The other exception is if the marks for the next leg are so difficult to see that they cannot be identified in time. In this case, if you can be absolutely certain that you have reached the correct turning point, it may be worth making the turn on to the planned heading, and looking for the marks directly ahead—as though using the boat itself as a hand-bearing compass. Do not, however, underestimate the advantages of using binoculars, especially at night. They can make all the difference between seeing and not seeing a critical mark.

Back Bearings
Steering by compass alone in the general direction of an unseen buoy or range can be unnerving in pilot waters, especially if there is a strong cross-wind or current setting the boat

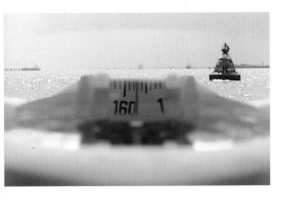

Fig 9–16 When using a back bearing, it is usually easier to sight along the correct bearing to see whether the mark is to the left or the right than to take a bearing of the mark and try to figure out the implications.

off track. A useful double-check can be made by taking bearings of a buoy or landmark astern.

If, for instance, your plan involves following a track of 045° from one buoy to the next, then as long as the first buoy is astern, on a bearing of 225°—the reciprocal (opposite) of the intended track—then the boat must be on track. In practice, using a back bearing is very similar to using the bearing of a single landmark ahead as a leading line; it is better to look along the correct bearing than to take a bearing of the mark in the usual way. One important difference is that if a back-mark is to the left of your line of sight, you need to come to starboard to get back on track.

A back bearing like this has the important advantage that, because you have just passed close to the object concerned, it is easy to make a very positive identification of it, but it is much more difficult for the helmsman to use as a point of reference than a mark that is ahead. To overcome this problem, then, once you are on track, it is a good idea to find some object—even one that is not on the chart, such as an oddly-shaped tree or a parked car—for the helmsman to aim for.

10 | Passage-making

The idea of simply setting off into the sunset to cruise wherever and whenever the fancy takes you, has a certain romantic appeal. Were one to try it, however, the chances are that the first night might be spent fighting a foul tide, and the second searching for a money exchange to get the right currency for wherever you've landed—or worse!

Cruise Planning Factors

Any journey, no matter how simple, requires some degree of planning. When you get up in the morning, you may not consciously think "I want to go down to the kitchen . . . that means going downstairs and through the dining room . . . I can't put the lights on, because that will wake the children, but I have to avoid the dog basket in the hall," but a plan along those lines must be in your mind. Almost all journey plans include:

- an objective;
- constraints—that limit your freedom of operation;
- hazards—to be avoided;
- aids—that will help you achieve your objective;
- a route—based on the other four.

In practice, the first phase of any passage plan is likely to involve gathering information: from charts, pilot books, almanacs, cruising guides, tide tables and tidal current tables, at the very least. For major cruises it may also be worth including additional guidebooks, ferry timetables, and perhaps some NGA *Sailing Directions*, if your plans include foreign waters.

Even at this stage—before the objectives have been decided—some of the constraints are likely to come into play. There is little point, for instance, in planning a Caribbean cruise from Key West if you only have a week to do it in, unless you are prepared to make other plans for getting the boat there and back. Time, speed and distance are important factors to consider. A very common mistake is to overestimate the average speed made good and the time that will actually be spent underway.

Cruise planning may well be carried out so far in advance that reliable weather forecasts are not available. Pilot books—especially U.S. Coast Pilots—often include weather statistics that can be used as a guide to the likely conditions, and in particular to how many days should be deducted from the time available to allow for bad weather. In setting objectives, it is also important to remember more mundane matters, such as the need to take on food, water and provisions.

Family vacations are often constrained by the need to get the boat home by a given date. A good overall plan for this type of cruise is to start with a short passage to "shake down" and get used to being at sea, followed by a longer trip to one of the most distant ports of call. This leaves most of the time available for the return journey, which can be broken up into short passages, giving the opportunity to skip one or two stopovers if time is running out.

The cruise plan usually boils down to a set of objectives—a list of ports of call—that break the cruise into a number of separate passages. Each passage can then be planned in more detail, usually working on larger scale charts. The breadth and depth of detail required depends largely on the speed of the boat concerned. It could be said that a sailboat has to be navigated from wherever it happens to be *toward* where it is trying to go, whereas a motorboat can be navigated from where it was, *to* its destination. To be more explicit, a sailboat is so much affected by current and wind that it cannot hope to stick rigidly to a set plan. Indeed, one of the commonest mistakes made by inexperienced navigators is to regard an "intended track" drawn on the chart as though it were a railway line, and devote too much time and effort to slogging up-current or upwind in order to stay "on the rails." For sailing yachts—and slow motorboats—it is far better to accept that you will have to reassess your situation from time to time, and adapt your passage plan accordingly. Fortunately, at speeds in the order of 5–10 knots, the slow boat navigator usually has the luxury of time in which to make decisions.

By contrast, a fast boat—at speeds of 20 knots plus—is relatively little affected by tidal currents, and small variations in wind speed or direction make almost no difference in the boat's speed. The chances of being able to stay close to the intended track are therefore good—and it is important to do so because there is little time available to adapt the plan, especially if lively motion or lack of navigation facilities are making chart work difficult. Navigation at speed is less a matter of decision-making than of monitoring progress to ensure that the passage is going according to plan. Of course, the fast boat navigator always has the option of slowing down if things go awry, but that makes the initial plan even less valid, and puts him in much the same situation as the slow boat navigator.

Sunrise and Sunset

The effect of sunrise and sunset is literally as clear as day. Simply operating the boat at night demands more skill and expertise; coastal navigation and piloting become more difficult; and unlit harbors are effectively closed to strangers altogether. Having said that, many people enjoy night passages, and for sailboats there is the strong possibility that a night at sea may be the only way to complete a passage longer than about 50 miles.

One positive feature of darkness is the operation of lighthouses, which can make it easier to identify parts of an unfamiliar coastline by night than by day. For this reason

CONSTRAINTS

Many different factors can limit your freedom of action, not necessarily preventing movement, but certainly influencing your decisions. These include:

- sunrise and sunset
- tidal height
- locks and bridges
- tidal currents
- weather and sea-state
- boat and crew strength
- traffic separation schemes
- domestic requirements
- fuel
- hazards and aids
- harbor regulations

it is common practice for cruising yachtsmen to time passages across long stretches of open water so as to make their landfall just before dawn, to have the benefit of the lighthouses as they approach the coast, and daylight to enter harbor.

The times of sunrise and sunset do not vary significantly from day to day or over short distances, so for passage planning during a cruise, detailed calculation is unnecessary; you are likely to have a good idea of when it gets dark. For advance planning the "lighting up times" given in many diaries are a rough guide, but more accurate times can be found in yachtsmen's almanacs. *Reeds* includes a table showing the time of sunrise and sunset at 5 day intervals throughout the year, and at different latitudes. Looking back at Height of Tide Example 2 in Chapter 5 (page 75), we were concerned with available daylight for anchoring near Portland, Maine on August 17. From the extract in Figure 10–1, it is easy to see that the time of sunset at 43° 39.6' North on August 17 must be somewhere between 1902 (sunset on Aug 14 at Lat. 42° N) and 1858 (sunset on Aug 19 at Lat. 44° N). So 1900 seems a reasonable estimate. On adjoining pages of the almanac, there are similar tables for other latitudes, and by interpolating between them, it is possible to come up with a reasonable estimate for any latitude. But the reason the sun appears to rise and set is because the Earth is spinning, not because the Sun is moving, so sunrise and sunset both happen later as you move westward. The simple rule is to subtract 4 minutes for every degree of longitude east of the zone's standard meridian; add 4 minutes for every degree west. With Portland at 70° 14' W and the Eastern Time zone Standard Meridian being 75° W, you should subtract 20 minutes (4 minutes × 5 degrees) to come up with a "standard time" of 1840. Finally, remember that you must add an hour to convert to DST, which means the clock time of Sunset in Portland, Maine on August 17 will be roughly 1940.

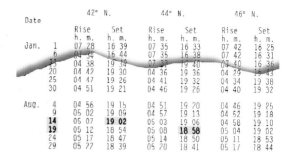

Fig 10–1 *Reeds Nautical Almanac gives the local mean time of sunrise and sunset for different latitudes, at five-day intervals.*

Tidal Height

The entrances of many natural harbors are partly obstructed by bars, formed where the out-flowing river water slows down on meeting the sea, and drops the sand and silt it has been carrying. The depths over such a bar can be considerably less than those inside the harbor, so it acts as a natural barrier, which can only be crossed when there is sufficient height of tide.

In onshore winds the shallowness of the water over a bar makes the waves higher and steeper, perhaps even to the extent of forming breakers. In such conditions, the troughs of the waves reduce the effective depth still further, so an extra margin for safety needs to be included in your tidal calculations. Breaking waves are particularly dangerous, but they are almost impossible to see from seaward, so it is essential to heed any relevant advice in the pilot book before tackling a bar in a fresh or strong onshore wind, especially on an ebb tide.

Bridges and overhead cables impose similar constraints, with the obvious difference that in this case you can only pass underneath when the tide has fallen far enough. The vertical clearance is marked on the relevant chart—remember that the charted clearance, like the elevation of a light, is measured from Mean High Water, so there will usually be more room than given on the chart. In addition, bridges are most often fitted with tide gauges, showing the available clearance.

Locks and Moveable Bridges

Locks and swinging or lifting bridges are subject to human control, rather than being governed solely by the height of tide, but the tide still has a part to play: Motorboats with a low vertical clearance may be able to pass under a bridge without it opening if the tide is low enough; and the opening times of locks are often related either to the time of high water or to a specified height of tide.

Tidal considerations apart, locks and bridges may open on demand at any time—during specified working hours, or at set times. It is worth checking with as many sources of information as possible, because policies can change—and a lockkeeper who has gone home for supper is unlikely to open up just for a yachtsman who quotes a ten-year-old pilot book at him!

The standard signal for requesting a bridge opening is a prolonged blast (4–6 seconds) followed by a short blast (1 second), which is also signal the bridge tender will sound when the bridge is about to open. The danger signal of 5 short blasts from the bridge tender indicates that the bridge is about to close (if already open) or that it will not open as requested. In the interest of general peace and quiet, it is preferred that skippers contact the bridge or lock tender via VHF radio. The only question is which channel to use. In some places it is the international distress and hailing frequency, channel 16. In others it's the "bridge to bridge" frequency, channel 13 (used by commercial shipping for close quarters vessel to vessel communication). In yet others, the required channel is 09, the now-recommended hailing channel for pleasure boats. Since bridge tenders only monitor one channel, using the correct one is critical. Your best bet is to consult the pilot books or cruising guides to see what is expected in any particular locale.

Locks and bridges in some places now also use the red, amber and green traffic lights we see at intersections ashore. In these cases, of course, the colors apply to vessel movement as they do to cars on land.

Tidal Currents

Around much of the coast, the tidal currents are strong enough to have a major effect on the speed over the ground of a displacement motor cruiser or a sailing yacht. This is particularly true when beating to windward, when the VMG (velocity made good) upwind is likely to be only about two-thirds of the boat's speed through the water (Figure 10–2).

A favorable current could, in many areas, double this, while a contrary one could bring the boat almost to a standstill. It makes sense, therefore, to plan a passage so as to make best use of favorable currents, and to minimize the effect of contrary ones. Tidal currents tend to be stronger around headlands and in narrow channels than in more open water, so these areas are sometimes described as "tidal gates"—because they effectively block the passage of low-speed boats altogether at certain times.

Tidal currents can also have a significant effect on sea-state: A fast-flowing current creates tide rips over a shallow, broken seabed, and makes the waves larger and steeper when it is flowing against the wind. Tide rips can be avoided either by going around them, or by passing through the area concerned at or near slack water, whereas wind-against-tide conditions can only be avoided by timing. Sea-state of course affects all boats, but its consequences are most pronounced for planning motorboats, which may be forced to reduce to displacement speed in wind-against-current conditions.

A good example of the way current can affect planning can be seen in the popular cruising grounds south of Cape Cod. Between Vineyard Sound and Buzzard's Bay there's a narrow passage, about which the *Coast Pilot*

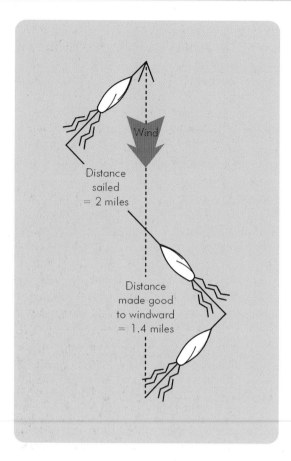

Distance
sailed
= 2 miles

Distance
made good
to windward
= 1.4 miles

Fig 10–2 The overall progress of a sailing yacht beating to windward is approximately two-thirds of her speed through the water, and will be significantly affected by tidal currents.

warns: *"The passage through Woods Hole, between numerous ledges and shoals, is marked by navigational aids. However, tidal currents are so strong that the passage is difficult and dangerous without some local knowledge. Buoys in the narrowest part of the channel sometimes are towed under, and a stranger should attempt passage only at slack water."* Even for powerful, fast sport yachts, making this passage at any other time invites trouble; it's difficult to stay within the channel and avoid the rocks when you can't see the buoys! So planning to arrive there at slack water can be well worth the effort.

Similar situations abound in other cruising areas as well.

Weather and Sea-state
The weather is much less predictable than the tide or currents, so even the best weather forecast can only be regarded as a guide. Nevertheless the weather plays such an important part in the comfort and safety of the boat and crew that it would be foolhardy to ignore the forecast. There are many possible sources of weather information.

During a cruise, for instance, daily local newspapers may be used as a source of weather maps, to keep an eye on changing weather patterns, while the apparently glib forecast of "another hot and sunny day on the beaches" from a local radio station is a strong hint that sea breezes are likely to develop in the afternoon. More useful forecasts tailored for marine use are available via your VHF, from NOAA Weather Radio (NWR).

Known as the "Voice of NOAA's National Weather Service," NWR uses 1000 transmitters, covering all 50 states, adjacent coastal waters, Puerto Rico, the U.S. Virgin Islands, and the U.S. Pacific Territories. Broadcasts are found on one of 7 frequencies usually designated as WX1 through WX7. The Canadian government operates a similar service on the same 7 frequencies. Cruising guides generally list the appropriate channel for any given area. When in doubt and you can receive more than one, listen for the clearest, strongest signal, which will indicate the nearest transmitter as they are all relatively low powered. Obviously, the closest transmitter will have the most accurate information for where you happen to be.

In addition to the NOAA broadcasts, Navtex and Wefax also provide detailed weather information by radio, but need dedicated receiving equipment to display their text messages (Navtex) or graphic images (Wefax), while the Internet offers a huge mass of information that can be accessed by anyone with a computer on board and a suitable communications link (such as a cell phone or satcom system).

Visibility

Visibility is usually classified as:

- good (over 5 miles);
- moderate (2–5 miles);
- poor (1,100 yards–2 miles) or
- fog (under 1100 yards).

Its effects are almost self-evident: Moderate visibility may affect coastal navigation by making visual fixes difficult or impossible; poor visibility is likely to have a serious effect on inshore navigation and piloting; while fog almost rules out any kind of visual navigation altogether. Visibility also plays a part in collision avoidance, so the risk of collision must be assumed to be greater in fog or poor visibility. It may well be worth thinking about adapting a passage plan to avoid shipping lanes or ferry routes if the visibility is forecast to be "poor."

Wind

Wind not only provides the motive power for sailing yachts, but also has a significant effect on the sea-state—something that affects everyone, sail or power. Generally speaking, increasing sea-states (i.e., larger waves) make conditions on board less comfortable, increase the power required to maintain any given speed, and may well set an upper limit on the speed that can be achieved or maintained. What constitutes "calm," "pleasant," "rough" or "survival" conditions, however, varies from boat to boat and crew to crew, so it is important to be realistic about the conditions your particular boat/crew combination can handle.

Although the wind creates most of the waves we encounter at sea, the size and length of the waves is related not only to the strength of the wind, but also to the depth and nature of the seabed, the direction and rate of the current, how long the wind has been blowing, and the fetch—the distance it has been blowing over clear water.

The effect of fetch can be dramatic, especially in an offshore wind. In a force 6—the strength at which strong wind warnings are issued— the typical wave height in open water is likely to be around 10 foot (3 meter), with many waves spontaneously breaking into foam at their crests. It is quite appropriately called "a yachtsman's gale," because few family cruisers would choose to be at sea in such conditions. Inshore, the "shelter" of the land to windward may lower the wind speed by only a few knots, but the reduced fetch is likely to keep the wave height down to a couple of feet. The implication of this, for motorboats especially, is that in wind strengths above about force 3 it may be worth planning a passage that hugs the coast, rather than one that hops from headland to headland.

Boat and Crew Strength

A 70-foot maxi-rater with a crew of fit professional sailors can race around the world, but it is pretty obvious that a 17-footer crewed by an eight-year-old and her 70-year-old grandfather could not. This—admittedly extreme—example proves that the boat and crew strengths impose limitations on the passage plan. Those constraints are, however, extremely difficult to quantify, simply because there are so many variables, but with experience of the boat and a knowledge of the individuals involved, most people find it becomes almost instinctive to set themselves some kind of weather and endurance limit. Having recognized your limitations, it is often possible to think of ways around them.

A crew of fit young adults, for instance, might sail to Florida from Newport in one hit. A 70-year-old couple would probably choose not to—but because they do not have to go back to work in two or three weeks, they could still go to Florida in a series of relatively short coastal "hops," with days in port in

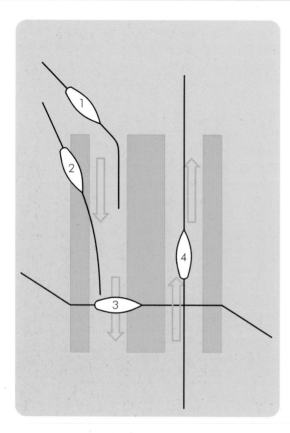

Fig 10-3 The rules governing traffic separation schemes are simple: (1) join and leave at the ends if possible; (2) otherwise, join at a shallow angle; (3) cross on a course—NOT a track—at right angles to the flow; and (4) travel in the appropriate lane. Small craft are well advised to stay out of TSSs whenever possible.

collision risks by channeling ships into clearly defined shipping lanes. Various special rules cover the behavior of yachts and small craft in Traffic Separation Schemes. From the passage planning point of view, the most significant are:

- If you are following a Traffic Separation Scheme, you must be in the right lane—just as you would on the road.
- If you are joining or leaving a separation scheme, you should aim to do so at the ends; otherwise join or leave it at shallow angle—like the ramps leading on and off interstate highways.
- If you are crossing a separation scheme—probably the most common situation for pleasure craft—you must steer a course at right angles to the traffic flow, without allowing for current or leeway.

Domestic Requirements

It may be tempting to dismiss domestic requirements as trivial. Nevertheless, details such as having fresh milk on board can make a major difference to the overall success of a cruise, so it is worth allowing for them in the planning process. Don't assume you can get going at 0830 and sail for 8 hours every day!

Fuel

The observation that "there are no gas stations at sea" is trite, but it makes the point that the distance you can cover under power is limited by your fuel capacity and consumption. As a working guide, one should never rely on being able to use more than 80% of your tank's capacity.

Consumption is a much more complicated calculation, with several different formulae in use. Any calculation is bound to be an approximation because it will be affected by several immeasurable factors, but as a crude rule of thumb:

between. A family with young children might shorten the cruise, but could still cope with some moderate-distance sailing by making most of the "boring" open ocean passages at night with the children asleep, perhaps with the assistance of another adult either to spread the watch-keeping while underway, or to entertain the children while the parents catch up on sleep the next day.

Traffic Separation Schemes

Traffic Separation Schemes have been set up in many busy sea areas, in order to reduce

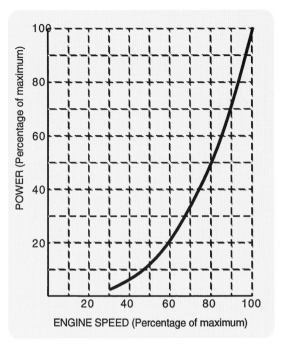

Fig 10–4 The power used—and hence the fuel consumption—is roughly proportional to the cube of the shaft speed.

n a diesel engine uses about 1 gallon per hour per 16–17 hp.

n a gasoline engine uses about 1 gallon per hour per 10–12 hp.

n a two-stroke engine uses about 1 gallon per hour per 6–8 hp.

The power used is approximately proportional to the cube of the shaft speed—shown by the graph in Figure 10–4.

As an illustration of how these calculations might work in practice, a motor cruiser with two 200 hp diesels would produce 400 hp at full power, and would therefore burn about 400 ÷ 16 = 25 gallons per hour. Reducing to cruising speed of, say, 80% of maximum revs reduces the power produced to just over 50% of maximum, reducing the fuel consumption to about 13 gallons per hour.

A sailboat powered by a 6 hp outboard would burn about 1 gallon per hour at full throttle, or about 0.5 gallons per hour at 80% of maximum rpm.

Hazards and Aids

Hazards, such as rocks and shoals, are generally fairly obvious—at least on the chart—though the height of tide and prevailing weather conditions need to be borne in mind to determine a sensible under-keel clearance. By day, in clear weather, above-water objects scarcely rank as hazards, because if you can see them it is easy enough to steer round them. In fog or at night, however, it is a different story: even unlit buoys and beacons—which by day would be classed as aids to navigation—become hazards to be avoided.

Aids and hazards need to be considered together, because it is the aids available that determine the safety margin that should be allowed around each hazard. The safety margin should never be less than the level of accuracy available—in other words, you should not aim to pass within 50 meters (164 feet) of a hazard if your navigational accuracy is "only" 100 meters (328 feet).

Figure 10–5 shows a shoal patch close to one side of a deep bay. A boat crossing the bay from east to west would have a good position fix rounding East Point, so it could safely aim straight for the Mussel Patch buoy, knowing that with only five miles to go, the buoy will be in sight before there is any serious risk of hitting the bank.

Without electronics, the navigator of an eastbound yacht is faced with a more complex decision, because on the 20-mile leg from West Head to Mussel Patch, an EP could easily be over a mile in error, making it quite possible to pass inshore of the buoy without seeing it. In good visibility (over 5 miles) it might still be safe enough to aim for the buoy, with a clearing bearing on East Point as a double-check. In moderate or poor visibility (1100 yards to

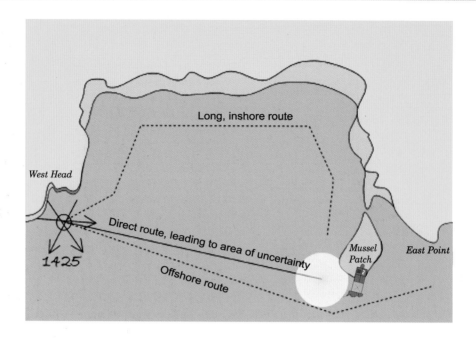

Fig 10–5 You should never approach a hazard more closely than the level of your navigational accuracy. With 20 miles since the fix, the navigator of an eastbound yacht in this situation could not guarantee to find the buoy before hitting the bank.

5 miles) this would be impossible, because East Point would be out of sight. One option would be to go inshore, to stay in sight of landmarks ashore. The alternative would be to aim at least a mile offshore of the Mussel Patch.

Harbor Regulations

In general, the movements of all vessels in U.S. ports and harbors are governed by the Inland Navigational Rules Act of 1980 (Inland Rules), which are nearly identical to (yet somewhat different from) the rules that apply at sea—the International regulations for the Prevention of Collisions at Sea (COLREGS, see page 13). Fortunately, both sets of rules are contained in the same book: *Navigation Rules Inland–International*, a copy of which is required to be aboard all vessels 12 meters (39.4 feet) or longer at all times The increasing size and speed of many commercial vessels, however, mean that in most ports Rule 9 assumes overwhelming importance: "*A vessel

of less than 20 m in length or a sailing vessel shall not impede the passage of a vessel which can safely navigate only in a narrow channel or fairway." While it may not be easy to decide exactly what constitutes "a narrow channel or fairway," it is fair to assume that a buoyed channel used by ships will be regarded as a narrow channel or fairway by ships' masters and by the harbor authorities! Staying out of it, if at all possible, not only conforms to the collision regulations, but is safer and less worrying for all concerned. Most busy harbors now make use of VHF radio to control vessel movements. Very few have the capacity—or the need—to handle incoming calls from yachts except in emergencies, but most recommend that all vessels equipped with VHF keep a listening watch on the port operation channel, and/or Channel 16 so as to be aware of shipping movements.

Since the sad events of 9/11/2001, port security has taken on greater importance. So, while a few ports formerly may have had their own "special regulations" that were enforced by local patrols, *every* port is now subject to provisions imposed by the Department of Homeland Security—in addition to any local ordinances that are probably now enforced more thoroughly than ever before. The most general rule is that all other vessels must stay at least 100 yards away from commercial ships, whether they are moored or underway. Further, under certain circumstances, certain channels or portions of ports may be closed to non-commercial traffic. For example, in the port of Miami, Florida, a major portion of the main ship channel, Government Cut, is closed to all traffic except ships, tugs and fuel barges whenever there are two or more cruise ships in port. Similar closures may be in effect in other ports, at various times, which means that "normal" travel routes may have to be revised, which further means that any given trip could take much longer that you would anticipate.

The increasing number of rules and regulations means that thorough research of regulations currently in effect (they can change quickly!) must now be an integral part of any cruising plan. Sources of information include booklets and brochures published by the various Harbor and Port Authorities, as well as charts, pilot books and cruising guides. It is worth remembering that pilot books, in particular, are seldom totally up to date and charts can give only very brief details, so be prepared to accept instructions from harbor patrol boats, the armed crews of which will often be quite adamant about curtailing your intended progress if you inadvertently try to enter a restricted area.

Most yachtsmen's pilot books are written primarily for sailing craft, so they tend to ignore the existence of speed limits. Motor cruiser navigators therefore need to keep their eyes open for warning notices posted on buoys, piles or harbor walls, and in any case try to keep their wake down when passing other craft.

Note the regulatory marks shown in the illustration of U.S. Aids to Navigation on page 168. The signs with an orange circle in the center will usually be posted where speed limits are in effect. "Idle Speed" means steerageway only. "Slow Speed" means displacement mode, settled in the water, not plowing and creating as little wake as possible. Sailboat skippers should have little problem complying with either; powerboat skippers need to exercise more care. A sign or buoy with an orange diamond usually marks a local hazard, while one with a diamond that contains a cross means "Keep Out!"

Bolt-holes

The chances of anything going badly wrong on the simple journey from bedroom to kitchen that introduced this chapter are fairly small. That is not the case at sea; a sailboat can be delayed by lack of wind, and miss a tidal gate as a result, or a motorboat might suffer engine trouble, so on any passage likely to last more than a few hours or to cover more than about 10 or 20 miles, it is a good idea to give some thought to bolt holes— harbors or anchorages in which to find shelter, carry out repairs, or simply await a favorable tide.

At the very least it is worth looking at what the pilot book has to say about any potential bolt-holes, to find out whether they are affected by any weather or tidal constraints, and whether the piloting involved is easy or difficult. Then, if things do go wrong, you can make a quick decision about where to head for, rather than having to hunt for the information. If you know circumstances are likely to be difficult—when short-handed, or on a boat with limited navigation facilities, for instance— it may be wise to take this "what if" planning a stage further, and prepare piloting plans for bolt-holes as well as for the intended destination, or even to amend the intended route so as always to be within easy reach of at least one safe harbor.

The Finished Plan

The object of all this research is to produce a plan of how the passage should go, which can be summed up by drawing the intended track on to a chart. Mark on it any critical timings such as tidal "gates" and useful information such as the name and number of the next chart. For night passages, many navigators like to draw circles showing the visible ranges of major lighthouses, while fast-boat navigators often highlight key landmarks and hazards by circling them with a thick soft pencil. The pages of the tidal current tables can usefully be labeled with the clock time to which they refer.

If you are going to be using an electronic position fixer, each waypoint should be clearly marked and labeled on the chart, written down on a separate list, and carefully "entered" into the navigator. Most electronic navigators are capable of displaying the range and bearing of one waypoint from the one before. Comparing this with the bearing and distance on the chart gives a useful cross-check that the positions entered by latitude and longitude were correct. Without this facility, it is almost essential to regard entering waypoints as a two-person job, with one reading from the list while the other keys in the position, then swapping roles so that one reads the stored data from the navigator while the other double-checks it on the chart.

Navigating on Passage— Traditional Methods under Sail/at Low Speed

Once on passage, the first requirement for any navigational decision is a knowledge of your present position, so fixing should become a regular routine. How often you should fix your position is largely determined by the proximity of hazards. As a very rough guide, the interval between fixes should be no more than the time

it would take you to reach the nearest hazard. Whatever fixing method you use there is always the possibility of gross errors, so it is essential to get into the habit of cross-checking by using a mixture of position-fixing methods, and by comparing each fix with an EP based on the fix before. If a position fix cannot be obtained, then of course you will have to fall back on EPs alone, but even these can often be cross-checked, roughly, by comparing the charted depth in the vicinity against the echo sounder.

Slow boat navigation often involves quite a lot of chartwork, so by the time you have worked out a few EPs, plotted a few fixes, and shaped a new course each time, the chart can quickly become very cluttered. This is especially true if you use the chart itself as a surface on which to jot down bearings, courses, log readings, and so on. It is much better to keep a notebook for rough jottings, and a proper deck log for everything of navigational significance. This need not be a pre-printed log book: an exercise book or even a loose-leaf binder will do, as long as you record the right information.

As a bare minimum, this means that whenever something significant happens—such as an alteration of course, change of sails, or a fix—you should record the time, log reading, course steered (since the last log entry) and "remarks." A simple test of whether your log-keeping is adequate is to ask yourself whether it would be possible to re-work all your chartwork using the information in the deck log alone, but there is also some merit in including columns for estimated leeway, wind, weather, and engine hours. Over the course of a season or two the deck log will then build up into a record of the boat's performance in various conditions that can be very useful in deciding which sails to set, or what the fuel consumption is likely to be.

Wind and Tide Routing

The shortest distance between two points is a straight line, but the straight-line route is not

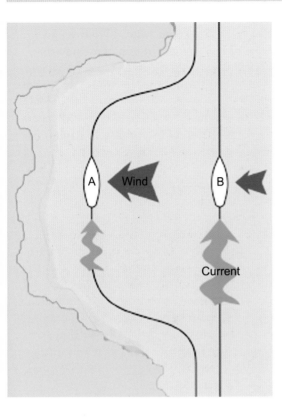

Fig 10–6 The optimum route may be influenced by wind and currents. Boat A has the advantage of a sea breeze but is out of the favorable current. Boat B has less wind but more current. Which is best depends to some extent on the boat!

necessarily the fastest or most efficient. Wind and tide routing involves adapting the straight-line route so as to maximize the effect of favorable currents, minimize the effect of contrary ones, and sail in the optimum wind.

A typical example might occur on a sunny afternoon when sailing across a bay, with a favorable current and a very light onshore breeze (Figure 10–6). One option would be to stay slightly offshore of the straight-line route, to make the most of the favorable current, but an equally valid alternative would be to go inshore—sailing farther and losing the current, but making the most of the sea breeze on the coast. Which of these two is actually better depends on a number of factors—not only the

strength of the current and the anticipated sea breeze, but also the characteristics of the boat. A lightweight, high-performance boat might well do best on the inshore route, while a long-keel, heavy-displacement cruiser will fare better offshore. It would almost certainly be a mistake for either of them to "hedge their bets" by taking the middle line—far enough into the bay to lose the current but too far offshore to pick up the sea breeze.

In different circumstances, however, that might well be the optimum route. Crossing the same bay against the current, the offshore route would have nothing to recommend it, while on a dull day with no possibility of a sea breeze there would be no merit in adding distance by going inshore.

Beating to Windward
Beating to windward under sail inevitably involves a significant departure from the straight-line route, with the boat's course largely determined by the direction of the wind. It is still, however, up to the navigator/skipper to decide which is the best tack to be on at any particular moment. If we sailed on waters with no current and perfectly consistent winds, "which tack?" would be an academic question: both tacks would be equally productive. Nor would there be much to be said in favor of short tacking to stay close to the straight-line route. If anything, it might be better to make fewer, longer tacks to avoid losing speed on each change of tack. In the real world, things are different: Not only do wind and current vary from place to place and from time to time, but they interact with each other.

Apparent Wind
The wind you feel, and which generates drive on the sails of a boat underway, is not the same as the "true wind" that would be registered by the wind indicator and anemometer of a stationary boat. Imagine, for a moment, a boat at anchor on a perfectly windless day. Her

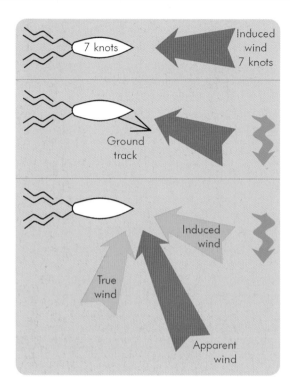

Fig 10–7 An induced wind is created by the boat's movement (top). It is parallel to the boat's ground track, so it is affected by the tidal current (middle). The apparent wind is a combination of the induced wind and the true wind (bottom).

anemometer reads zero, and her wind indicator points nowhere in particular. Now imagine that she weighs anchor and starts motoring at seven knots.

Because she is now moving through still air, her crew will feel the sensation of wind, and her instruments will show a 7-knot breeze, dead ahead. Much the same would happen if she was drifting in a strong current instead of motoring: The crew and instruments would register an "induced wind," equal in speed to the boat's speed over the ground, but in the opposite direction.

If it was not a calm day, but there was instead a true wind of ten knots, then this would be felt as well as the induced wind; the two would combine to produce what is usually

called the "apparent wind." What follows from all this is that the apparent wind that creates drive from the sails and determines the boat's close-hauled course is dependent on six factors:

- True wind speed
- Boat's speed
- Tidal current speed
- True wind direction
- Boat's course
- Tidal current direction

Faced with so many interrelated variables, even the most conscientious navigator might be forgiven for throwing in the towel and deciding to "tack when we've all finished our tea!" Fortunately, however, racing navigators have developed a number of strategies to simplify the decision, some of which can usefully be adopted by cruising sailors.

The Cone and Corridor Strategies

The cone strategy is a simple device that is mainly intended to hedge your bets, to avoid the temptation to hang on to one tack for so long that you risk being caught by an unexpected wind shift when sailing toward a destination to windward. Prepare it by drawing a line on the chart, extending directly downwind from your intended destination. Then add two more lines, at an angle of 15°, one on each side of the downwind line, so as to form a "cone" or funnel-shaped approach. Start by sailing close-hauled into the funnel, then tack whenever you reach one of the limiting lines, so as to stay within the approach cone.

One drawback of the cone approach is that on a long passage the first few tacks may be so long that a fresh and enthusiastic crew becomes bored, while at the end of the trip the tacks are so short that a tired crew becomes irritated. A variation is to modify the cone into a "corridor," with limiting lines drawn parallel to the downwind line, but a mile or two away from it.

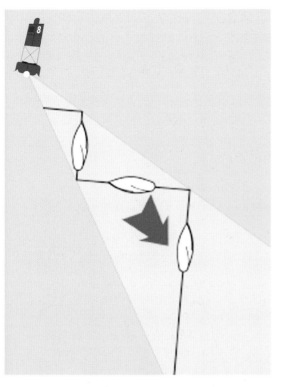

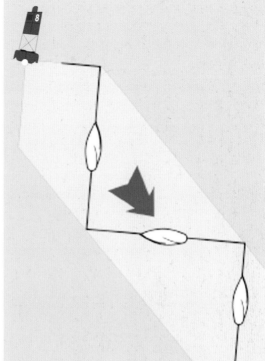

Fig 10–8 A cone strategy can be used when beating to windward, to avoid being caught out by wind shifts radiating outward from the waypoint

Fig 10–9 A corridor strategy uses the same principle as the cone strategy, but gives more evenly-spaced tacks.

Electronically-assisted Cone and Corridor

The cone and corridor strategies both lend themselves particularly well to electronic navigation. In the case of the cone strategy, the edges of the cone are defined by straight lines. In Figure 10–8, the cone's edges are 320° and 290°. Using the Bearing to Waypoint display of an electronic navigator makes staying inside the cone a simple matter of tacking whenever the bearing to waypoint increases to 320° or reduces to 290°.

The corridor strategy is more difficult to set up, but is even easier to use. Essentially, you need to set up a waypoint somewhere on the downwind line, so that the navigator regards the downwind line as one leg of your route. Then, once you've crossed the downwind line "tell" the navigator to skip the extra waypoint,

and guide you to the next one—the one you were really interested in all along. Finally, switch to the Cross Track Error display, and tack whenever the cross track error reaches the limit you have set yourself.

The purpose of the initial jiggery-pokery with the extra waypoint is simply to make sure that the cross track error is measured from the downwind line, rather than from the line between your two genuine waypoints. On many electronic navigators there are easier ways of achieving the same effect; it is well worth reading the manual.

Steer Toward Wind Shifts

The cone and corridor strategies are both pessimistic, damage-limitation plans, aimed at minimizing the risk of being caught by an unexpected wind shift. If, however, you have good reason to expect a wind shift, and you know which way it is likely to go, it is possible to adopt a much more constructive approach by using a strategy aimed at taking advantage of the shift.

The idea is very simple indeed: You set off on the tack that takes you as close as possible to the direction of the forecast wind. This means that if the wind is expected to veer (e.g. shift clockwise as from west to north-west) you should initially favor port tack: if it is expected to back (e.g. shift counter-clockwise as from west to south west) you should opt for starboard tack.

Lee-bowing the Current

The lee bow strategy is intended to make sure that the shifts of apparent wind caused by changing tidal currents are always in your favor.

Although the principle is somewhat complicated, applying it is simple: You should choose the tack that puts the current on the lee bow of the boat. Having the current on the lee bow creates an induced "current wind" on the windward quarter, which moves the apparent wind farther aft—allowing the boat to point slightly closer to the true wind. The effect is most pronounced in light winds and strong currents, and especially when wind and current are at right angles to each other.

The lee bow strategy is simple and effective, but it needs to be applied with some caution, especially if it conflicts with the "steer toward wind shifts" policy; a shift in the true wind that is large enough to have been forecast is almost certain to be more significant than the apparent shift created by a lee bow current.

Lay Lines

Despite a name that sounds as though it has something to do with crop circles or parapsychology, a lay line is simply a line that represents the optimum close-hauled track to a windward mark. In other words, once you have crossed the lay line, you can lay the mark without having to tack again.

In non-tidal water, finding the lay line is reasonably straightforward, as long as you know your boat's tacking angle in the prevailing conditions. Suppose, for example, that your tacking angle is 90°, and that you make 5° leeway. If your close-hauled course on port tack is 310°, then on starboard tack it should be 310° − 90° = 220°. The 5° of leeway will give a water track of 220° − 5° = 215°. With no current, the ground track will also be 215°, so when your destination (or waypoint) is bearing 215° or less, it is time to put in your last tack.

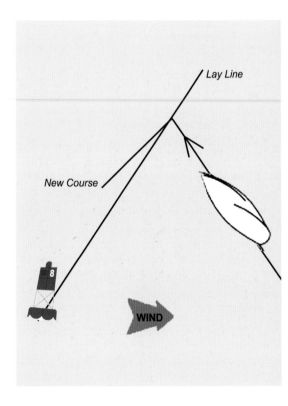

Fig 10–10 The lay line is the line of approach that will just reach a windward destination on one tack. In non-tidal waters, it is a line drawn through the destination, parallel to the boat's predicted water track.

In tidal waters, the situation is a little more complicated, because you will have to work out your likely ground track allowing for the tidal current. One way of doing this is to work out an EP as though you had already tacked, using your estimate of the new water track and speed. The process of working out an EP gives you the expected ground track, which can be measured and transferred across the chart to pass through your intended destination, when it becomes the lay line (Figure 10–11).

A neater method, but one that is slightly less easy to remember, is shown in Figure 10–12:

1. Estimate your new water track and boat speed as before.

2. Find the rate and direction of the tidal current from the tidal current tables.
3. Draw a line from your destination, pointing directly up-current.
4. Choose a suitable time interval (such as one hour), and measure along the current line the distance the boat would drift with the current in that time.
5. From the end of this measured distance, draw a line along the reciprocal (opposite) of your expected water track.
6. Measure along this line a distance corresponding to the distance you would expect to cover through the water in your chosen time interval.
7. Join your intended destination to this point with a straight line. This represents your lay line.

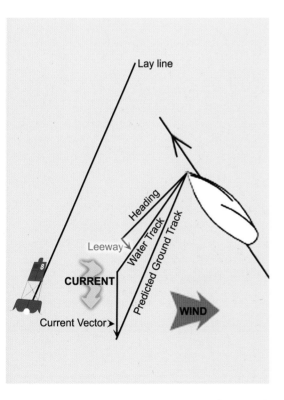

Fig 10–11 In tidal waters, the lay line must be adjusted to allow for the tidal current: it is parallel to the boat's predicted ground track.

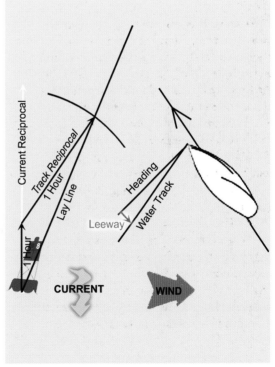

Fig 10–12 The lay line can be found by a technique similar to those used for plotting an EP and shaping a course (see text).

Navigating on Passage— Traditional Methods at High Speed

In all but the calmest conditions, the motion of a planing motorboat makes the traditional routine of plotting EPs, taking fixes, and shaping courses almost impossible. Unless you are prepared to rely entirely on electronics, this means that navigation at speed has a lot in common with piloting, with buoy-hopping very much the favored technique. In other words, the plan for a high speed passage should, ideally, consist of a number of relatively short, straight "legs" from buoy to buoy.

The big difference between this and a piloting plan is that the distances involved in a coastal or offshore passage may be very much greater. You can't expect to see a buoy (even a large one) at a range of more than a mile or two, but there is no great secret about finding a buoy that is too far away to see; it is simply a matter of traveling in the right direction for the right distance. The navigator's main task, therefore, is to check the compass and log. In practice, however, it is much easier to steer accurately by aiming for some fixed object ahead, so if there is land visible beyond the buoy—especially if it has some conspicuous landmark—it is worth steering toward it, and using the compass as an occasional check. Equally, as most motor cruisers' logs show speed much more clearly than distance travelled, it is a good idea to work out your estimated time of arrival at the next mark, based on speed and distance, rather than relying on the distance reading itself.

Allowing for Tidal Current

Many people make the mistake of assuming that the speed of a planing boat renders it completely immune to the effects of current. That is not the case, though on a passage made up of very short legs or at very high speeds it may seem to be so, because the effect of the current over a short period will be so small.

Over longer distances or at lower speeds, however, it becomes more noticeable; on a ten-mile "hop" between buoys, a three-knot current setting across the intended track is enough to push a twenty knot boat far enough off track for it to pass out of sight of the second buoy. If you have a decent chart table, it's quite possible to use the classic method of working out a course to steer (page 20) to good effect. On a RIB or open cockpit sport cruiser, it may be better to use the One in Sixty Rule. Whichever you choose, it's worth working out your speed over the ground as well as your course to steer.

Estimating Time to Go

The reason speed over ground is important is because it allows you to estimate when you can expect to reach your next waypoint. This reduces the risk of overshooting and, conversely, stops you worrying about having not seen a buoy when, in reality, you have not yet reached it.

The basic arithmetic is simple: You don't need to be a mathematical wizard to work out that if you are doing 20 knots and have 10 miles to go it will take half an hour. Without a calculator the problem seems much more difficult if, for instance, you are traveling at 23 knots and have 17 miles to go. One solution is to think in terms of tenths of an hour—or 6 minute intervals.

It is easy to see that in 6 minutes, a boat traveling at 23 knots will cover 2.3 miles, and that in half an hour it will cover 11.5 miles. Combining these two gives:

$$11.5 + 2.3 = 13.8 \text{ miles in 36 minutes}$$

$$13.8 + 2.3 = 16.1 \text{ miles in 42 minutes,}$$

$$16.1 + 2.3 = 18.4 \text{ miles in 48 minutes} \ldots$$
and so on.

From this, it is obvious that it will take about 45 minutes to cover the distance. (The right answer, incidentally, is 44 minutes 21 seconds!)

Reaching a Waypoint

Shortly before reaching a waypoint, then, the navigator should check on the planned track, and use current calculations to work out the new course to steer.

At the waypoint—assuming it is marked by a buoy or nearby landmark—he or she should check that it really is the right one, either by reading the name off the buoy or, if it is a waypoint in the open sea, by slowing down to take a traditional fix. At this stage it is useful to record the time and the new course to steer; it is too easy to forget the exact time at which you passed a buoy, or to get confused between the course to steer, the intended track, and the course the helmsman is actually steering! Finally, as you leave the waypoint and have a better idea of the speed you are likely to achieve on the next leg of the route, work out the estimated time of arrival at the next waypoint, and if necessary reassess the course to steer.

The High-speed Log

Some kind of record of what has taken place is just as important in high-speed navigation as it is at the more sedate pace of a sailing yacht, yet the factors that make chartwork difficult—the lively motion and (often) the lack of space—also make it difficult to maintain a traditional deck log. There are a number of possible alternatives, each with advantages and disadvantages.

The Pre-written Log

As a high speed passage has to be planned in considerable detail, and with the expectation that it will go almost exactly according to plan, there is no reason why most of the information that would traditionally be recorded en route should not be written down in advance. Much of it—including positions (waypoints), intended tracks, and possibly even courses to steer—are part of the plan anyway. To use the written plan as a pre written log, it is only necessary to leave spaces for the details such as times, log readings, speeds and actual courses steered that cannot be planned in advance.

The Log-on-Chart

The log-on-chart method is exactly what it says it is: The most important pieces of information that would traditionally be recorded in a separate logbook are written directly on the chart itself. It is important to be methodical and as neat as possible, otherwise the chart quickly becomes an unintelligible mess. But if you can discipline yourself to stick to a system, such as writing the time, log reading and course to steer alongside each waypoint as you pass it, the intended track and distance to run alongside the track, and the estimated time of arrival alongside the next waypoint, it has the dual advantages of keeping all the navigational information together and reducing the amount of paper that has to be kept under control.

The Tape Recorded Log

The use of a pocket dictating machine in place of a written log is the most controversial option, and is based on the assumption that everything will happen exactly according to plan, and that the log is kept only as a last resort—to be referred to if an expected buoy doesn't show up on time. The obvious drawbacks are that it is difficult to find specific pieces of information quickly, and that a machine intended for use in an office environment is unlikely to be 100% reliable at sea. On the credit side, in very lively boats, or when operating short-handed at very high speeds, it may be the only means of keeping any sort of log at all.

Between Waypoints

Between waypoints the fast-boat navigator, as well as continuing to keep an eye on the boat's speed and course, is mainly concerned with monitoring its position relative to the intended track. Traditional position-fixing may not be practical, or necessary: the information required is not "Where am I?" but "Am I on track?" and "How am I progressing?"

Answering the question "Am I on track?" requires only a single position line, as long as that position line lies along, or nearly parallel to, the intended track. Any kind of position line will do, such as a depth contour line, a radar range from a coastline or feature passing abeam, or a visual bearing of a landmark almost directly ahead or astern. The position line does not even have to be plotted on the chart; if you know, for instance, that your intended track follows the 10-meter (33-foot) contour, and the echo sounder reading (corrected for the height of tide) is 8 meters (26 feet), then it is reasonably obvious that you need to turn out toward deeper water in order to get back on track. Similarly, if your intended track lies 2 miles off the coast but the radar shows the coastline to be 2½ miles away, then you need to turn inshore until the coastline touches the 2 mile range ring.

For this purpose, visual bearings can be taken without using a hand-bearing compass, simply by pointing the boat at the landmark for a few seconds, and reading the heading from the steering compass. This has the advantage of being easier to read, generally more stable, and corrected (or correctable) for deviation. Assuming you have chosen your intended track and landmark carefully, so that the landmark lies very close to the intended track or on a continuation of it, then the bearing should be the same as the intended track. If the measured bearing is low—240°, for instance, when it should be 250°—then you need to steer lower still, to (say) 230°, to get back on track. If the measured bearing is higher than it should be, then the opposite applies, and you need to steer higher still to regain your intended track.

Using a back bearing, such as the buoy you have just left, is more difficult; it is likely to involve using a hand-bearing compass, and the bearing should be the reciprocal of the intended track (track ± 180°). The rules for getting back on track are reversed, too: If the bearing is high, you steer lower, and vice versa.

Monitoring progress also requires only a single position line—this time roughly at right angles to the intended track. Again, any kind of position line can be used, including depth contours that cross the intended track, radar ranges of objects ahead or astern, or visual bearings. In this case, visual bearings are often the easiest, because it is usually possible to keep an eye open for conspicuous landmarks, and to note when they pass abeam. With experience, and at ranges up to two or three miles, it is possible to do this accurately enough by eye. At longer ranges it is again possible to use the boat's steering compass, rather than a hand-bearing compass, by sighting along some fixed part of the boat such as a seat-back or bulkhead, and adding or subtracting 90° to or from the compass reading when the landmark crosses your line of sight.

Using Electronics

A navigator who chooses to rely entirely on traditional tools and techniques is likely to find that quite a significant proportion of his time and effort has to be devoted to finding out where he is—either by taking and plotting fixes or by working up EPs. Electronics, of course, can do that particular job almost continuously with considerable accuracy and precision and without human intervention.

This does not, however, mean that the navigator has nothing to do. The electronic navigator still needs to go through the same planning process as his traditional counterpart. His preparation may well need to be somewhat more thorough, because he may need to mark up waypoints on the chart and store them in the GPS or chart plotter.

Of course, he reaps the benefit once the boat is underway. Even here, though, electronic systems can only provide information; it is still up to the human skipper or navigator to make decisions.

Waypoint Arrival

Of course, it is important to be certain that waypoints have been entered correctly, but there is another more subtle piece of information that an electronic navigator needs if it is to guide you along the planned route; you have to tell it how to decide when you have reached a waypoint. Some of the more sophisticated devices offer a range of alternatives, but most use waypoint arrival distance as the main criterion. This is usually found in one of the menus dealing with alarm settings, because arrival at a waypoint usually triggers an audible alarm, as well as switching the instrument's attention to the next waypoint.

The waypoint arrival distance can be set to anything from zero to several miles. If it is set to a very small distance, then it may be almost impossible to get close enough to the waypoint to convince the navigator that you have actually arrived. On the other hand, if the waypoint arrival distance is too large, then the navigator will switch to the next waypoint too early, and you will find yourself cutting the corner. The appropriate setting depends on how precisely you need to follow your planned route and on the accuracy you can expect from your position fixer. It is seldom necessary or desirable to use an arrival distance of much less than about 0.05 mile, or greater than about 0.25 mile.

Monitoring Progress

The apparent precision of an electronic display makes it tempting to try to steer by the cross track error display, aiming to keep it to zero. This is particularly true if you are using the popular "rolling road" or "highway" display, but it's akin to driving a car by looking out of the driver's door at the white line: It is almost invariably better to be guided primarily by the bearing to waypoint display, and to steer by compass, referring to the cross track error display at intervals to see if there is a clear and continuing tendency for the boat to slide off

track in one particular direction.

Finally, remember that while traditional navigation usually involves a range of different tools and techniques, electronic navigation tends to put all your eggs in one basket, in which errors can pass unnoticed, and in which the whole system can fail if a single wire breaks or a fuse blows. To guard against this it's important to keep some kind of backup system going, ready to take over if things go wrong. This could, perhaps, be a second electronic system, but for most people it's more likely to be traditional navigation. It is a good idea to get into the habit of using traditional methods to cross-check your electronics at regular intervals—by noticing, for instance, when you cross a range or depth contour, or when you pass a headland or buoy. Keep a deck log of some sort, whether it's in the form of notes added to the passage plan, a log-on-chart system, or a tape recorder.

Getting Lost, and "Finding Yourself"

Logs sometimes under- or over-read, compass deviation can change without being noticed, and electronics can fail—and all human beings make mistakes occasionally. So there can be very few experienced navigators who have not, at some stage, been "uncertain of their position."

There are two distinct types of being "lost," of which by far the most dangerous is being misplaced—being convinced (wrongly) that you know where you are when you are really somewhere quite different. This is the kind of "lost" that leads to boats running onto rocks, to yachts being pounded onto lee shores, and to motor cruisers leaving their running gear on sandbanks. It happens when you can see something, but convince yourself that it is something else, or "fudge" a fix by adding a few degrees to one of the bearings because you would rather believe that you remembered the wrong numbers than accept that you have just taken a bearing of the wrong object. It is important never to believe that what you can see is what you want to see, unless you have some real evidence to support it.

The other kind of "lost" is a gradual realization that something is "not quite right," usually brought about by not seeing something when you expect to, by seeing something you were not expecting, or by a succession of larger-than-usual cocked hats that don't quite agree with your EP.

Example 1

A fleet of yachts was racing across the Celtic Sea to the Fastnet Rock. They had just cleared Lands End when the weather forecast predicted that the SW wind would shift to the NW in about 12 hours time. On one of the leading boats the PC plotter incorporated weather routing software that took this shift into account, and suggested a route well north of the rhumb line. Most of the fleet, however, carried on along the rhumb line.

In this case, the skipper overruled the plotter because she had reservations about the reliability of the weather forecast, and was unwilling to jeopardize a good position by breaking away from the main fleet.

The first job is to prevent the situation getting worse. Generally, this means slowing way down, if possible reducing your speed over the ground to zero by anchoring or by altering course and speed to stem the current. Once you know you are not rushing toward an unseen hazard you have time to think and to study the chart.

The main exception to this general advice is if staying where you are would increase the danger. If, for instance, you are already in

Example 2

A motor cruiser was due to leave Alderney, bound for St. Peter Port, Guernsey. Her PC plotter suggested that the optimum time to leave Alderney was at about the time of local low water.

Her skipper decided to overrule the plotter, because its plan would have taken him through the Alderney Race when the SW tide was at its strongest, and likely to be producing rough conditions against a SW wind. Also, arriving at St. Peter Port soon after LW, he would not have been able to go straight into the marina.

Example 3

A large cruise ship left Bermuda bound for Boston, Massachusetts. Her integrated bridge system automatically compared the output from the GPS with a DR position, calculated automatically by means of log and compass inputs.

About an hour after leaving Bermuda the antenna cable became disconnected from the GPS, which automatically switched to DR mode. The integrated bridge system was then comparing the DR position that had been calculated by the GPS set with the DR position that it had calculated for itself. Not surprisingly, there was no difference between the two, so it did not trigger its position fix alarm.

Thirty-four hours later, the ship ran aground, having recently passed several buoys, and within sight of a lighthouse. The Marine Accident Investigation Branch (MAIB) report of the incident pointed out that "a fundamental rule of navigation is always to check the primary method of navigation by an independent source."

Example 4

A 28-foot yacht was approaching Plymouth, England after a channel crossing. It was late in the season, it was dark, and there was a force 7–8 wind blowing. Four of the five man crew succumbed to seasickness, leaving the skipper effectively singlehanded for the last 4 hours of the passage. He had GPS, but no chart plotter, and was not able to leave the cockpit to plot his position on the chart, so he resorted to local knowledge and eyeball navigation.

The yacht grounded on unlit rocks just off the eastern entrance to Plymouth Sound, and quickly broke up. Four of the crew survived, but the owner/skipper did not. The GPS set was subsequently recovered, and the position data it had recorded was used by accident investigators to reconstruct the yacht's movements during her final few minutes.

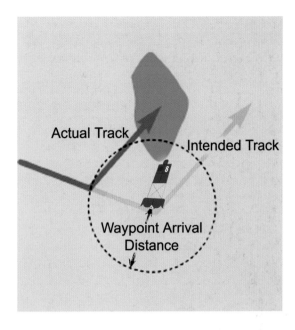

Fig 10–13 It is important to be aware exactly what an electronic navigator's waypoint arrival alarm means, especially if it is linked to an autopilot.

shallow water and the tide is falling or the weather deteriorating. In that case, it may be better to turn and head back the way you came until the boat is in a safer position. Having stabilized the situation, it is time to take stock of your assets. Foremost among these is your last reliable fix; from this, it should be possible to work out an EP. This is why keeping some form of deck log is so important, because without a record of the time of the fix, and the courses and distances since, it is impossible to produce an EP. The EP may not be right (if it is, then you are not really lost!), but it is a good basis to work from, because you can now set about deciding why it is wrong.

You may, for instance, have noticed that the log has stopped working, in which case it would be reasonable to assume that you have

travelled farther than the EP suggests; or you may have a "gut feeling" that the helmsman has been allowing the boat to yaw farther one way than the other; or that your estimate of leeway could have been optimistic. This should narrow down your possible position to somewhere within a more or less definite area. If, for some reason, you have no deck log, you still need to try to narrow down your position somehow, even if it is based on little more than rough guesses such as "I think we must have been drifting north-east for almost an hour after the mainsail blew out" or "That must have been the Fire Island ferry that passed us." Limiting the possibilities should make it possible to start using more conventional navigational clues, such as visual bearings of landmarks. A visual bearing of an unidentified church crossed with one of an unidentified headland does not provide a fix, but plotting the bearings on every possible church and headland in your general vicinity will narrow down your possible position still further. Some of these false fixes can then be eliminated by using other clues, such as the depth of water, or their proximity to other landmarks. Once all the available clues have been used, you will have to move in order to gather more information, but by this stage you should have a relatively limited number of possible positions. Choose a course that would be safe from any of the possibilities, and set off—this time keeping a meticulous log, so that you can plot an EP based on each of the tentative "fixes." After a while you may be rewarded by a new and easily identifiable landmark. If not, try taking bearings of the same objects as you used before, comparing each of the new "fixes" with the "EP" based on the corresponding old "fix." A new "fix" ' that agrees with the corresponding "EP" is probably right. It is still a matter of eliminating the impossible, however, not a question of convincing yourself that the "best" of several dubious possibilities must be right.

Finding yourself calls for more skill and ingenuity than not getting lost in the first place. There are no hard-and-fast rules, other than to make sure you have used every piece of information available to you. It calls for clear thinking, so it is important not to panic, but work methodically, and avoid distractions. Above all else, though, it is essential to avoid any temptation to bend the facts to support your supposition about where you are. Giving in to that temptation only makes matters worse because you will then be misplaced, rather than merely uncertain of your position. If necessary, you must be prepared to accept defeat. Approaching Nantucket, for instance, where there are numerous shoals extending several miles offshore in many directions, it would be reckless to try to locate a harbor entrance without having a good idea of where you are.

If you cannot find yourself, the only option might well be to head back to the mainland, where you stand a better chance of being able to go close enough to identify landmarks without running into danger.

Landfalls

Making a landfall after a passage in open water is always a special moment, though electronics have removed much of the excitement from the occasion. One waypoint is just like any other, and the mere fact that one is within sight of land makes very little real difference. For the traditional navigator, however, there is always a sense of uncertainty about a landfall. The satisfaction of finding land and the anticipation of arrival is mixed with some of the anxiety that is associated with being lost, and an almost overwhelming temptation to believe that what you can see is what you were expecting to see.

In some ways, the navigational tasks associated with making a landfall are very similar to those involved in finding yourself, but you start off with a number of inbuilt advantages—including an EP that you believe to be reliable, rather than one which has been proved wrong! Another big advantage is that you have no real choice about where you get lost, whereas you can plan a landfall in advance so as to make the job relatively simple. The easiest possible landfall is on a safe stretch of coastline with a few conspicuous and readily-identifiable features. In this case, the best plan is usually to aim straight for the most conspicuous feature, because that way, even if your EP is a few miles out, you can still expect to see your chosen target before you get close enough to have to worry about knowing exactly where you are.

At the other extreme are flat or featureless coastlines, with off-lying hazards. In this case, when land first appears, it can be almost impossible to identify anything with certainty.

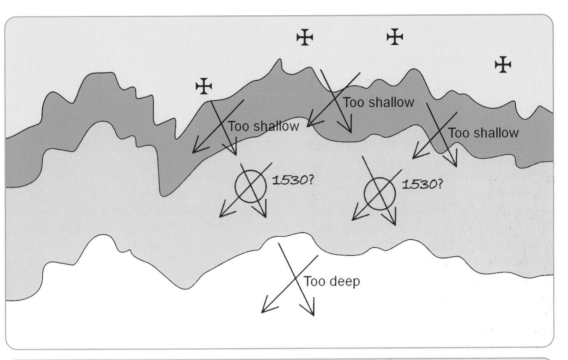

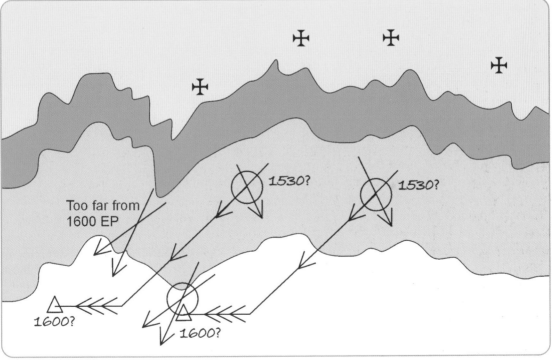

Fig 10–14 Finding yourself, once lost, is often a matter of gathering every available clue and eliminating the positions that are impossible. It is important, however, to be very careful not to eliminate possibilities just because you don't like them, or to "bend" facts to suit what you believe.

If your destination is not directly ahead of you, you will literally not know which way to turn. The solution is to "aim off," usually toward a position a few miles up-current of your final destination. Then at least you know which way to go, and can close the coast at an angle, looking for identifiable features while using a depth contour as a clearing line to stay away from possible hazards. This approach does not work if you are approaching a coastline made up of deep bays, because by "aiming off" you could find yourself heading into the wrong bay! In this case, it may be better to make sure of getting the right bay by aiming for the middle, and rely on seeing the headland on one side or the other as you go in.

Fog

Navigating in fog is, even with electronic aids, more difficult, dangerous, and unpleasant than under almost any other conditions. By far the best way of dealing with it, if you have the choice, is not to go out in it. Being caught out in fog is a very different matter: Heading for port is only one option, and not necessarily the best.

Staying offshore carries with it the risk of colliding with a ship or of running out of fuel, water, food, or stamina before the fog lifts. Going inshore reduces the risk of collision, but increases the chance of going aground. Heading for port is a high gain/high risk option, combining an increased risk of collision with other vessels using the harbor with the risk of going aground on your way inshore, but offering virtually guaranteed comfort and safety once you are in. A low risk alternative is to head for shallow water, and anchor. Which of these strategies is best depends on the boat and crew, the type and density of other traffic, the navigation aids available, and the weather—in particular, the type of fog and its likely duration.

Having decided on a strategy, navigation in fog is almost easier than in good visibility, simply because there is less information available. Electronic position fixers, of course, are unaffected, as is radar, but for the traditional navigator, the primary task is to maintain a meticulous EP. There are limits, however, to the accuracy that can be expected of an EP, particularly if it has to be maintained for several hours, and it may deteriorate to such an extent that it can no longer be relied upon for inshore navigation.

Buoy Hopping

The accuracy of an EP depends to a very great extent on the time that has elapsed since the last fix: An EP that is based on a fix 15 minutes ago is likely to be four times as accurate as one that has been run for an hour. So, in well-marked waters, one fairly obvious way of making safe progress inshore in fog is to amend the passage plan by breaking it down into very short "hops" from one buoy to the next.

If a buoy does not show up when it is expected, it is futile to try searching for it, or to press on in the hope of finding the next one. As time goes by, the quality of your EP will be getting worse, not better, so having failed to find one buoy virtually guarantees not finding the next, so you will end up completely lost. In that situation it is better either to anchor or to head offshore.

Contours

Echo sounders work just as well in fog as in any other conditions, so depth contours can be a valuable source of position lines—possibly enough to allow a passage to be continued into harbor when it would otherwise be impossible. They are especially useful in areas where the seabed has a gentle, reasonably consistent slope, because this means that a pair of contours—such as the 5-meter and 10-meter contours—can be used as the boundaries of a corridor, which can be followed by zigzagging between the two. The angle between the legs of the zigzag depends on how straight the contours are, but should typically be about 30°. Zigzagging between contours is far more satisfactory than trying to follow the twists and turns of a single contour; it is less nerve wracking, it is unlikely to increase the total distance travelled by very much and it allows an EP to be maintained with a reasonable degree of accuracy.

Do I Need to Navigate?

Unless you are prepared to trust to luck to decide whether you end up parked on a sandbank, wrecked on a rock, or roaming the seas like some latter-day Flying Dutchman, the answer to this question is an emphatic "Yes." That is not to say, however, that you always need to use the "formal" methods covered in this book, any more than you would use an topographical map and compass to get to your corner shop.

Navigation is only a part of effective skippering, and there are times when it is a relatively low priority. A good example of this would be on a short-handed sailboat traveling from Montauk to Cape May in bad weather. Trying to keep a reliable EP going is doomed to failure, because the boat cannot be steered accurately and the log may well be over- or under-reading by 10%. In the open ocean it hardly seems worth making yourself sick over, because there is nothing around to hit—you'll be in reasonably deep water until you near the Jersey shore and your main concern should be avoiding other traffic—not natural hazards— which requires keen situational awareness rather than an accurate knowledge of your position.

In theory, you could estimate the extent of all the possible errors and use this information to define an area on the chart which you know must include the boat's position. This area, which is usually oval in shape and expands with the passage of time, is sometimes called the "pool of errors." You may not know where you are in the pool, but as long as you are not sharing it with a hazard, that does not matter. Working out the size and shape of the pool of errors would be difficult and time-consuming,

but in practice it is enough to have a rough idea of it—enough to be able to say, for instance, that "if we keep going generally southeast, we should see Provincetown about lunch time," as opposed to "if we steer 350° we shall reach Gloucester at 0845." This kind of navigation is not to be recommended, because it has obvious risks, but as long as you have assessed the risks it may at least be acceptable.

The other situation in which formal navigation can safely be abandoned could hardly be more different: It is when you are in familiar waters and good conditions. To stop familiarity breeding contempt, however, it is worth running through a mental checklist:

- Am I sure of continuing good visibility and daylight?
- Do I have complete confidence in my local knowledge of landmarks and hazards?
- Is there enough deep water around me to make a knowledge of my precise position irrelevant?
- Have I allowed for the state of the tide and the direction and rate of the tidal current?

Do I Need a Passage Plan?

A significant change in international law came into effect in 2002, when some of the requirements of the Safety of Life at Sea convention were extended to vessels of less than 150 tons, including private pleasure craft. One of its regulations (Number 34) requires the master of vessel to ensure that the intended voyage has been planned using appropriate charts and publications, according to official guidelines and recommendations.

The U.S. Coast Guard does not expect small craft skippers to produce written passage plans, and certainly does not intend that official "approval" has to be obtained before setting off on a passage. In fact, the USCG will *not* accept "Float Plans" whether they're offered on paper, over the radio or by telephone. But it nonetheless recommends preparation of a suitable passage plan, which should include:

- an up-to-date weather forecast
- tidal predictions
- an assessment of the limitations of the boat and crew
- navigational dangers
- a contingency plan
- details left with a responsible person ashore

In regard to that last point, small-craft operators should always prepare a written "Float Plan" before starting on an extended trip and leave it with a yacht club, marina, friend, or relative. The float plan should include:

- A full description of the vessel including her name, type, LOA, rig, color of hull and accessories (such as white hull and flying bridge with a red Bimini Top), radio call sign, registration and/or sail number
- A complete list of every person on board including names, ages, addresses and, if applicable, the physical limitations or special medical requirements of any POB who has them
- A detailed itinerary with an anticipated date and time of arrival at each stop, updated as required throughout the voyage
- For motorboats, the type of power, fuel capacity and normal rage as well as the cruising speed at which this range is attained

It is advisable to use a checking-in procedure by telephone for each stopping point specified in the float plan to confirm arrival and, if necessary, make adjustments to the itinerary. This entire process is vital for determining if a boat is overdue and will assist materially in locating a missing craft in the event that search and rescue operations become necessary.

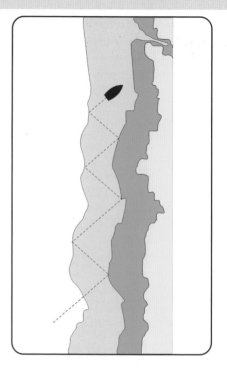

Fig 10–15 In poor visibility, well-defined contours may be the best way to continue the passage to a safe harbor. Aim off to one side of the harbor, then zigzag between two contours along the coast.

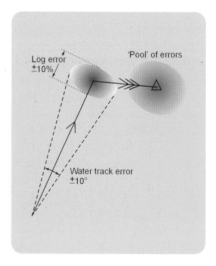

Fig 10–18 As the time since your last fix increases, your position becomes less accurate—it is somewhere inside an ever-expanding "pool of errors"—but as long as you are not sharing that pool with a hazard, you are safe. In extreme conditions, it may be more practical to estimate the size of the pool of errors than to be meticulous about plotting a position.

Appendix

I Depths

Depths in Fairways and Areas		Supplementary national symbols: a, b
Plane of Reference for Depths → H		
20	Limit of dredged area	
21	7.0 m — Dredged channel or area with depth of dredging in meters	7.0 m — 7.0 meters
22	24 FEET OCT 1983 — Dredged channel or area with depth and year of the latest control survey — 30 FEET APR 1984	Dredged to 7.2m (1978) — 7.2m (1978)
23	Maintained depth 7.2m — Dredged channel or area with maintained depth	Maintained depth 7.2m — 7.2m
24	29 23 3 / 22 8 / 30 18 7 / 21 — Depth at chart datum, to which an area has been swept by wire drag. The latest date of sweeping may be shown in parentheses	10₈ / 10₂ / 9₆ (1980) / 11 9₅
25	Sand and mud / Unsurveyed / 11 / 13 / 12 17 / 10 / 13 / 22 rky 20 — Unsurveyed or inadequately surveyed area; area with inadequate depth information	Inadequately Surveyed (see Note) / Inadequately Surveyed (see Note)

A portion of a page from Section 1 of *Chart No. 1* showing the various ways depths are indicated on NOAA Charts

165

U.S. AIDS TO NAVIGATION SYSTEM
on navigable waters except Western Rivers

LATERAL SYSTEM AS SEEN ENTERING FROM SEAWARD

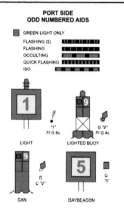

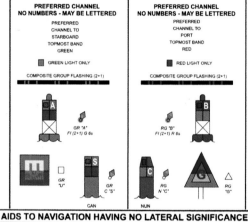

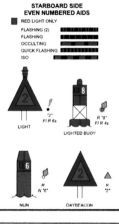

PORT SIDE
ODD NUMBERED AIDS

GREEN LIGHT ONLY
FLASHING (2)
FLASHING
OCCULTING
QUICK FLASHING
ISO

"1"
Fl G 6s
LIGHT

G "9"
Fl G 4s
LIGHTED BUOY

G
C "V"
CAN

9
DAYBEACON

PREFERRED CHANNEL
NO NUMBERS - MAY BE LETTERED

PREFERRED
CHANNEL TO
STARBOARD
TOPMOST BAND
GREEN

GREEN LIGHT ONLY

COMPOSITE GROUP FLASHING (2+1)

GR "A"
Fl (2+1) G 6s

GR
"U"
CAN

GR
C "S"

PREFERRED CHANNEL
NO NUMBERS - MAY BE LETTERED

PREFERRED
CHANNEL TO
PORT
TOPMOST BAND
RED

RED LIGHT ONLY

COMPOSITE GROUP FLASHING (2+1)

RG "B"
Fl (2+1) R 6s

RG
N "C"

RG
"G"

STARBOARD SIDE
EVEN NUMBERED AIDS

RED LIGHT ONLY
FLASHING (2)
FLASHING
OCCULTING
QUICK FLASHING
ISO

"2"
Fl R 6s
LIGHT

R "8"
Fl R 4s
LIGHTED BUOY

6
R
N "6"
NUN

R
"2"
DAYBEACON

AIDS TO NAVIGATION HAVING NO LATERAL SIGNIFICANCE

ISOLATED DANGER
NO NUMBERS - MAY BE LETTERED

WHITE LIGHT ONLY
Fl (2) 5s

BR "A"
Fl (2) 5s

LIGHTED   UNLIGHTED

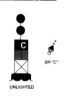

SAFE WATER
NO NUMBERS - MAY BE LETTERED

WHITE LIGHT ONLY   MORSE CODE
Mo (A)

RW "N"
Mo (A)
LIGHTED
AND/OR SOUND

RW
"A"
MR

RW
SP "B"
SPHERICAL

RW "N"
UNLIGHTED
AND/OR SOUND

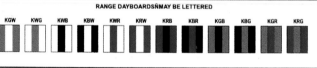

RANGE DAYBOARDS ÑMAY BE LETTERED

KGW KWG KWB KBW KWR KRW KRB KBR KGB KBG KGR KRG

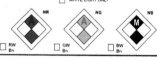

DAYBOARDS - MAY BE LETTERED

WHITE LIGHT ONLY

NR   NG   NB

RW
Bn

GW
Bn

BW
Bn

SPECIAL MARKS - MAY BE LETTERED

YELLOW LIGHT ONLY
FIXED
FLASHING

Y
C "A"
UNLIGHTED

Y
N "C"

Y "A"
Bn

SHAPE OPTIONAL--BUT SELECTED TO BE APPROPRIATE
FOR THE POSITION OF THE MARK IN RELATION TO THE
NAVIGABLE WATERWAY AND THE DIRECTION
OF BUOYAGE.

Y "B"
Fl
LIGHTED

Aids to Navigation marking the Intracoastal Waterway (ICW) display unique yell w symbols to distinguish them from aids marking other waters. Yellow triangles △ indicate aids should be passed by keeping them on the starboard (right) hand of the vessel. Yellow squares ▢ indicate aids should be passed by keeping them on the port (left) hand of the vessel. A yellow horizontal band ▭ provides no lateral information, but simply identifies aids as marking the ICW.

TYPICAL INFORMATION AND REGULATORY MARKS

INFORMATION AND REGULATORY MARKERS

WHEN LIGHTED, INFORMATION AND REGULATORY
MARKS MAY DISPLAY ANY WHITE LIGHT RHYTHM
EXCEPT QUICK FLASHING, Mo(A), AND FLASHING (2)

W
Bn   DANGER   NW

MOORING
BUOY
WHITE WITH BLUE BAND
MAY SHOW WHITE
REFLECTOR OR LIGHT

SWIM   AREA
BOAT
EXCLUSION
AREA
EXPLANATION MAY BE PLACED
OUTSIDE THE CROSSED DIAMOND
SHAPE, SUCH AS DAM, RAPIDS,
SWIM AREA, ETC.

ROCK   DANGER
THE NATURE OF DANGER MAY
BE INDICATED INSIDE THE
DIAMOND SHAPE, SUCH AS ROCK,
WRECK, SHOAL, DAM, ETC.

SLOW
NO   WAKE
CONTROLLED
AREA
TYPE OF CONTROL IS INDICATED
IN THE CIRCLE, SUCH AS SLOW,
NO WAKE, ANCHORING, ETC.

MULLET LAKE
◀ BLACK RIVER
INFORMATION

FOR DISPLAYING INFORMATION
SUCH AS DIRECTIONS, DISTANCES,
LOCATIONS, ETC.

BUOY USED TO DISPLAY
REGULATORY MARKERS

5
MPH
MAY SHOW WHITE LIGHT
MAY BE LETTERED

PLATE 1

U.S. Aids to Navigation: IALA System B

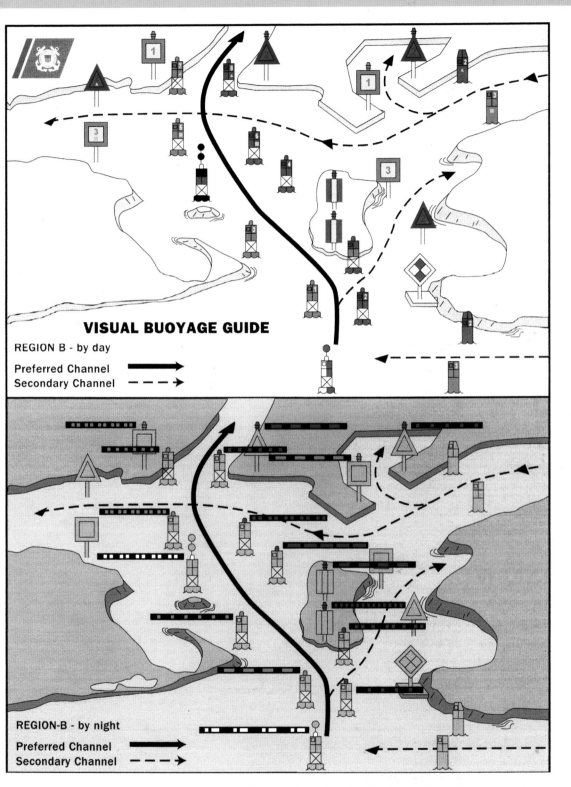

VISUAL BUOYAGE GUIDE

REGION B - by day

Preferred Channel

Secondary Channel

REGION-B - by night

Preferred Channel

Secondary Channel

A Visual Buoyage Guide, showing the appearance of various channel markers by day and by night and illustrating their respective relationships to the channels they mark

167

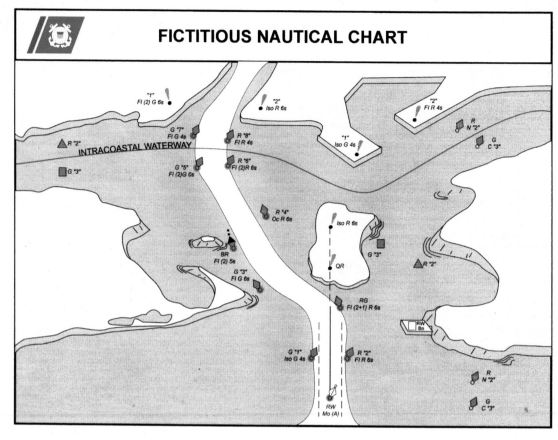

A fictitious chart of the area shown in the Visual Buoyage Guide

Useful Web Sites

This alphabetical list is by no means all inclusive, but it can be a good place to start when looking for navigation material and information online.

Bluewater Books & Charts:
http://www.bluewaterweb.com/

Canadian Notices to Mariners (NOTMAR):
http://www.notmar.gc.ca/

Landfall Navigation (Navigation Products):
http://www.landfallnavigation.com/

Maptech (Electronic & Paper Charts, Publications and Software):
http://www.maptech.com/

National Ocean Service:
http://oceanservice.noaa.gov/

NGA Publications and Notices to Mariners:
http://www.nga.mil/portal/site/maritime/

NOAA ON-Line Chart Viewer:
http://www.nauticalcharts.noaa.gov/mcd/OnLineViewer.html

NOAA Tides and Currents:
http://tidesandcurrents.noaa.gov/

Nobeltec (Electronic Charts & Navigation Software): http://www.nobeltec.com/

Reed's Nautical Almanac:
http://www.reedsalmanac.com/

USCG Local Notices to Mariners:
http://www.navcen.uscg.gov/LNM/default.htm

Weems & Plath (Trad-Nav Instruments):
http://www.weems-plath.com/

Index